Aligning Tests wit

Reflections on using the Council of Europe's draft Manual

Also in this series:

Aligning Tests with the CEFR

Reflections on using the Council of Europe's draft Manual

Edited by
Waldemar Martyniuk
Jagiellonian University in Krakow, Poland

CAMBRIDGE
UNIVERSITY PRESS

CAMBRIDGE UNIVERSITY PRESS
Cambridge, New York, Melbourne, Madrid, Cape Town, Singapore,
São Paulo, Delhi, Dubai, Tokyo, Mexico City

Cambridge University Press
The Edinburgh Building, Cambridge CB2 8RU, UK

www.cambridge.org
Information on this title: www.cambridge.org/9780521176842

First published 2010

Printed in the United Kingdom at the University Press, Cambridge

A catalogue record for this publication is available from the British Library

Library of Congress Cataloging-in-Publication Data
Aligning tests with the CEFR : reflections on using the council of Europe's draft
manual / edited by Waldemar Martyniuk.
    p. cm.
  Includes bibliographical references.
  ISBN 978-0-521-17684-2
1. Second language acquisition—Ability. testing. 2. Language and languages—
Ability testing. I. Martyniuk, Waldemar. II. Title.

  P118.75.A48 2010
  418.0076—dc22
  2010023939

ISBN 978-0-521-17684-2 paperback

Contents

Acknowledgements

I would like to express my thanks to all contributors to the volume for developing and writing up their original presentations given at the Cambridge Colloquium in December 2007 and for their willingness to make subsequent revisions in line with the editorial suggestions.

The volume could not have reached publication without the professional assistance of the editors of the SiLT series, Mike Milanovic and Cyril Weir, as well as Lynda Taylor of Cambridge ESOL acting on their behalf. I am grateful to them for their support throughout the editing process.

I am also grateful to the whole team at the Language Policy Division of the Council of Europe in Strasbourg led by Joe Sheils for enabling me to become actively involved in the work of this great organisation.

Waldemar Martyniuk

The publishers are grateful to the copyright holders for permission to use the copyright material reproduced in this book, and to Trinity College London for the use of data, diagrams and tables previously published in Papageorgiou 2007.

Series Editors' note

This Series Editors' note is longer than usual, given the importance of the impact that the Common European Framework of Reference for Languages (CEFR) is having on language education in Europe. There is growing interest worldwide in establishing comparability between assessment tools and external standards, whether these are technical standards relating to matters of quality assurance, or descriptions of performance levels that offer benchmarks for comparison. Such standards tend to be influential since they provide policy makers with tools that can be used for gathering baseline data, for benchmarking and for evaluating current practices. External standards are of particular benefit to governments which have educational or test reform initiatives. Given the scope for abuse or at least misuse of the CEFR in this context we feel that an in-depth consideration of the issues involved is an important preface to this volume.

The CEFR levels referred to in this volume are not 'standards' in the true sense of the concept; they form a useful framework of reference and offer a helpful metadiscourse. The word 'standard' is not used in the title of the CEFR, and the introductory notes heavily downplay the notion that the CEFR offers 'standards', though the message is mixed: for example, on page xiii, towards the end of the fourth paragraph (Council of Europe 2001) we read:

> It is already clear however, that a set of common reference levels as a calibrating instrument is particularly welcomed by practitioners of all kinds who, as in many other fields find it advantageous to work with stable, accepted standards of measurement and format.

The CEFR is a widely used, common framework of reference based on six broad reference levels and an 'action-oriented' approach to language teaching and learning. Within a relatively short period of time it has become highly influential in Europe and beyond as a helpful way of articulating objectives for language teaching and learning. The CEFR has certainly helped to raise awareness of language issues and has provided a useful focus for researchers, policy makers, assessment providers, and teachers.

However there is some concern that the CEFR has been adopted or interpreted as a fixed standard or set of standards, even though it perhaps was not originally designed as such. Over time, the pressure has grown, often from government, for test providers and examination boards to link their examinations to a particular external standard, namely the CEFR. The case of Taiwan (see Wu and Wu in this volume) is a good example of this.

In response to perceptions and expectations that the CEFR could and should offer a set of stable and acceptable standards for testing and assessment purposes, the Council of Europe set about providing a 'toolkit' of resources to inform and facilitate the process of aligning tests to the framework. This initially included a draft pilot Manual for *Relating language examinations to the CEFR* and a technical reference supplement to this (Council of Europe 2003, 2004), with a later revised version of the Manual (2009). The Council also provided forums where practitioners could share their reflections on the use of the draft Manual and their experience in using the different linking stages as suggested within it. Examples of such forums include a seminar entitled 'Reflections on the use of the Draft Manual for Relating Language Examinations to the CEFR: Insights from Case Studies, Pilots and other projects' held in Cambridge in December 2007. This *Studies in Language Testing* (SiLT) volume contains many of the papers that were first delivered at that meeting. It provides a number of perspectives on the process and outcomes of attempts to align examinations to the Common European Framework of Reference (CEFR) using the Manual provided by the Council of Europe. Waldemar Martyniuk, the Editor of this volume, outlines the content and focus of these papers in his editorial introduction below.

The Association of Language Testers in Europe (ALTE) and Cambridge ESOL in its own right, and also as a founder member, have encouraged the development of the 'toolkit' to allow users to make better use of the CEFR for their own purposes, and have overseen or been directly involved with a number of initiatives to assemble the necessary resources for the toolkit. These include:

- Co-ordinating the development of a *Users' Guide for Examiners* (1996) – now under revision by ALTE again as a manual for test development and examining (2010).
- Developing the EAQUALS/ALTE European Language Portfolio (ELP), both in hard copy and electronic forms (from 2000).
- Providing support for the authoring and piloting of the draft Manual for relating examinations (since 2002/03).
- Contributing to benchmarking materials and examples of test items and tasks to accompany the CEFR (from around 2004).
- Developing content analysis grids for speaking and writing materials (based on ALTE projects dating back to 1992); and
- Specifically as Cambridge ESOL, playing a co-ordinating role in developing Reference Level Descriptions for English – The English Profile Programme (since 2005). The Profile in English will contribute significantly to the usefulness of the CEFR as a practical tool.

Cambridge ESOL's involvement with the Council of Europe has an even longer history dating back to 1980 when the concept of a multi-level system of Cambridge examinations began to emerge in light of Wilkins' work on proficiency levels (see Wilkins in Trim 1978) and starting with the addition of a Threshold Level test (Preliminary English Test – PET) to the well-established First Certificate in English (FCE) and Certificate of Proficiency in English (CPE) examinations. In 1990 the revised Waystage and Threshold specifications (which had been partly sponsored by Cambridge) formed the basis of the test specifications for the new Key English Test (KET) and updated PET, and further additions and revisions to existing examinations saw the process of convergence taking place to achieve this goal, as noted by North (2008:31−32).

From the early 1990s Cambridge ESOL, both in its own right and also as part of ALTE, worked to develop an empirically derived common scale that allowed for the systematic ordering of its examinations according to level (see the Series Editor's note in *Studies in Language Testing* Volume 1, 1995) as well as the comparison of examinations across languages on the ALTE 5-level system. In the Cambridge context, the empirical underpinning for the system was achieved by introducing an item banking approach which involves assembling a bank of calibrated items – that is, items of known difficulty. Designs employed for collecting response data ensure a link across items at all levels. The Cambridge ESOL Common Scale, a single measurement scale covering all Cambridge ESOL levels, has been constructed with reference to these objective items. The Common Scale thus relates different testing events within a single frame of reference, greatly facilitating the development and consistent application of standards.

Since the inception of the Common Scale many millions of candidates at all proficiency levels have taken the Cambridge examinations and their responses have allowed the scale to be incrementally refined based on analyses of this data within the framework. (See the paper for the Council of Europe by North and Jones (2009) to accompany the revised Manual; also Maris (2009) for discussion of test equating using IRT in the context of standard setting in the collection of papers edited by Figueras and Noijons (2009).) As part of ALTE, Cambridge contributed to the development of the ALTE 5-level system. Underpinning this work is a system of test content analysis and the application of an item banking approach that is applied to the examinations of a number of ALTE members.

It is important, nevertheless, to constantly remind ourselves that the CEFR itself is deliberately *underspecified* and *incomplete* (see Milanovic 2009). It is precisely this feature which makes it an appropriate tool for comparison of practices across many different contexts in Europe and beyond. On the one hand it is useful as a common framework with six broad reference levels, but on the other it is not applicable to all contexts without user intervention in order to *adapt it flexibly* to suit local purposes.

The three main authors of the CEFR, Daniel Coste, Brian North, and John Trim, made this point very clearly in the text itself and they have all repeated it on numerous occasions in subsequent presentations on the framework and its principles. So, for example, in the introductory notes for the user, the following statement is emphatically made: 'We have NOT set out to tell practitioners what to do or how to do it' (Council of Europe 2001:xi). This is reiterated throughout the text by the use of the phrase: 'Users of the framework may wish to consider and where appropriate state . . .' (e.g. page 40).

Subsequent work on the 'toolkit' has also followed this lead. For example, the authors of the Manual for *Relating language examinations to the CEFR* stress this point when they state that the Manual is not the only guide to linking a test to the CEFR and that no institution is obliged to undertake such linking.

More recently, in his plenary paper presented at the Council of Europe Policy Forum on use of the CEFR (Strasbourg 2007), Coste (2007) described how contextual uses which are seen as deliberate interventions in a given environment can take 'various forms, apply on different levels, have different aims, and involve different types of player'. In his view: 'All of these many contextual applications are legitimate and meaningful but, just as the Framework itself offers a range of (as it were) built-in options, so some of the contextual applications exploit it more fully, while others extend or transcend it.'

When considering test alignment questions, this fundamental principle must be borne in mind because there are important implications which follow on from this. For example, it is important to remember that the CEFR is not intended to be used prescriptively and that there can be no single 'best' way to account for the alignment of an examination within its own context and purpose of use. As Jones and Saville (2009:54−55) point out:

> . . . some people speak of applying the CEFR to some context, as a hammer gets applied to a nail. We should speak rather of referring a context to the CEFR. The transitivity is the other way round. The argument for an alignment is to be constructed, the basis of comparison to be established. It is the specific context which determines the final meaning of the claim. By engaging with the process in this way we put the CEFR in its correct place as a point of reference, and also contribute to its future evolution.

A particular concern relates to the status of the 'illustrative scales of descriptors' as they are called, and their recent uses in overly prescriptive ways (i.e. against the intentions of the authors), especially in the context of standard setting. In one of the pre-publication drafts of the framework document entitled *Learning, Teaching, Assessment. A Common European Framework of Reference* (Strasbourg 1998), these scales were included in the appendix as examples and did not occur in the body of the text. The only scales to be included in the main text were the common reference levels (later to become Tables 1, 2 and 3 in the published version, Council of Europe 2001:24–29).

This original layout of the text in the 1998 draft visibly reinforced the different status and function of the general reference levels and the more specific *illustrative* scales. This approach underlined the very tentative nature of the illustrative scales, many of which were uncalibrated and indeed were underrepresented, particularly at the higher C-levels. Given the vigour with which some people have recently attempted precise alignment using these scales, despite their obvious and clearly stated deficiencies, it is dangerous to give the illustrative scales too much prominence.

In Chapter 8 of the 1998 draft version which was entitled 'Scaling and Levels' the tentative status of the illustrative scales was made clear in the following paragraph (page 131):

> The establishment of a set of common reference points in no way limits how different sectors in different pedagogic cultures may choose to organise or describe their system of levels and modules. It is also to be expected that the precise formulation of the set of common reference points, the wording of the descriptors, will develop over time as the experience of member states and of institutions with related expertise is incorporated into the description (1998:1,310).

Since the publication of the CEFR in its finalised form in 2001, the second point in this paragraph, emphasising the tentative nature of the illustrative scales, has tended to be forgotten or at least downplayed by some users. This may be in part due to the way that the final text was edited. Many of the less well validated illustrative scales remained in the final text, but for pragmatic reasons the authoring group decided to incorporate them into the main text rather than keep them in the appendix. Four appendices were used to illustrate several projects involving the development of scale descriptors; Appendix B (Council of Europe 2001:217) was used to describe the development of the 'illustrative scale descriptors' which was part of the Swiss research project conducted by North (published in 2000 as a book based on his PhD).

But the points made by the authors in 1998 still remain true; in other words, the functional and linguistic scales were there to illustrate the broad nature of the levels rather than to define them precisely. While some of the scales might prove stable across different contexts, there should not be an expectation that they all will. This has important implications for the use of the 'illustrative scales of descriptors' in alignment procedures; for example, given their status, individual scales should only be used with great care in any kind of standard-setting exercise. Indeed it is hard to see how, over and above a very general approximation to the levels, standard setting using the current scales can be considered an entirely satisfactory procedure.

North himself (2007) notes that the 'fluency' scale was useful in linking the ALTE 'Can Do' project to the framework (based on values from the Swiss project he had conducted) but that other scales were not robustly calibrated, and there were significant gaps at the A1 and C levels (see North's presentation made at the 23rd ALTE conference, Sèvres, April 2007 – available from the ALTE website: www.alte.org).

Somewhere along the way, these very real concerns expressed by a principal author of the scales have been lost or ignored. Indeed, given the origins and status of the scales it is perhaps unfortunate that there has been a somewhat one-sided reading of the text of the CEFR, as noted by Coste (2007), another of its original authors: 'In various settings and on various levels of discourse . . . people who talk about the Framework are actually referring only to its scales of proficiency and their descriptors.' Trim echoes this view in Saville (2005) – *An interview with John Trim at 80.*

In any case, it is important to note that the illustrative scales in the CEFR are precisely that. They are underspecified at the upper levels at least and uncalibrated in many instances. They should be viewed and used with caution, particularly in standard-setting exercises, since they are likely to prove misleading at best and quite damaging at worst.

Embedded procedures rather than one-off exercises

If the CEFR is to have a lasting and positive impact in the context of assessment, then its principles and practices need to be integrated into the routine procedures of assessment providers so that alignment arguments can be built up over time as the professional systems develop to support the claims being made (for examples of how this can be done, see O'Sullivan, and Khalifa, ffrench and Salamoura in this volume). This entails working with the text of the CEFR *as a whole* and *adapting it* where necessary to suit specific contexts and applications. It is unlikely that any single study or report can provide satisfactory evidence of alignment. On the contrary, a single standard-setting exercise should *not* be taken as sufficient evidence of alignment and examination providers should seek to provide multiple sources of evidence accrued over time.

Standard-setting events which are conducted as one-off procedures simply do not provide enough evidence for consistent interpretation of any level system. If necessary, alignment arguments should remain tentative and be modified later in light of additional evidence as and when it becomes available. This should be expected rather than be seen as a problem.

In relation to assessment, therefore, alignment arguments and assessment standards need to be maintained in the long term using a range of techniques and professional processes, including:

- item banking to establish common measurement scales and to allow for both item-based and person-based equating to be employed in test construction and in the monitoring of standards over time
- routine test validation processes to quality assure test outcomes
- iterative cycles of test development and revision.

More specifically, this means that the recommendations found in the Manual on how to use the CEFR and other 'toolkit' resources supplied by the Council of Europe for alignment purposes (e.g. familiarisation activities with stakeholders and standard-setting exercises of different types, whether task- or person-based) need to be *integrated within the standard procedures* of the assessment provider rather than seen as 'one-off events'. Chapter 7 of Khalifa and Weir (2009) in the *Studies in Language Testing* series provides an informative account of how these linking devices are embedded in Cambridge ESOL standard procedures.

Manual procedures and the Cambridge ESOL test cycle

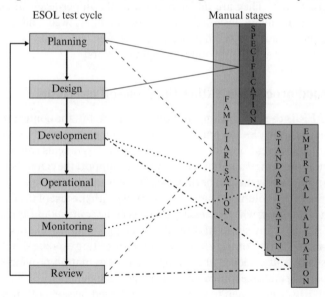

Such an approach is relevant across a broad range of contexts from classroom testing to the work of an examination board like Cambridge ESOL or other members of ALTE which interact with (literally) thousands of stakeholders to develop, administer, mark and validate many different types of examination within a consistent but evolving frame of reference. In 2010, for example, many hundreds of administrations of different language examinations by

Cambridge and other ALTE partners will take place, most of which include the assessment of four skills (including face-to-face Speaking tests). Given the complexity of these operations, the arguments for alignment to external reference points need to be developed on a case-by-case basis and must be one part of the broader validity argument which is needed to support the appropriate uses of each examination.

Finally we would like to return to the underspecification of the CEFR and to consider what this means for relating particular language examinations to the framework. It is important to recognise that the CEFR is *neutral* with respect to language and, as a common framework, it must by necessity be underspecified for all or any specific language(s). This means that specialists in the teaching or assessment of a given language (e.g. Cambridge ESOL for English) will need to determine the linguistic features which increasing proficiency in the language entails (i.e. the user/learner's competences described in Chapter 5 of the CEFR). Such features are peculiar to each language and so the CEFR must be adapted to accommodate the language in question.

ALTE's testing systems have developed alongside the CEFR over the past two decades. Many of them are now able to provide rich data and analysis to help refine the CEFR as it applies to a number of European languages. This is an important role for responsible assessment organisations to engage in and very much in keeping with the original intentions of the Council of Europe. The aim is to facilitate understanding and collaborative activities rather than to regulate or dictate to others what they should or should not do. An example of this in practice is the English Profile (EP) programme (see also *Research Notes* 33). It seeks to transpose the CEFR into English so that it becomes immediately relevant and useful to that language to curriculum designers, teachers assessment organisations and so on. Similar projects are under way in France, the Czech Republic, Germany, Spain, Georgia, Greece, Portugal and Italy to name but a few. ALTE members are involved in all cases where the country has an ALTE partner.

A major objective of the EP programme is to analyse learner language to throw more light on what learners of English can and cannot do at different CEFR levels, and to address how well they perform using the linguistic exponents of the language at their disposal (i.e. using the grammar and lexis of English). One of the main inputs to this analysis is provided by the Cambridge Learner Corpus which contains 35 million words of learners' written English from levels A1 to C2 of the CEFR. The EP research team is already providing evidence of 'criterial features' of English which are typically found in the writing of learners at the different CEFR levels. Of course this data alone does not provide an adequate sample and so part of the EP programme involves the collection of additional data from learners within the 'EP Network', including more written data and also focusing on spoken English as well (see Green forthcoming).

Examination boards and other institutions offering high-stakes tests need to demonstrate how they are seeking to meet the demands of validity in their tests and, more specifically, how they actually operationalise criterial distinctions between the tests they offer at different levels on the proficiency continuum. Cambridge ESOL, for example, has commissioned a number of 'construct volumes' in the SiLT series to assemble and present additional evidence that the examinations offered by the board are well grounded in the language ability constructs they are attempting to measure. An explicit socio-cognitive test validation framework has been developed which enables examination providers to furnish comprehensive evidence in support of any claims about the soundness of the theoretical basis of their tests (see Geranpayeh and Taylor (Eds) forthcoming in this series, Khalifa and Weir (2009), Shaw and Weir (2007), Taylor (Ed.) forthcoming, and Weir (2005)). The series develops a theoretical framework for validating tests of second language ability which then informs an attempt to articulate the Cambridge ESOL approach to assessment in the skill area under review. The perceived benefits of a clearly articulated theoretical and practical position for assessing skills in the context of Cambridge ESOL tests are essentially twofold:

- Within Cambridge ESOL – this articulated position will deepen understanding of the current theoretical basis upon which Cambridge ESOL assesses different levels of language proficiency across its range of products, and will inform current and future test development projects in the light of this analysis. It will thereby enhance the development of equivalent test versions and tasks.
- Beyond Cambridge ESOL – it will communicate in the public domain the theoretical basis for the tests and provide a more clearly understood rationale for the way in which Cambridge ESOL operationalises this in its tests. It will provide a framework for others interested in validating their own examinations and thereby offer a more principled basis for comparison of language examinations across the proficiency range than is currently available.

Cambridge ESOL is now in a position to begin a systematic and empirically based approach to specifying more precisely how the CEFR can be operationalised for English, and this in turn will lead to better and more comprehensive illustrative descriptors (particularly at the bottom and top of the scale) (Green forthcoming). In this way the CEFR will become the useful tool that it was intended to be.

In conclusion, we would like to reiterate our support for the principles and practices of the CEFR and for what we see as the main strength of the CEFR so far, its use as a communication tool (Taylor 2004). Within the common framework of levels, ALTE members have attempted to make the interpretation of examination results as transparent and meaningful as possible and the development of functional descriptors ('Can Dos') has been useful in promoting better communication between stakeholders.

However, as noted above, it is also important to draw attention to some limitations and uses of the framework for which the CEFR was not designed. Some of these limitations were acknowledged by the original authors and some others have also been noted in the literature over the past few years (see, for example, Alderson, Figueras, Kuijper, Nold, Takala and Tardieu (2006), Fulcher (2004, 2004a), Green (forthcoming), Milanovic (2009) and Weir (2005a)).

Weir (2005a) argues that although it contains much valuable information on language proficiency and advice for practitioners, in its present form the CEFR is not sufficiently comprehensive, coherent or transparent for uncritical use in language testing. First, the descriptor scales take insufficient account of how variation in terms of contextual parameters may affect performances by raising or lowering the actual difficulty level of carrying out the target 'Can Do' statement. In addition, a test's cognitive validity – a function of the processing involved in carrying out these 'Can Do' statements – must also be addressed by any specification on which a test is based. Failure to explicate such context and cognitive validity parameters – i.e. to comprehensively define the construct to be tested – vitiates current attempts to use the CEFR as the basis for developing comparable test forms within and across languages and levels, and hampers attempts to link separate assessments, particularly through social moderation.

Weir emphasises that it is crucial that the CEFR is not seen as a prescriptive device but rather a heuristic, which can be refined and developed to better meet our needs. For the language testing constituency in particular it currently exhibits a number of serious limitations such that comparisons based entirely on the scales alone might prove to be misleading, given the insufficient attention paid in these scales to issues of validity. The CEFR as presently constituted does not enable us to say tests are comparable let alone equip us to develop comparable tests.

Taylor (2004:4) advises a cautious approach in general in using any comparative framework. She argues that:

> . . . while they promise certain benefits they can also carry inherent risks. This is because all frameworks, by definition, seek to summarise and simplify, highlighting those features which are held in common across tests in order to provide a convenient point of reference for users and situations of use. Since the driving motivation behind them is usefulness or ease of interpretation, comparative frameworks cannot easily accommodate the multidimensional complexity of a thorough comparative analysis; the framework will focus on shared elements but may have to ignore significant differentiating features. The result is that while a framework can look elegant and convincing, it may fail to communicate some key

differences between the elements co-located within it. The result is likely to be an over simplification and may even encourage misinterpretation on the part of users about the relative merits or value of different exams.

Taylor (2004:5) concludes that:

> . . . there is no doubt that comparative frameworks can serve a useful function for a wide variety of test stakeholders: for test users – such as admissions officers, employers, teachers, learners – frameworks make it easier to understand the range of assessment options available and help users to make appropriate choices for their needs; for applied linguists and language testers frameworks can help define a research agenda and identify research hypotheses for investigation; for test providers frameworks not only help with product definition and promotion, but also with planning for future test design and development. However, we need to understand that they have their limitations too: they risk masking significant differentiating features, they tend to encourage oversimplification and misinterpretation, and there is always a danger that they are adopted as prescriptive rather than informative tools. They need to come with the appropriate health warnings!

As responsible assessment providers, ALTE members seek to provide leadership in the field of language testing, and it is important for them to address these issues explicitly. That is why organisations like Cambridge ESOL have attempted to make their stance very clear. By working collaboratively with the CEFR, the shortcomings of the illustrative scales and linguistic content can be addressed more effectively, with data being collected to enable well-informed refinements to be made as our understanding increases.

This volume therefore offers interesting insights into the application of the CEFR to language examinations and a small sample of the work that is now starting to take place. As such the papers provide a number of perspectives ranging from narrow to broad. ALTE suggested the event that led to this volume and Cambridge ESOL offered to publish the proceedings in the SiLT series precisely in order to help open up the debate on the use of the CEFR and to encourage further research along the lines illustrated here.

Michael Milanovic
Cyril J Weir
February 2010

Bibliography

Alderson, J C, Figueras, N, Kuijper, H, Nold, G, Takala, S and Tardieu, C (2006) Analysing tests of reading and listening in relation to the Common European Framework of Reference: the experience of the Dutch CEFR Construct Project, *Language Assessment Quarterly* 3 (1), 3–30.

Coste, D (2007) *Contextualising uses of the Common European Framework of Reference for Languages*, paper presented at Council of Europe Policy Forum on use of the CEFR, Strasbourg 2007. www.coe.int/T/DG4/Linguistic/Source/ SourceForum07/ D-Coste_Contextualise_EN.doc

Council of Europe (2001) *Common European Framework of Reference for Languages: learning, teaching, assessment*, Cambridge: Cambridge University Press.

Council of Europe (2003) *Relating language examinations to the Common European Framework of Reference for Languages: learning, teaching, assessment (CEF). Manual: preliminary pilot version*, DGIV/EDU/LANG 2003, 5, Strasbourg: Language Policy Division.

Council of Europe (2004) *Reference Supplement to the Preliminary Pilot Version of the Manual for Relating Language Examinations to the Common European Framework of Reference*, Strasbourg: Language Policy Division.

Council of Europe (2009) *Relating language examinations to the Common European Framework of Reference for Languages: learning, teaching, assessment (CEFR). A Manual*, Strasbourg: Language Policy Division.

Figueras, N and Noijons, J (2009) (Eds) *Linking to the CEFR levels: Research perspectives*, Strasbourg: Council of Europe.

Fulcher, G (2004) Deluded by artifices? The Common European Framework and harmonization, *Language Assessment Quarterly* 1 (4), 253–266.

Fulcher, G (2004a) *Are Europe's tests being built on an unsafe framework?*, an article for the *Guardian* weekly TEFL supplement, in association with the BBC World Service, 18 March.

Geranpayeh, A and Taylor, L (Eds) (forthcoming) *Examining Listening: Research and practice in assessing second language listening, Studies in Language Testing*, Cambridge: University of Cambridge ESOL Examinations/ Cambridge University Press.

Green, A B (forthcoming) Requirements for Reference Level Descriptions for English, *English Profile Journal* 1 (1).

Jones, N and Saville, N (2009) European language policy: assessment, learning and the CEFR, *Annual Review of Applied Linguistics* 29, 51–63.

Khalifa, H and Weir, C J (2009) *Examining Reading: Research and practice in assessing second language reading, Studies in Language Testing 29*, Cambridge: University of Cambridge ESOL Examinations/Cambridge University Press.

Maris, G (2009) Standard setting from a psychometric point of view, in Figueras, N and Noijons, J (Eds) *Linking to the CEFR levels: Research perspectives*, Strasbourg, Council of Europe, 59–66.

Milanovic, M (2009) Cambridge ESOL and the CEFR, *Research Notes* 37, 2–5.

North, B (2000) *The development of a common framework scale of language proficiency*, New York: Peter Lang.

North, B (2007) *The CEFR levels: key points and key problems*, paper presented at the 23rd ALTE Conference, Sèvres.

North, B (2008) The CEFR levels and descriptor scales, in Taylor, L and Weir, C J (Eds) *Multilingualism and Assessment: Achieving transparency, assuring quality, sustaining diversity – Proceedings of the ALTE Berlin Conference, May 2005, Studies in Language Testing 27*, Cambridge: University of Cambridge ESOL Examinations/Cambridge University Press, 21–66.

North, B and Jones, N (2009) *Further material on maintaining standards across languages, contexts and administrations by exploiting teacher judgment and IRT scaling*, Strasbourg: Council of Europe.

Saville, N (2005) An interview with John Trim at 80, *Language Assessment Quarterly* 2 (4), 263–288.

Shaw, S and Weir, C J (2007) *Examining Writing: Research and practice in assessing second language writing, Studies in Language Testing 26,* Cambridge: University of Cambridge ESOL Examinations/Cambridge University Press.

Taylor, L (2004) Issues of test comparability, *Research Notes* 15, 2–5.

Taylor, L (Ed.) (forthcoming) *Examining Speaking: Research and practice in assessing second language speaking, Studies in Language Testing 30,* Cambridge: University of Cambridge ESOL Examinations/Cambridge University Press.

Trim, J (1978) *Some possible lines of development of an overall structure for a European unit/credit scheme for foreign language learning by adults,* Strasbourg: Council of Europe.

Weir, C J (2005) *Language testing and validation: an evidence-based approach,* Basingstoke: Palgrave Macmillan.

Weir, C J (2005a) Limitations of the Council of Europe's Framework of reference (CEFR) in developing comparable examinations and tests, *Language Testing* 22 (3), 281–300.

Wilkins, D (1978) Proposal for levels definition, in Trim, J (1978) *Some possible lines of development of an overall structure for a European unit/credit scheme for foreign language learning by adults,* Strasbourg, Council of Europe, 71–78.

From the Editor of this volume

In December 2007 a 2-day Colloquium was held at the University of Cambridge, UK. Organised by the Association of Language Testers in Europe (ALTE) on behalf of the Council of Europe's Language Policy Division, and hosted by University of Cambridge ESOL Examinations (Cambridge ESOL), the Colloquium was intended as a concluding event for the piloting phase of the preliminary version of the Manual for *Relating Language Examinations to the Common European Framework of Reference for Languages* (CEFR), first released by the Council of Europe in 2003. Following the event a call for contributions was sent out to a broad range of institutions and individuals involved in the piloting and willing to share their experiences in using the preliminary version of the Manual. In this volume we present a selection of studies offered for publication in response to this call.

The studies range from the linking of a single test to the CEFR (e.g. Kantarcıoğlu, Thomas, O'Dwyer and O'Sullivan; Kecker and Eckes; Kollias and Downey; O'Sullivan; Khalifa, ffrench and Salamoura), through CEFR-linking of suites of examinations at different levels (e.g. Barni, Scaglioso and Machetti; Dávid; Papageorgiou; Szabó; Wu and Wu) to large-scale multilingual projects undertaken by specialist research institutes (e.g. Jones, Ashton and Walker; Noijons and Kuijper).

Some studies are modest in their aims and restricted to one section of the examination(s) (e.g. Dávid; Wu and Wu), whilst others involved a thorough validation of all papers (Kecker and Eckes; Khalifa, ffrench and Salamoura). Some apply one or two of the sets of procedures proposed in the Manual (e.g. Papageorgiou), others undertook a systematic piloting of familiarisation, specification, standardisation, and empirical validation procedures suggested in the pilot Manual (e.g. Kecker and Eckes; Noijons and Kuijper). Several papers offer a more thoughtful approach to how CEFR linking should become part of the iterative cycle of exam development (e.g. Jones, Ashton and Walker; O'Sullivan; Szabó). All of them include some reflections on their use of the Manual in addition to their findings.

In their introductory text, **Brian North** – co-ordinator of the piloting phase and of the revision of the Manual that followed – **Waldemar Martyniuk** and **Johanna Panthier** provide the background to the development of the Manual; they outline the procedures suggested for linking and present a broader context for the use of the CEFR and the Manual as part of the Council of Europe's language policies. Following the Introduction is a detailed report on the 2007 Cambridge Colloquium in which **Lynda Taylor** – who served as Moderator for the Colloquium – gives the background to the event and summarises the content of the presentations given and the issues discussed.

In **Section One** studies on linking single tests to the CEFR are presented.

O'Sullivan presents a project that aimed to confirm the linking of a single test, City & Guilds' Communicator, to the CEFR but which led to the embedding of the Manual-based processes and systems developed for the project (including assessment training; CEFR familiarisation as well as inter- and intra-organisational structures) into City & Guilds procedures at a broader level. **Kecker** and **Eckes** describe following the Manual's procedures for familiarisation, specification, standardisation, and empirical validation to examine the relation between the TestDaF (Test of German as a Foreign Language) and the CEFR levels. For the external validation, the German section of DIALANG served as an external criterion measure for the receptive skills data, with teacher judgements being used for the productive skills. **Khalifa**, **ffrench** and **Salamoura** report on a standard-maintaining project in connection with a test that already has a long relationship with the CEFR, the Cambridge ESOL First Certificate in English (FCE). Their paper demonstrates how the procedures proposed by the Manual can be constructively used and extended not only to build a linking argument but also, and more importantly, to maintain it. **Kantarcıoğlu**, **Thomas**, **O'Dwyer** and **O'Sullivan** describe linking Bilkent University's Certificate of Proficiency in English examination (COPE) to the CEFR, reporting initial findings from the familiarisation, specification, standardisation and empirical validation stages of the project and reflecting on the use of the Manual. **Downey** and **Kollias** report their experience in linking the content of the Hellenic American University's Advanced Level Certificate in English (ALCE) examination to the CEFR descriptors by following the Manual's Specification and Standardisation procedures.

Section Two includes studies on linking a suite of exams to the CEFR.

Szabó provides an overview of how the Hungarian 'European Consortium for the Certificate of Attainment in Modern Languages' (ECL) examination system implemented a project to align ECL exam levels with the CEFR. He discusses potential problems and practical difficulties with special regard to empirical validation and to aligning examinations in lesser-taught languages. **Papageorgiou** reports on linking the Trinity College London GESE and ISE international examinations to the CEFR. He focuses on the problems judges faced during the familiarisation and standardisation training and the impact of the linking project on the design of the examinations concerned. **Barni**, **Scaglioso** and **Machetti** report experience with the Manual's standardisation procedures followed by the University for Foreigners in Siena's CILS – Certification of Italian as a Foreign Language – in relating its examinations at different levels to the CEFR, with particular emphasis on the A1 module 'Adults in Italy'. **Dávid** describes linking the Grammar and Vocabulary papers of the Hungarian Euro Examinations for English to the CEFR through all four sets of procedures in the Manual. The study used many-faceted Rasch analysis of ratings of illustrative DVD samples and CEFR illustrative descriptors to replicate the measurement scale that the illustrative scales in the CEFR are based on. **Wu** and **Wu** describe a project relating the reading comprehension part of the Taiwanese General English Proficiency Test to the CEFR, in the context of the adoption of the CEFR for English qualifications in Taiwan. The impact of using the CEFR as a common framework of reference in a non-European country like Taiwan is also discussed.

Two large-scale multilingual projects are presented in **Section Three**.

Jones, **Ashton** and **Walker** argue that the Manual should encourage methodological innovation and that CEFR linking procedures should be seen as integral to test construction and administration, rather than a one-off exercise. They report on using the CEFR to impose consistency across languages in developing a 'Languages Ladder', a new voluntary recognition system linked to the English 'Asset Languages' lifelong learning project. **Noijons** and **Kuijper** report on following the Manual's content specification and standardisation procedures in relation to the Dutch state school-leaving examinations of reading comprehension in the foreign languages of French, German and English. The project identified what the mean minimum reading comprehension level of candidates at different types of secondary school should be in terms of the CEFR and compared this to the official cut-off scores for the tests.

This compendium of case studies and reflections on the use of the Council of Europe's draft Manual for relating exams to the CEFR is offered to the profession with the intention to share insights and experiences gathered during the piloting phase of the tool and – more importantly – to provide a reference for and encourage international co-operation on ensuring best possible quality and transparency in language assessment.

Waldek Martyniuk
December 2009

Introduction
The Manual for *Relating language examinations to the Common European Framework of Reference for Languages* in the context of the Council of Europe's work on language education

Brian North, Waldemar Martyniuk and Johanna Panthier

The Council of Europe and language education

Intergovernmental co-operation programmes in the area of language education have been carried out by the Language Policy Division (formerly the Modern Languages Section) of the Council of Europe in Strasbourg for almost five decades, and by the European Centre for Modern Languages (ECML) in Graz, Austria, since it was established by a Partial Agreement in 1994.

The Division is responsible for designing and implementing initiatives for the development and analysis of language education policies aimed at promoting linguistic diversity and plurilingual education. The Division is particularly engaged in developing tools and standards to help member states elaborate transparent and coherent language policies. These instruments, which are disseminated and used not only throughout Europe but all over the world, are making a vital contribution to the establishment of a European education area for modern languages and serve as benchmarks for other bodies and institutions, including the European Union. The Division's programmes cover all languages – mother tongue/first language/language(s) of education as well as foreign, second or minority languages – and address the needs of all of the 48 states that have ratified the European Cultural Convention[1]. The Division also provides a forum for debate on policy development and assists member states in reviewing their policies with a view to enhancing plurilingual and intercultural education.

Early programmes of international co-operation in Strasbourg focused on the democratisation of language learning for the mobility of persons and ideas, and on the promotion of the European heritage of cultural and linguistic diversity. Projects assisted member states in implementing reforms aimed at developing learners' communication skills and encouraged innovation in language teaching and teacher training, with an emphasis on a learner-centred approach. While continuing to promote innovation for successful communication and intercultural skills, more recent projects have increasingly addressed the social and political dimensions of language learning, focusing on language education for democratic citizenship, diversification in language learning, improving coherence and transparency in language provision, and the language education rights of minorities. The European Year of Languages (2001) led to further initiatives to support member states in developing policy responses to the new challenges to social cohesion and integration. The results of these projects have been embodied in a Resolution[2] and a number of Recommendations[3] of the Committee of Ministers and Parliamentary Assembly of the Council of Europe (PACE).

The recent priorities of the Council of Europe were established by the Heads of State and Government of the Member States of the Council of Europe at their Third Summit (Warsaw 2005). They confirmed the core objective of preserving and promoting human rights, democracy and the rule of law. All activities must contribute to this fundamental objective. The Heads of State and Government committed themselves to developing those principles and, in propagating these values, they resolved to enhance the role of the Council of Europe as an effective mechanism for pan-European co-operation in all relevant fields.

The Language Policy Division's medium-term programme 'Language Policies for Democratic Citizenship and Social Inclusion' (2006–09) provides a follow-up to the priorities established by the Heads of State and Government. Its activities include the development of European standard setting and other instruments to promote social inclusion, intercultural dialogue, human rights and democratic citizenship through language education. The Division assists member states in the renewal of policies for these purposes and is involved in education policies for national/official and minority languages as well as foreign languages. It has recently launched new projects on language policies for the integration of adult migrants and on policies and European reference standards for competence in the languages of school education, with a special focus on policies for disadvantaged and migrant children. Further information is available at: www.coe.int/lang and www.coe.int/portfolio

The work of the Language Policy Division is supported by implementation activities at the European Centre for Modern Languages (ECML) for the 34 states of the Enlarged Partial Agreement in Graz, Austria. The two units, which – together with the European Charter for Regional or Minority Languages – form the Department of Language Education and Policy, have distinct but complementary missions and working methods. The Centre in Graz, in accordance with its Statutes, has as its mission the implementation of language policies and the promotion of innovative approaches to the learning and teaching of modern languages. To respond to this mission the ECML organises international language education projects primarily targeting teacher trainers, researchers and key multipliers in the field. These essentially aim to raise awareness on critical issues, provide training to language education practitioners and facilitate networks of specialists. The ECML offers educational facilities at its premises in Graz, including a resource centre housing the collection of reference works and papers of Dr John Trim, who was Project Director for the programmes of the Language Policy Division in Strasbourg from 1971 to 1997. The ECML's third medium-term programme 'Empowering Language Professionals' (2008–11) includes 20 projects organised in four main thematic strands:

- Evaluation
- Continuity in language learning
- Content and language education
- Plurilingual education.

Further information is available at: www.ecml.at

The Council of Europe's *Common European Framework of Reference for Languages: Learning, Teaching, Assessment* (CEFR)

The purpose of the CEFR

The *Common European Framework of Reference for Languages: learning, teaching, assessment* (CEFR) (Council of Europe 2001) was developed between 1993 and 1996 by a Council of Europe international working party following the recommendation of an intergovernmental symposium *Transparency and Coherence in Language Learning in Europe* held at Rüschlikon, near Zurich, Switzerland, in November 1991. One of the aims of the CEFR was to introduce common reference points, in the form of the 'common reference levels'. It was hoped that, in time, the existence of such common reference points would help to relate courses and examinations to each other and thus achieve the 'transparency and coherence' that had been the subject of the Rüschlikon symposium.

The CEFR is not a harmonisation project. The aim of the CEFR is to provide a mental framework that enables people to say where they are, not a specification telling them where they ought to be. Right at the very beginning of the CEFR, the authors emphasise:

> We have NOT set out to tell practitioners what to do or how to do it. We
> are raising questions not answering them. It is not the function of the
> CEF to lay down the objectives that users should pursue or the methods
> they should employ (Council of Europe 2001: xi Note to the User).

There is no conflict between on the one hand a common framework desirable to organise education and encourage productive networking, and on the
other hand the local strategies and decisions necessary to facilitate successful
learning in any given context. The aim of the CEFR is to facilitate reflection,
communication and networking. The aim of any local strategy ought to be
to meet needs in context. The key to linking the two into a coherent system
is flexibility. The CEFR is a concertina-like reference tool that provides categories, levels and descriptors that educational professionals can merge or
sub-divide, elaborate or summarise, adopt or adapt according to the needs
of their context – whilst still relating to the common hierarchical structure. It
is for users to choose activities, competences and proficiency stepping-stones
that are appropriate to their local context, yet can be related to the greater
scheme of things and thus communicated more easily to colleagues in other
educational institutions and to other stakeholders such as learners, parents
and employers.

The common reference levels

The CEFR levels (A1–C2) did not suddenly appear from nowhere. The
first reference to a possible set of 'Council of Europe levels' – based around
Waystage, Threshold Level and similar such concepts – was in a presentation by David Wilkins (author of *The Functional Approach*) at the 1977
Ludwigshafen symposium (Trim 1978). This symposium had represented
the first – unsuccessful – attempt to move towards a common European
framework in the form of a unit–credit scheme linked to common levels. The
six CEFR common reference levels correspond both to the seven levels suggested by Wilkins in 1977 (minus the top level) and (with the addition of A1)
to the five levels adopted in 1991 by ALTE – the Association of Language
Testers in Europe – in which Cambridge ESOL was a founding member. The
illustrative descriptors for these levels were developed in a 1993–96 project
by two members of the CEFR Working Party (North 2000a, North and
Schneider 1998, Schneider and North 2000), who co-ordinated the research
work supported by the Swiss National Science Foundation.

It is perhaps worth emphasising the salient features of the levels, as
illustrated by the empirically calibrated descriptors:

Level A1 is the point at which the learner can:

- *interact in a simple way, ask and answer simple questions about
  themselves, where they live, people they know, and things they have,*

initiate and respond to simple statements in areas of immediate need or on very familiar topics, rather than relying purely on a rehearsed repertoire of (tourist) phrases.

Level A2 reflects the Waystage specification with:

*   the majority of descriptors stating social functions: *greet people, ask how they are and react to news; handle very short social exchanges; ask and answer questions about what they do at work and in free time; make and respond to invitations; discuss what to do, where to go and make arrangements to meet; make and accept offers*
*   plus descriptors on getting out and about: *make simple transactions in shops, post offices or banks; get simple information about travel; ask for and provide everyday goods and services.*

Level B1 reflects the Threshold Level, with two particular features:

*   maintaining interaction and getting across what you want to communicate: *give or seek personal views and opinions in an informal discussion with friends; express the main point he/she wants to make comprehensibly; keep going comprehensibly, even though pausing for grammatical and lexical planning and repair are very evident, especially in longer stretches of free production*
*   plus coping flexibly with problems in everyday life: *deal with most situations likely to arise when making travel arrangements through an agent or when actually travelling; enter unprepared into conversations on familiar topics; make a complaint.*

Level B2 reflects three new emphases:

*   effective argument: *account for and sustain opinions in discussion by providing relevant explanations, arguments and comments; explain a viewpoint on a topical issue giving the advantages and disadvantages of various options*
*   holding your own in social discourse: *interact with a degree of fluency and spontaneity that makes regular interaction with native speakers quite possible without imposing strain on either party; adjust to the changes of direction, style and emphasis normally found in conversation*
*   plus a new degree of language awareness: *correct mistakes if they have led to misunderstandings; make a note of 'favourite mistakes' and consciously monitor speech for them.*

Level C1 is characterised by access to a broad range of language that results in fluent, spontaneous communication:

*   *express him/herself fluently and spontaneously, almost effortlessly; has a good command of a broad lexical repertoire allowing gaps to be readily*

overcome with circumlocutions; there is little obvious searching for
expressions or avoidance strategies – only a conceptually difficult subject
can hinder a natural, smooth flow of language

• *produce clear, smoothly flowing, well-structured speech, showing*
  controlled use of organisational patterns, connectors and cohesive devices.

Level C2 represents the degree of precision and naturalness typical of highly
successful learners:

• *convey finer shades of meaning precisely by using, with reasonable*
  accuracy, a wide range of modification devices

• and *a good command of idiomatic expressions and colloquialisms with*
  awareness of connotative level of meaning.

Relating language examinations to the CEFR – the purpose of a Manual

North and Schneider (1998:243) emphasised that the production of a
common scale was only the first step in the implementation of a common
framework, and that ensuring a common interpretation through standardised performance samples and monitoring data from tests was necessary. The
process of standardising the interpretation of the levels has been supported
by the development of the draft Manual *Relating Language Examinations*
to the Common European Framework of Reference for Languages: Learning,
Teaching, Assessment (CEFR) (Council of Europe 2003). The Manual was
developed following a seminar hosted by the Finnish authorities in Helsinki
in July 2002. The drafting and piloting of the Manual was a response by
the Council of Europe to the need to assist examination providers to relate
their examinations to the CEFR. It was conceived as a contribution to the
co-operative endeavour of improving the transparency of and comparability
between language qualifications in Europe. It was intended as a continuation
of the work of the Council of Europe's Language Policy Division in developing planning tools which provide reference points and common objectives
as the basis for a coherent and transparent structure for effective teaching/
learning and assessment relevant to the needs of learners as well as society,
and that can facilitate intercultural understanding and personal mobility.

The primary aim of the Manual is to help the providers of examinations to
develop, apply and report transparent, practical procedures in a cumulative
process of continuing improvement in order to situate their examination(s)
in relation to the Common European Framework of Reference (CEFR).

The approach developed offers guidance to users to:

• describe the examination coverage, administration and analysis
  procedures

- relate results reported from the examination to the 'common reference levels of language proficiency' of the CEFR
- provide supporting evidence that reports the procedures followed to do so.

Following the best traditions of Council of Europe action in developing language education policy, however, the Manual has wider aims to actively promote and facilitate co-operation among relevant institutions and experts in member countries. The Manual aims to:

- contribute to competence building in the area of linking assessments to the CEFR
- encourage increased transparency on the part of examination providers
- encourage the development of both formal and informal national and international networks of institutions and experts.

Relating an examination or test to the CEFR is a complex endeavour. The existence of such a relation is not a simple observable fact, but is an assertion for which the examination provider needs to provide both theoretical and empirical evidence. The procedures by which such evidence is put forward can be summarised by the term 'validation of the claim'.

The approach adopted

The pilot version of the Manual presents four inter-related sets of procedures that users are advised to follow in order to design a linking scheme in terms of self-contained, manageable activities. The activities carried out in all four sets of procedures contribute to the validation process.

Familiarisation: a selection of activities designed to ensure that participants in the linking process have a detailed knowledge of the CEFR. This familiarisation stage is necessary at the start of both the Specification and the Standardisation procedures.

In terms of validation, these procedures are an indispensable starting point. An account of the activities taken and the results obtained is an essential component of the validation report.

Specification: a self-audit of the coverage of the examination (content and task types) profiled in relation to the categories presented in the CEFR. As well as serving a reporting function, this exercise also has a certain awareness-raising function that may assist in further improving the quality of the examination concerned.

These procedures assure that the definition and production of the test have been undertaken carefully, following good practice. Content specification grids are available to help when implementing them (see below).

Standardisation: suggested procedures to facilitate the implementation of a common understanding of the 'common reference levels' presented in the CEFR.

These procedures assure that judgements taken in rating performances reflect the constructs described in the CEFR, and that decisions about task and item difficulty are taken in a principled manner on the basis of evidence from pretesting as well as expert judgement. Samples of oral and written production illustrating the CEFR levels and calibrated items to test comprehension skills are available to support the standardisation procedures (see below).

Empirical Validation: the collection and analysis of test data and ratings from assessments in order to provide evidence that both the examination itself and the linking to the CEFR are sound. Suggestions and criteria are provided for adequate and credible validation appropriate for different contexts.

These procedures assure that the claims formulated through Specification and Standardisation ('test-under-construction') can indeed be confirmed when the examination is administered in practice ('test-in-action'). This scheme was adopted (a) because these categories are a good way of grouping linking methodologies found in the literature, (b) because they reflect the classic stages of quality management (design, implementation, evaluation), (c) because such broad concepts could thus be applied equally to formal, high-stakes assessment situations (examinations) and to lower-stakes school and teacher assessments.

Relating examinations to the CEFR can best be seen as a process of 'building an argument' based on a theoretical rationale. As noted above, the central concept within this process is 'validity'. **Therefore, before an examination can be linked to an external framework like the CEFR (external validity), it must demonstrate the validity of the construct, and the consistency and stability of the examination (internal validity).**

The approach adopted in this process is an inclusive one. The recommended procedures encourage alignment of examinations to the CEFR with differing degrees of rigour appropriate to different testing contexts. The Manual aims to encourage the application of principles of best practice even in situations in which modest resources and expertise are available. First steps may be modest, but the aim is to help examination providers to work within a structure, so that later work can build on what has been done before, and a common structure may offer the possibility for institutions to more easily pool efforts in certain areas.

Not all examination providers may consider they can undertake studies in all of the areas outlined above. Some institutions in 'low-stakes' contexts may decide to concentrate on Specification and Standardisation, and may not be able to take the process to its logical conclusion of full-scale Empirical Validation as outlined in internationally recognised codes and standards for testing and measurement[4]. However, it is highly recommended that even less well-resourced examination providers should select techniques from all areas. The linking of a qualification to the CEFR will be far stronger if the claims based on test specifications and their content are supported by both standardisation of judgements and empirical validation of test data. Every examination provider – even examination providers who have only limited resources or countries that have decentralised traditions – can demonstrate in one way or another through a selection of techniques both the internal quality and validity of their examination and its external validity: the validity of the claimed relationship to the CEFR.

Piloting the Manual

In addition to the 'Sounding Board' of 16 experts employed as consultants during and after the development process, the Manual was piloted at different levels of intensity: (a) through formal feedback – without necessarily employing the techniques in a project, (b) through trialling procedure, (c) in documented case studies such as those published in this volume. In 2005–06, 40 institutions from 20 countries registered for the pilot phase of the Manual following an international seminar organised by the Language Policy Division in Strasbourg. The feedback indicated that the structure (familiarisation, specification, standardisation, validation) worked well. It was also felt to be a very effective way to mediate the CEFR, though several users reported on the difficulty of following the suggested procedures without a full set of calibrated performance samples and test items for the standardisation training, and for incorporation in cross validation studies. The other main points made were the following:

- The Manual appeared to be a good way to critically review and evaluate the content and the statistical characteristics of an exam. Some respondents found the specification forms labelled A1–A21 time-consuming, whilst others stressed their awareness-raising value.

- Some stressed that the CEFR cannot be a test specification because, since it is a policy reference document, it lacks the necessary detail. Others felt that the Manual – and the content specification grids now associated with it – provided a good way of developing CEFR-based tests.

- The procedures proposed by the Manual should be integrated into the test development and production process and used to assist the maintenance of standards from year to year, not just for a one-off study.

- Standardisation training and standard setting should be split, presented in different chapters. Standardisation training with illustrative examples can in fact be seen as Familiarisation.
- Standard-setting techniques should also cover data-based candidate-centred procedures (only procedures for external validation are proposed in the pilot version).
- The Manual would be improved if shortened and made more user-friendly with chapter outlines and a representation of different entry points and routes. The 'didactic' approach taken in 'Standardisation training' could be adopted elsewhere.

Supporting materials

The work of institutions that piloted the preliminary draft of the Manual was supported by a set of multilingual reference materials. Up-to-date documents and links are available on the website www.coe.int/portfolio. They include:

Reference Supplement

- Quantitative and qualitative considerations in relating certificates and diplomas to the CEFR.
- Different approaches in standard setting.

Content Analysis Grids

- CEFR content analysis grid for listening and reading (sometimes referred to as 'the Dutch CEFR Grid'): Appendix B1 of the revised version of the Manual (Council of Europe 2008). The Grid can be accessed at: www.ling.lancs.ac.uk/cefgrid
- CEFR content analysis grids for speaking and writing, developed by ALTE: Appendix B2 of the revised version of the Manual (Council of Europe 2008).

Illustrative Descriptors

- The collated set of descriptors from the CEFR.
- The descriptor bank from the European Language Portfolio, documenting the relationship between those descriptors and the original CEFR descriptors.
- A collation of C1/C2 descriptors (in English) from the CEFR and related projects that indicates which descriptors were calibrated to CEFR levels and which were not.

Illustrative Samples

- A *Guide* for the organisation of a seminar to calibrate examples of spoken performances in line with the scales of the CEFR[5]. This is based on the experiences gathered during a seminar organised in Sèvres, France, by the Centre International d'Etudes Pédagogiques (CIEP) and Eurocentres aimed at calibrating samples of oral performances in French to the CEFR levels[6].

- Documentation complementing the samples of spoken performance is available on the website mentioned above.
- DVDs showing samples of spoken performance are available from the Language Policy Division and the respective language institutes at the time of writing for English, French, Italian and Portuguese.
- Illustrative samples of written performance are available on the above-mentioned website at the time of writing for English, French, German, Portuguese and Italian.
- Illustrative items for listening and reading for English, French, German, Italian and Spanish are available on a CD-ROM from the Language Policy Division.
- A DVD for German is published with its documentation by Langenscheidt as Bolton, Glaboniat, Lorenz, Müller, Perlmann-Balme and Steiner (2008).
- Samples of spoken performance in English, French, German, Italian and Spanish by teenage learners in France calibrated at a Council of Europe cross-language rating seminar (CIEP, June 2008) are available on a DVD from the Language Policy Division, the CIEP and other partners, as well as on www.ciep.fr/publi_evalcert
  In addition:
- A collection of papers presented at a colloquium on *Standard setting research and its relevance to the CEFR* organised on behalf of the Language Policy Division jointly by the Dutch Institute for Educational Measurement (Cito) and the European Association for Language Testing and Assessment (EALTA) is published as Figueras and Noijons (Eds 2009).

Recommendation on the use of the Council of Europe's Common European Framework of Reference for Languages (CEFR) and the promotion of plurilingualism

In July 2008, the Committee of Ministers representing the 47 member states of the Council of Europe adopted Recommendation CM/Rec(2008)7 on the use of the Council of Europe's Common European Framework of Reference for Languages (CEFR) and the promotion of plurilingualism[7]. Under the measures recommended for implementation there is a set related to the use of the CEFR in the area of assessment. When national, regional and local education authorities decide to use the CEFR, they are *inter alia* invited to:

4.5. ensure that all tests, examinations and assessment procedures leading to officially recognised language qualifications take full account of the relevant aspects of language use and language competences as set out in the CEFR, that they are conducted in accordance with internationally recognised principles of good practice and quality management, and that the procedures to relate these tests and examinations to the common reference levels (A1−C2) of the CEFR are carried out in a reliable and transparent manner;

4.6. ensure that full information regarding the procedures applied in all tests, examinations and assessment systems leading to officially recognised language qualifications, particularly those used to relate them to the common reference levels (A1−C2) of the CEFR, is published and made freely available and readily accessible to all the interested parties;

4.7. encourage all other bodies responsible for foreign/second language assessment and certification to adopt measures that guarantee the provision of fair, transparent, valid and reliable tests and examinations in conformity with the principles set out in paragraph 4.5 above and to publish their procedures, particularly those used to relate these tests and examinations to the CEFR common reference levels (A1−C2) as outlined in paragraph 4.6 above;

4.8. extend such recognition as is appropriate to language qualifications, including those certified in other member states, which satisfy the above criteria;

4.9. encourage all bodies, official and unofficial, responsible for foreign/second language assessment and certification to adopt measures that give special attention to:

4.9.1. the evaluation and recognition of receptive and productive competences, as appropriate to the needs of learners, in all languages and at all levels, in particular at lower levels, as contributions to each individual's developing plurilingual profile;

4.9.2. forms of assessment which value the plurilingual capacities of learners and recognise the full range of their plurilingual repertoire;

4.9.3. dimensions of language learning and use which go beyond proficiency itself ensuring that they are taken into consideration and recognised through adequate means of evaluation, such as portfolios.

In the Explanatory Notes attached to the recommendation special attention is being given to the challenges and responsibilities related to the use of the CEFR:

The Council of Europe's *Common European Framework of Reference for Languages* is rapidly becoming a powerful instrument for shaping language education policies in Europe and beyond. The task of relating language policies, language curricula, teacher education and training, textbook and course design and content, examinations and certification systems to the CEFR is currently being undertaken by a growing number of public and private stakeholders in all of the Council of Europe member states. Most of these stakeholders recognise the real reference value of the document and apply the principles on which it was based most appropriately. There are instances of use, however, that indicate that reference may be made to the CEFR as a Council of Europe document merely for the purpose of recognition on 'the educational market' without real application of its basic values and concepts. In some other cases the CEFR may be referred to in an attempt to introduce one normative curriculum for a uniform language education in Europe – contradictory to the intention of the authoring team and to Council of Europe principles – and indeed to the very nature and content of the CEFR itself!

To ensure a coherent, realistic and responsible use of the CEFR the following principles are being strongly underlined and recommended for consideration:

1 The CEFR is purely descriptive – not prescriptive, nor normative.

2 The CEFR is language neutral – it needs to be applied and interpreted appropriately with regard to each specific language.

3 The CEFR is context neutral – it needs to be applied and interpreted with regard to each specific educational context in accordance with the needs and priorities specific to that context.

4 The CEFR attempts to be comprehensive, in that no aspects of language knowledge, skills and use are deliberately left out of consideration.
It cannot, of course, claim to be exhaustive. Further elaboration and developments are welcomed.

5 The CEFR offers a common language and point of reference as a basis for stakeholders to reflect upon and critically analyse their existing practice and to allow them to better 'situate their efforts' in relation to one another.

6 The use of the CEFR should contribute to increased transparency of processes and procedures, improved quality of provision and comparability of outcomes.

7 The use of the CEFR should contribute to the promotion of the basic educational values for which the Council of Europe stands, such as social inclusion, intercultural dialogue, active democratic citizenship, language diversity, plurilingualism, learner autonomy and lifelong learning.

Measures recommended for language assessment and certification

The Recommendation CM/Rec(2008)7 invites the authorities to take responsibility for the appropriate use of the CEFR as a reference in officially recognised language qualifications systems. Most specifically they are asked to ensure that procedures for relating official language examinations to the principles and reference levels of the CEFR are carried out in a reliable and transparent manner. This means that authorities need to be able to account for the quality of their assessment procedures and qualifications with reference to the principle of good practice that exist in the field of language assessment in general and as set out in internationally recognised Codes of Practice (listed as Appendix II to the Recommendation). The procedures for accounting for the validity of the examinations and their relationship to the CEFR should be made available to all interested parties. All institutions responsible for language assessment and certifications should be reminded by the authorities that using the CEFR as a reference means adopting measures that guarantee comprehensibility, quality and transparency of actions. Language qualifications that satisfy these criteria should be given appropriate recognition in all member states.

The Manual for relating examinations to the CEFR is used as an important reference tool in the explanatory notes attached to the Recommendation. It is pointed out that:

> Increasing educational, vocational and professional mobility make the portability of qualifications a matter of increasing urgency. Portability is only possible if the user institutions have confidence in the reliability and validity of the qualification a candidate for employment or admission to a college or university brings from his or her country of origin. Since it is not feasible for each particular institution or individual employer to research the value of each qualification offered, they are likely to take a cautious view. This may well result in well-qualified candidates being rejected, which then acts as an obstacle to freedom of movement. There is thus a strong demand for a reliable method of establishing and making readily available to all interested parties the actual value of qualifications across national boundaries. It is therefore not at all surprising that it should be in the area of the assessment of language proficiency that the CEFR has aroused the greatest interest. Examining bodies and educational institutions, as well as individuals working in the field have shown themselves willing to work together in a serious way to link the examinations with which they are concerned to the common reference levels of the CEFR in a valid and reliable manner. Their cooperation has led to the production of a Manual for helping examination providers to relate their examinations to the CEFR. This Manual covers a range of procedures which can be used in *building an argument* supported by evidence

and explanations to account for the extent to which an examination or examination system is aligned to the principles and levels of the CEFR. It has a reference supplement which includes technical information and is also supported by examples of test tasks for reading and listening comprehension and samples of written and spoken performance to illustrate language proficiency at the successive reference levels of the CEFR. The exemplar tasks, the spoken samples (which are available on CD-ROMs and DVDs) and written samples (available online) do not represent prototypes or models to be copied but are intended to be used as reference material in test development or benchmarking exercises. As in the case of the CEFR itself, the Manual is not intended to be prescriptive or to suggest that a single set of procedures needs to be followed to account for the relationship between an examination and the CEFR. It provides an accessible knowledge base to help policy makers and practitioners to achieve their own goals in a coherent and transparent way and to situate and explain their own efforts in relation to others.

As pointed out in the Explanatory Notes, the mere statement that an examination or a qualification is set at a particular level 'will not of itself carry conviction'. Unsupported and uncorroborated claims can too easily lead to all claims being discredited. For this reason, the Council of Europe regards it of primary importance that all such claims should be fully supported by proper documentation that is made publicly available. It is, of course, recognised that transparency is limited by the requirements of secrecy in the case of certain technical processes and of confidentiality in the case of some information in respect of individual candidates. However, secrecy should be kept to a necessary minimum, and the fact that some information is withheld 'should itself be openly stated and reasons given'.

Case studies on piloting the Manual

As noted in the explanatory part of the Recommendation CM/Rec(2008)7, a substantial number of case studies have been reported, which show that, if undertaken with due care, examinations can be linked to the common reference levels in a valid and reliable way. The case studies also made it clear that linking procedures need to be reviewed periodically, as examinations evolve over time. Authorities are therefore invited, in the interests of portability, to see that the language qualifications they award are linked to the common reference levels of the CEFR in a fully responsible manner, taking international experience fully into account. In this way, it is intended that sufficient mutual trust and confidence can be built up to justify the reciprocal recognition of language qualifications across national boundaries. A selection of these case studies presented in this volume may serve as a reference in this process.

The Language Policy Division of the Council of Europe is pleased to offer the profession this compendium of case studies concerning the use of the preliminary pilot version of the Manual for *Relating language examinations to the Common European Framework of Reference for Languages* (Council of Europe 2003). It takes the opportunity to express its gratitude to all those who took an active part in the piloting of the original document. Making their experience available to others they have contributed to fostering coherence and transparency in language testing and comparability of certifications, thus promoting mobility and intercultural understanding among citizens. This kind of 'unforced co-operation' among professionals has been an outstanding feature of Council of Europe projects, an intergovernmental organisation that fully respects the principle of subsidiarity in education matters.

This publication will form an important part of the 'tool-kit' being built around the Common European Framework of Reference for Languages (CEFR), including the revised Manual, the 'Reference Supplement' to the Manual, the samples illustrating the CEFR levels, the case studies on the use of the CEFR, the General Guide for Users (of the CEFR), the 'Reference level descriptions' for specific languages, the European Language Portfolio, etc.

All these documents and many others, including the report on a Policy Forum on *The CEFR and the development of language policies: challenges and responsibilities*, are available on the Language Policy Division's website www.coe.int/lang

The CEFR and related 'tool-kit' as well as all the other outcomes of the Council of Europe programmes in the field of languages are rooted in the nature, aims, values and *modus operandi* of the Council of Europe itself. Quality, coherence and transparency in language learning, teaching and assessment are objectives designed to serve learners as language users and active, responsible citizens in interacting and participating fully in our democratic societies.

Notes

1. http://conventions.coe.int/Treaty/Commun/QueVoulezVous.asp?NT=018&CM=2&DF=13/12/2005&CL=ENG
2. www.coe.int/t/dg4/linguistic/20thsessioncracow2000_EN.asp#TopOfPage
3. See: www.coe.int/t/dg4/linguistic/Conventions_EN.asp#TopOfPage
4. ALTE (Association of Language Testers in Europe)
   Code of Practice: www.alte.org/quality_assurance/index.php
   Principles of Good Practice: www.alte.org/quality_assurance/code/good_practice.pdf
   Quality Management System: www.alte.org/quality_assurance/quality.php
   ILTA (International Language Testers' Association)
   Code of Ethics: www.iltaonline.com/code.pdf
   Code of Practice: www.iltaonline.com/ILTA-COP-ver3-21Jun2006.pdf

EALTA (European Association for Language Testing and Assessment)
Code of Practice: www.ealta.eu.org/guidelines.htm
General – not specific to language testing:
The Standards for Educational and Psychological Testing (1999), developed jointly by: American Educational Research Association (AERA); American Psychological Association (APA) ; National Council on Measurement in Education (NCME): www.apa.org/science/standards.html
5. *Guide for the organisation of a seminar to calibrate examples of spoken performances in line with the scales of the CEFR*, by Sylvie Lepage and Brian North, Council of Europe, Language Policy Division, Strasbourg, May 2005 (DGIV/EDU/LANG (2005) 4).
6. S*eminar to calibrate examples of spoken performances in line with the scales of the CEFR, CIEP, Sèvres, 2−4 December 2004*, report by Brian North and Sylvie Lepage, Council of Europe, Language Policy Division, Strasbourg, February 2005 (DGIV/EDU/LANG (2005) 1)
7. www.coe.int/t/dg4/linguistic/Source/SourceForum07/Rec%20CM%202008-7_EN.doc

References

Bolton, S, Glaboniat, M, Lorenz, H, Müller, M, Perlmann-Balme, M and Steiner, S (2008) *Mündlich: Mündliche Produktion und Interaktion Deutsch: Illustration der Niveaustufen des Gemeinsamen europäischen Referenzrahmens*, Berlin: Langenscheidt.

Council of Europe (2001) *Common European Framework of Reference for Languages: learning, teaching, assessment*, Cambridge: Cambridge University Press.

Council of Europe (2003) *Relating Language Examinations to the Common European Framework of Reference for Languages: Learning, Teaching, Assessment (CEFR), Manual − Preliminary pilot version*, DGIV/EDU/LANG (2003) 5, Strasbourg: Council of Europe.

Council of Europe (2008) *Relating Language Examinations to the Common European Framework of Reference for Languages: Learning, Teaching, Assessment (CEFR), A Manual*, Strasbourg: Council of Europe.

Figueras, N and Noijons, J (Eds) (2009) *Linking to the CEFR levels: Research perspectives*, Arnheim, Cito, EALTA.

North, B (2000a) *The Development of a common framework scale of language proficiency*, New York: Peter Lang.

North, B and Schneider, G (1998) Scaling Descriptors for Language Proficiency Scales, *Language Testing* 15 (2), 217–262.

Schneider, G and North, B (2000) *Fremdsprachen können – was heisst das? Skalen zur Beschreibung, Beurteilung und Selbsteinschätzung der fremdsprachlichen Kommunikationsfähigkeit*, Chur/Zürich:

Trim, J L M (1978) *Some Possible Lines of Development of an Overall Structure for a European Unit/Credit Scheme for Foreign Language Learning by Adults*, Strasbourg: Council of Europe, Appendix B.

Wilkins, D A (1978) Proposal for Levels Definition, in Trim (1978), 71–78, Appendix C.

The Cambridge Colloquium on using the preliminary pilot version of the Manual for relating language examinations to the CEFR – summary of discussion

Lynda Taylor
Consultant to University of Cambridge ESOL Examinations, UK

Background to the Colloquium

In December 2007 a 2-day Invited Colloquium was held at the Carvonius Centre, in the University of Cambridge, UK. Organised by the Association of Language Testers in Europe (ALTE) on behalf of the Council of Europe's Language Policy Division, and hosted by University of Cambridge ESOL Examinations (Cambridge ESOL), the event was intended as a forum for language testers from across Europe to reflect upon and share their experiences of using the preliminary pilot version of the Manual for relating language examinations to the CEFR, initially released in 2003. The Council of Europe was eager to draw upon the experience of those who, following the Manual's original launch, had registered to conduct case studies, pilots, etc., as well as to gather insights from others who had engaged with the content of the publication during the period 2004–07. At the time of the Colloquium in December 2007, the draft Manual was undergoing a revision at the hands of the Authoring Group and a revised version was planned for publication during 2008. For this reason, as well as participants from educational and examining institutions across Europe, three members of the Manual's Authoring Group were invited to attend the Colloquium (Brian North, Sauli Takala, Norman Verhelst).

The anticipated benefits of the event for Colloquium participants were thus:

- to provide an opportunity to share experiences about the Manual in its draft form for those who had actively used it in their own contexts
- to learn about the main lines of revision in progress, based upon feedback received to date, and to provide a final general review prior to publication

- to help participants in finalising their own case studies in order to write them up with a view to possible publication at a later stage

- to provide the Council of Europe with input which might lead to further guidance on appropriate uses of the Manual in a variety of contexts.

Participants in the Colloquium

Nearly 50 participants attended the Cambridge Colloquium. They represented at least 10 European countries as well as a wide variety of European and other languages (the Asset Project in the UK, for example, is concerned with 23 heritage and community languages other than English). In addition, participants represented a diversity of assessment contexts and providers, including: primary and secondary school-based education; adult education; further and higher education in colleges and universities; teacher training and development; examination boards; and government ministries and departments.

Programme overview

The overall programme format for the 2-day Colloquium was structured around a series of six 90-minute sessions, each one designed to focus on a theme or section of the draft Manual. A session included three short presentations, each lasting 15 minutes with an additional 5 minutes allowed for questions, followed by a 30-minute plenary discussion. The plenary discussion was facilitated by a Moderator, whose role was to identify from the presentations those questions and issues that lent themselves to open discussion amongst the full group of participants. Full documentation of the Colloquium can be viewed at: www.alte.org/further_info/cambridge07.php

The Colloquium opened with an official welcome to Cambridge from Michael Milanovic, Manager of ALTE and Chief Executive of Cambridge ESOL. This was followed by an introduction from Johanna Panthier of the Council of Europe's Language Policy Division, who explained the context for and the aims of the Colloquium. The remainder of this summary paper describes in brief the general focus of each of the six sessions, the specific questions and issues arising out of the individual presentations and the plenary discussion based upon them.

Session 1 – summary of content and issues arising for plenary discussion

The three short presentations in Session 1 highlighted some general issues and challenges encountered in trying to apply the Manual's procedures in specific assessment contexts, and thus set the scene for the particular topics to be discussed in the later plenary sessions.

Lisbeth Salmonsen and Eli Moe, from the University of Bergen, reported some of the benefits and difficulties they had experienced in using the Manual with the Norsk spraaktest (test of Norwegian as a second language). In their reflections they noted the large amount of useful information contained in the Manual, but commented that its emphasis tended to be more on qualitative approaches for content linking than on quantitative approaches, and that it was not always clear to them which of the various methods referred to it might be most appropriate to select. They recommended the Kaftandjieva (2007) Supplement B as a valuable additional resource for guidance on quantitative methods, but called for more specific advice on matching method to context, together with exemplar case studies of actual implementation. A further concern centred upon the difference between conceptualising the CEFR framework as a mental construct, with undoubted heuristic value, and conceiving of it as an empirical construct. This was exemplified in the difficulty of assigning actual test items and tasks to CEFR levels, either through the process of expert judgement or by empirical methods, and they posed the additional question of whether certain item or task types might actually be more or less suitable for certain levels. The Nordic experience also raised the complex issue of comparability between languages, i.e. the language of instruction and the target language to be learned. Different interpretations of CEFR level requirements had been observed even within the Nordic family of languages. It was recognised that features of the linguistic and instructional contexts needed to be taken into account, since different, albeit related, linguistic, socio-linguistic and socio-pragmatic contexts are likely to privilege certain aspects over others, both in terms of task input design and the nature of the productive outcome, e.g. for an extended writing task.

Reflections on the Nordic experience were followed by reflections on two separate case studies conducted in Hungary. Gábor Szabó noted the influence of the CEFR as a positive force for encouraging the development of language assessment, including growing technical improvement and professionalisation. At the same time, however, he noted the extent to which the CEFR, though not legally binding, is steadily assuming a pseudo-official power and authority to shape assessment policy and language testing practice. Reporting on challenges encountered in the empirical validation process to link one of Hungary's examination systems – the one offered by the European Consortium for the Certificate of Attainment in Modern Languages (ECL) – to the CEFR, he identified the lack of representative tasks for each of the levels as a major constraint on the exercise. This, he suggested, imposes serious limits on attempts to provide evidence of CEFR test or task linkage by means of test-centred validation procedures, especially as some of the limited set of representative tasks which do exist are themselves open to variable interpretation in terms of their CEFR level, with only limited evidence to support their classification. Recommendations for future action were proposed, including: increased co-operation and collaboration to develop and share tasks, to address the issue of availability; and the identification of transparent, consensus-based criteria for endorsing tasks as representative reference points, to address the issue of acceptance and acceptability. Candidate-centred methods were recommended in contexts where a test-centred approach was not well-supported (see Szabó in this volume). In a second Hungarian project, Gergely Dávid, of Euro Examinations in Budapest, described the application of CEFR-linking procedures to grammar and vocabulary tests. He highlighted the relative underspecification of these categories at the different CEFR levels and the tendency for local European standards to develop among users, e.g. item writers, in the absence of a clearly shared understanding of established benchmarks or yardsticks. Reflecting on the various sections of the Manual, he commented on the formative training function of the Familiarisation stage, and, like Szabó, noted the limitations of currently available performance samples for the process of Standardisation of judgements. The standard-setting section of the Manual was considered to be the least accessible (see Dávid in this volume).

Plenary discussion following these three presentations from Norway and Hungary revolved around the following issues:

- the need to increase the range of linking methods and procedures available, especially in relation to quantitative approaches
- the need for more guidance on selecting appropriate linking procedures, and for more advice on the contextual factors involved
- the nature of the training and support needed by judges through and following the Familiarisation phase
- the need for more and better representative tasks at each CEFR level, especially for the less frequently taught languages in Europe, e.g. Hungarian
- the nature of texts, tasks and items, and the process of assigning them to CEFR levels
- the implications of (under)specification within the CEFR descriptive scheme for some categories, e.g. grammar and vocabulary
- the value of published accounts of locally contextualised and sensitive case studies, and the potential for co-operation and collaboration in this area
- issues of comparability: across languages; across linguistic and social contexts; between local and national standards; between European and CEF standards
- the nature and implications of the CEFR's socio-political/legal 'power'.

Session 2 – summary of content and issues arising for plenary discussion

The presentations in Session 2 drew on experiences of using the Manual in Turkey, Slovakia and the Netherlands.

Carole Thomas and Elif Kantarcıoğlu reported on a 3-year project to link Bilkent University's in-house English proficiency exam to the CEFR B2 level. They reflected on the usefulness of the Manual as a means of gaining a clearer understanding of the test's level and as a tool for quality management and improvement, as well as test recognition and currency. Their experience of the Familiarisation stage had raised questions about: group dynamics and management; the success and limitations of activities offered; the supplementary activities needed; schedules and timings; how to deal with the variable background knowledge of participants; and how to evaluate the sufficiency of familiarity with the CEFR at the end of the Familiarisation process. Reflections on the Specification phase centred upon the accessibility and user-friendliness of the various forms and grids offered (A1−A22), in particular assumptions about shared knowledge of terminology; the addition of a glossary was suggested. The appropriate level of agreement needed among judges in order to validate claims was also a matter for concern, along with the desirability of confirmation by other external experts. Reflections on the Standardisation phase echoed earlier concerns from Norway and Hungary about the range and quality of the exemplar samples. The presenters also proposed the helpful addition of checklists itemising what is involved in the preparation of this and other stages (see Kantarcıoğlu, Thomas, O'Dwyer and O'Sullivan in this volume).

Jana Bérešová, of Trnava University in the Slovak Republic, described the context for linking the Maturita test to the B1 and B2 levels as part of a language teacher training project for assessment purposes within the national language education reform programme at secondary up to school-leaving level. She highlighted the considerable time needed for adequate training and familiarisation of personnel within this process. She also commented on the impact of internationally and locally produced teaching materials and tests, which resulted in variable perceptions of levels and standards among those being trained. Issues of cross-linguistic comparability and translation effects emerged as other key variables that influenced outcomes.

Angela Ashworth and Hans Veenkamp, from the Language Centre at the University of Groningen in the Netherlands, reported on their piloting of the Manual procedures in two testing projects. The first concerned Familiarisation and Standardisation workshops for teachers and the collection of local samples of calibrated material for levels B1−C2 for the productive skills. The second involved the revision of the Language Centre's own English test for international students, master's candidates and researchers.

Their experience led them to adapt and localise the CEFR descriptors as a means of contextualising these within their own high-stakes, high-level EAP/ESP assessment context, and also as a way of countering the vagueness experienced in the Dutch Grid. They focused on creating locally produced tasks and performances and generated a localised version of an assessment grid, using parallelism as a means of linking their revised descriptors to the CEFR. Their reflections identified the strengths of the Manual as its provision of expert and comprehensive procedures to be followed and its practical suggestions. Suggestions for possible improvements included: clearer guidelines for localisation options; improved presentational aspects, e.g. greater signposting; the addition to the document of useful links to other relevant work.

Plenary discussion following these three presentations revolved around the following issues:

- The Familiarisation stage: Who does it? How is it managed? Are more activities needed? Is more time needed? How familiar is 'familiar enough'?
- The Specification stage, including: perceived user-friendliness of Forms A1–A22; assumptions of prior knowledge or familiarity with related terminology and discourse.
- The Standardisation phase, including: the potential role and value of domain-specific samples, e.g. for ESP/EAP; a possible checklist of things to remember for purposes of preparation beforehand.
- Approaches to validating all the above phases: Who does it, and how?
- The role and impact of internationally and locally published teaching and test materials, and the notion of the CEFR 'brand'.
- The Manual's potential as a useful tool for quality assurance within a quality management system.
- Issues of the Manual's target audience and purpose, including presentational features which might be enhanced.

Session 3 – summary of content and issues arising for plenary discussion

The presentations in Session 3 described the experiences of two UK examining boards in using the Manual with English examinations produced by them.

Rachel Roberts, from City and Guilds, and Barry O'Sullivan, of Roehampton University, explained the background to the City and Guilds Communicator Linking Project, a series of studies to align to the CEFR the board's International ESOL examinations, developed in 2001–04 and offered at six levels. They described using the CEFR descriptive scheme, the 'blue book' (Council of Europe 2001), as a reference tool for test development along with the activities in the Manual. Work in progress on the linking project at the time of the 2007 Colloquium was restricted to a focus on the test at B2 level. The presenters commented on the considerable cost involved in undertaking such an alignment project, in terms of resources, time and enthusiasm, and they also emphasised the importance of embedding the procedures within the core test development process, rather than seeing alignment as a one-off activity or outcome for a test product. While broadly following the recommendations of the pilot Manual, procedures were implemented in a more iterative way than the linear approach implied in the draft version. The need for all staff involved in the project to receive Familiarisation training was highlighted, and they also stressed the distinction between the procedures of standard setting and benchmarking, with the benchmarking stage introduced only at the end of the Standardisation phase as a natural conclusion at this point. Within these phases they noted the relative small spread that emerged in level assignment for the productive skills, where agreement between judges seemed easier to achieve, compared with a wider spread for reading and listening, where lower levels of consistency were apparent. Associated with this, the definition of the 'least able' candidate was found to be important. They noted differentiation between internal and external judging groups, but also the tendency for exam stakeholders to agree with internal 'expert' claims. Specific issues raised included how best to account for items and tasks that 'don't fit' the CEFR levels, as well as the operational constraints that exist for examining bodies and the nature of decision making processes involving experts. Since a key aim of the exercise had been the promotion of organisational change, the presenters offered reflections on practical, real-world factors that needed careful management, e.g. composition of the expert panel, i.e. an appropriate balance of insiders/outsiders, local and external; group dynamics; an impartial chair to arbitrate. Time needed to work through the procedures was also a practical issue though it was observed that less time was needed as the process went on and as participants became familiar with the approach. Final reflections touched upon the nature of linking claims: How strong can claims be? Do only evidence-based claims have value? What constitutes evidence? Is the linking process like a computer game, where progression to the next level is only possible once a previous level has been achieved, i.e. must evidence for initial and earlier phases of the Manual procedures be demonstrated before progression to empirical studies? (See O'Sullivan in this volume.)

Hanan Khalifa, Angela ffrench and Angeliki Salamoura reported on a Cambridge ESOL case study to confirm the alignment of the FCE examination with the CEFR's B2 level, building upon the historical, conceptual and empirical links that already exist between Cambridge ESOL exams and the CEFR. They explained how the work in progress was contextualised within a larger project to update features of the FCE exam in 2008. They also stressed the importance of embedding the Manual's methodology into the core assessment processes for routine test production so as to assist international awarding bodies in their commitment to and maintenance of quality standards. Focusing upon the Familiarisation and Standardisation phases, they offered reflections on the effectiveness of the Manual's procedures in relation to pre-, during and post-event activities for workshops involving a group of internal and external participants. Although FCE was the target level (B2) for consideration in the case study, the group was encouraged to take into account the adjacent levels, B1 and C1, so as to tease out the criterial features at the level thresholds. Different data collection methodologies were described, both qualitative and quantitative, and outcomes from the analysis of participant feedback were briefly touched upon. One conclusion from the exercise was that both Manual-based and supplementary activities were found to be valuable (see Khalifa, ffrench and Salamoura in this volume).

Plenary discussion following these two presentations revolved around the following issues:

- The potential for contextualising and embedding the Manual procedures for CEFR alignment in an institutional context (e.g. examining body), rather than regarding them as a one-off exercise.
- The potentially non-linear, iterative nature of implementation of procedures.
- The strength of linking claims: Are only evidence-based claims of value? What sort of evidence – psychometric, cognitive, what else? When is there sufficient/insufficient evidence? Who decides?
- The types of data collection that are possible/desirable; the types of follow-up analysis that are possible/advisable; their contribution to the evidence base.
- The role and value of feedback from participants in the process.
- How to extend the knowledge, skills and attitudes (KSA) to all those involved, e.g. a cascade model.
- The amount of time needed and the level of other resources required.
- The external validation process concerning linking claims – who does it, when and where?

Session 4 – summary of content and issues arising for plenary discussion

Session 4 began with a presentation from the test agency in Germany responsible for producing TestDaF, the test of German as a foreign language. Gabriele Kecker and Thomas Eckes, from the TestDaF Institut, Hagen,

Germany, reported on using the Manual guidelines to run a series of work-shops piloting the Familiarisation and Standardisation phases, including standard-setting and benchmarking studies, for all four sections of the test (two receptive and two productive papers) at the B2/C1 level. They made use of the Council of Europe supplementary materials, i.e. German reading and listening items on CD, adopting a modified Angoff approach for two rounds of judgement. Consensus, consistency and measurement approaches were used to evaluate rater agreement. Reflecting on their experience, they noted the time-consuming nature of the standardisation and benchmarking phases and speculated on whether this could take the form of 'homework' rather than being done in the workshop session. They also recommended mentioning the CEFR grids in the Manual (see Kecker and Eckes in this volume).

The second presentation in this session was given by Brian North, member of the Manual's Authoring Group, who updated Colloquium participants on the project to revise the Manual. He reported that valuable feedback had been received to date. The Manual was generally regarded as good way to review a test, and though the forms and checklists were sometimes felt to be onerous, they were seen as a useful mechanism for awareness-raising. The basic scheme of the Manual, with its current chapter outline, would be retained but some presentational changes were foreseen to increase the user-friendliness of the document. Further editing would be undertaken to achieve a more unitary style. There was a proposal to split the Standardisation training and the Standard-setting training and provide illustrative examples in Familiarisation. Wider coverage of standard-setting techniques was also anticipated. The recommendation that all stages, including external validation, needed to be covered would be strengthened. Outstanding issues still to be resolved concerned: (a) guidance on cross-language linking, involving multilingual development panels and cross-language benchmarking activities (such as those done for the Asset Languages Project); (b) guidance on standard-setting methods, particularly where 'safe' reference tests were not available.

Plenary discussion following these two presentations revolved around the following issues:

- the extent to which the various procedures (familiarisation, standardisation, etc.) have the desired outcome(s), and how this can be quantified
- rater issues in judging procedures, e.g. rater dependence; the paradox of raters as 'independent experts' versus 'scoring machines', and the implications of excluding raters from analysis
- the need for more guidance on appropriate procedures and also appropriate interpretation, especially when different procedures produce different results

- the need for more explicit justification for certain procedures advocated in the Manual, e.g. form-filling for content analysis
- issues of practical feasibility and manageability, when multiple methods are offered and/or advised; balancing recommendations to 'do as much as you can' against 'do as much as you need to'; implications for external validation, and evaluators of the evidence available to underpin claims
- the challenges of undertaking cross-language linking research.

Session 5 – summary of content and issues arising for plenary discussion

Session 5 contained two presentations on further case studies conducted in the UK and the Netherlands, both with a strong multilingual dimension. Neil Jones, Karen Ashton and Tamsin Walker reported on use of the preliminary pilot Manual to align the suite of language proficiency exams which make up Asset Languages, a 6-level assessment framework for 25 languages designed to be organically embedded within England's National Languages Strategy launched in 2002. They stressed the significant challenges of working with a multilingual assessment framework in a real-world project and described their use of the Manual as critical, selective and pragmatic for this reason. They reported finding the Familiarisation and Specification stages useful together with some of the forms. The approach to standard setting in the Manual, however, was felt to be idiosyncratic and it was suggested this section might benefit from greater reference to the wider literature in this area. Finally they highlighted issues of audience and purpose for the Manual (see Jones, Ashton and Walker in this volume).

Henk Kuijper and José Noijons, from the Dutch National Institute for Educational Measurement, Cito, described the background context and aims of a cross-foreign language linking project in association with the CEFR to achieve more comprehensive CEFR-related tests. The four Manual stages – Familiarisation, Specification, Standardisation, and Empirical Validation – were followed as recommended in the document. The key forms used for the Specification stage were A10 and A19, based upon Chapters 4 and 5 of the Manual, but these were supplemented with extensive use of the Dutch Grid. The presenters noted the absence of certain features in the scheme for describing certain tasks, and commented on the inadequate accounting for socio-linguistic, strategic and pragmatic competence. The high agreement of judges from all walks of life in assigning tasks and items to levels was observed, though some task features raised cross-linguistic issues (see Noijons and Kuijper in this volume).

Plenary discussion following these two presentations revolved around the following issues:

- the challenges of real-life application in a real-world context, especially in conditions of 'patchiness', i.e. when there is an incomplete matrix or insufficient data
- the need to recognise the difference between applying the procedures in a new as opposed to an existing assessment framework
- the relationship between notions of overall language proficiency level, and levels for individual skill areas (i.e. 'flat' as opposed to 'spiky'/'jagged' profiles: should the Manual offer more advice on this issue?)
- task as determinant of level, relating once again to the importance of the reference tasks
- more guidance on task description for specification purposes: should the Dutch Grid be incorporated into the Manual?
- the influence of cross-language variation on linguistic features
- insufficient coverage within the descriptive scheme of sociolinguistic, strategic and pragmatic competence
- the setting of cut-scores and the issue of relating these to the CEFR, including the challenge of developing a clear and meaningful relationship between 'pass'/'fail' reports and CEFR levels – how to align, and when, within national education systems
- the importance of distinguishing between notions of 'equatedness' and 'equivalence' – causes of differentiation: is more explanation needed in the Manual?

Session 6 – summary of content and issues arising for plenary discussion

A final case study, also with a multi-lingual focus, was presented in Session 6 by Francesca Parizzi, of the Università per Stranieri di Perugia, Italy; Gilles Breton, of CIEP, France; and Michaela Perlmann-Balme, of the Goethe-Institut, Germany. The presenters reported first on the process of producing the Council of Europe DVDs with exemplar oral performances at different CEFR levels in French, Italian, German, and Portuguese, including issues concerning recording format and other technical matters. The second part of their presentation reflected upon the various approaches adopted during the benchmarking conferences for the ratings and the formulation of the descriptors.

Plenary discussion following this presentation revolved around the following issues:

- the value of practical guidance for conducting benchmarking studies, especially the sharing of reports on such studies, thus providing guidelines to aid preparation and management by others undertaking similar exercises

- the differing backgrounds of the experts involved, and the potential impact of this: should some sort of 'descriptive scheme' be devised?
- the 'plus' levels of the CEFR framework: how to find them? what is their function?
- selecting the CEFR scale(s): which one(s) to use? which to avoid?
- the nature of benchmarking samples: should they be test performances? or 'natural/naturalistic' samples?
- production challenges and the impact of interventions; identification of a prototype, or a cluster of tasks/samples?
- is the aim to rate *a person* or *a performance*? the 'coat-hanger' concept versus task/context dependence

Conclusion

The Colloquium ended with a round-up session after lunch on the second day and some closing words from Johanna Panthier. It was generally agreed by the participants that the event had fulfilled its original aim of providing a useful forum in which language testers from across Europe could reflect together and share their experience of relating examinations to the CEFR. In addition, the open and vigorous exchange of views, and the positive and cooperative manner in which this was conducted during the Colloquium, modelled a welcome and refreshing alternative approach when compared with the unhelpfully iconoclastic attitude towards the CEFR that sometimes characterises academic debates in this area.

Section One
Linking single tests to the CEFR

1 The City & Guilds Communicator examination linking project: a brief overview with reflections on the process

Barry O'Sullivan
Roehampton University, London, UK

Abstract

This chapter presents an overview of the Communicator linking project, a joint project between City & Guilds of London (the examination developers) and the Centre for Language Assessment Research (CLARe), Roehampton University, London. The project, which has taken almost two years to complete, was designed to establish empirical evidence of a link between the examination and the Common European Framework of Reference for Languages (CEFR) level B2.

The project was designed to follow the linking methodology suggested in the draft Manual (Council of Europe 2003), though in reality the operationalisation of the suggested procedures meant that a number of changes were necessitated. These changes, together with the main outcomes of the project are presented here along with reflections on the whole process. While City & Guilds embarked on the project with the main aim of establishing a link between the Communicator and CEFR level B2, it quickly became clear that an unintended benefit to participation in the project would reach beyond the Communicator itself. The lessons learned during the process have fed into the rest of the City & Guilds International ESOL suite and more recently into the broader organisation. The embedding of the processes and systems developed for the project (including assessment training; CEFR familiarisation as well as inter- and intra-organisational structures) has been the true 'added value' of the exercise.

Purpose and context of the project

Background

City & Guilds was established in 1878 and has a long history of assessment of English for specific and more recently for general purposes. City &

Guilds' ESOL examinations consist of two English proficiency suites, each set at six different levels. One suite is focused on speaking (Spoken ESOL), and the other on the other sub-skills (International ESOL, referred to here as IESOL). Development of the suite started in 2001 with the examinations launched in 2004. The decision was made early on in the development process to align the levels of the examinations with the levels of the CEFR.

Since the draft Manual for relating examinations to the CEFR (Council of Europe 2003) – henceforth referred to as the Manual – was not in existence during the development phase, the organisation embarked on a series of internal activities to ensure alignment to the external standards (the CEFR). However, with the publication of the Manual the logical step for the organisation was to set up a formal linking project.

The awareness that a linking project would be resource intensive led to the decision to focus on aligning the most popular level in the examination suite, B2. This chapter therefore deals with the CEFR mapping project for the IESOL examination at 'Communicator' level (B2).

Goals

The project was initially intended to provide evidence in support of a link between the Communicator and the CEFR. With this in mind, the project planned to include all four stages described in the Manual (Council of Europe 2003).

City & Guilds was also keen that the project would contribute to the professional development of its ESOL staff and to the overall quality of its examinations. With this in mind, the project described in this report is planned to be the first in a series, the end result of which will be the linking of all examinations in the IESOL suite to the relevant CEFR levels.

Relevance to national policy

All examinations in the IESOL and Spoken ESOL suites are accredited by the Qualifications & Curriculum Authority (QCA) in the United Kingdom, though the evidence they require of test level and quality is nothing like that expected in a Manual-driven linking project. The QCA is certainly aware of the importance of test level, and has joint-funded a project in which the levels in the CEFR were mapped to the levels in the National Qualifications Framework for England, Wales and Northern Ireland (West and Reeves 2003). However, limitations in the methodology of that project (links were established only through a comparison of descriptors) and in the whole approach to validation taken by the QCA calls into question the value of their accreditation of examinations in the UK. We can only hope that projects such as this will help raise the standards expected of tests in general in the UK and of the organisations that develop and monitor these tests.

The Communicator examination

The Communicator is a comprehensive test of reading, writing and listening skills in English. It is taken by non-native speakers of English worldwide for a variety of purposes, including as a precursor to language or academic study and for those who require externally recognised certification of their levels in English. For more information on the City & Guilds ESOL suite of examinations visit their website at: www.cityandguilds.com/cps/rde/xchg/cgonline/hs.xsl/3450.html

Reliability and validity evidence

The Communicator examination, like the other examinations in the IESOL suite, has been developed with direct reference to the CEFR and has used Weir's (2005) validation frameworks as its theoretical basis. The main value in using the frameworks is that the notion of validity is integrated into the development model from the planning stages. New items and tasks are written based on item writer guidelines that have been developed from the specifications, thus establishing a link between the items and the CEFR from the beginning. In addition, all tasks and items are routinely trialled and analysed from qualitative and quantitative perspectives to ensure quality and appropriateness of level, while *a posteriori* analysis of all tasks and items is routine.

Project design

Scope

The Communicator linking project was designed to follow the methodology described in the Manual (Council of Europe 2003).

Participants

Table 1 outlines the participants and their role at each stage of the project.

The critical review

In order to establish that the examination was of high quality and accuracy (in terms of level) a critical review panel was established. The rationale for including this element in the linking process was that we wished to avoid

Table 1: Participants

Stage	CLARe	City & Guilds	External
Critical Review	1 Chair	3 Panel	3 Panel
Familiarisation		2 Leaders	
		9 Group participants	
Specification	1 Form Completion	3 Form Completion	1 Reviewer
Standardisation	1 Judge	3 Judges	8 Judges
	1 Judge	3 Judges	8 Judges
	2 Judges	3 Judges	6 Judges
Validation	1 Planning and Delivery	3 Delivery	Teachers (x13)
			Learners (x330)

making any assumptions about the quality of the examination and felt that a critical review of all aspects of the examination would help the project. Test papers are typically written to reflect a specification, which itself is written to reflect current thinking on the language and on validation theory. Unless the developers are aware of the need to constantly reflect on the specification, so that it is fine-tuned to reflect changes in the language and in our understanding of validity and validation over time, it can relatively quickly become dated. Since it is not uncommon for the paper to 'slip', or move away from the specification in some way (e.g. task types can simply be copied or cloned with no regard for underlying assumptions regarding performance or the scoring system can drift, so that the critical boundary can shift up or down) there is a sort of double jeopardy here. It is unlikely that the changes in the test paper will happen to move with our understanding of the changes in the language and validity, so it is clear that the paper will become dated relatively quickly.

Most examination boards rely exclusively on internal quality assurance systems to ensure that the impact of any slippage is minimised. This approach, however, is likely to be negatively affected by the fact that the very people who are charged with maintaining quality may have had some significant input into the examination and will almost certainly have some loyalty to the organisation or brand. This can quite easily lead to complacency, in that the organisation will argue that since the systems are in place the examinations must be satisfactory, even though the systems themselves may be suspect. It is vital, therefore, that the critical review panel should not just reflect the opinions of internal stakeholders, but that it should include external experts who do not have any stake in the examination or the organisation. This means that the outcomes from the panel discussions are likely to be impartial and objective.

On a more practical level, including such a stage will go a long way towards ensuring that the evidence emerging from the standardisation and validation stages of the project will support the linking argument rather than question the integrity of the examination. In other words, there is no point in even starting on a linking project if you cannot be sure that the examination is of a high enough quality. We need unbiased evidence, hence the critical review.

The panel consisted of a Chair (from CLARe), three representatives from City & Guilds, including the chief examiner for Communicator, and three independent judges from outside both organisations. Participants had extensive experience with the CEFR and with assessment at the B2 level, while external panel members were also experienced teachers at the B2 level. Panel members were asked to review a set of Communicator tasks for all three papers and to make judgements in relation to overall level, appropriateness and quality. The first iteration of the review was carried out prior to the meeting, with each panel member given the test specifications and a set of tasks (up to three versions of every task in each paper) and asked to comment on how well these reflected the demands of the specifications, on how appropriately the tasks (and the specifications) reflected the target level (CEFR B2), and finally on the overall quality of the tasks (in terms of content and replicability). The data emerging from these comments was collated and analysed for emerging themes by the Chair and formed the basis of the discussions and later judgements' iterations during the critical review event.

The main outcome of the meeting was the recognition that the papers were likely to result in an overall level B2 performance. However, it was also felt that some minor changes to the specifications were required to ensure that the level could be more systematically achieved (i.e. to ensure that the tasks were more easily replicated in future test versions). Task versions, based on these recommendations, were re-specified and trialled. Results from the trials indicated that the mean scores achieved by learners on the tasks were very similar to those achieved for the Council of Europe recommended tasks for B2 (the participants had been asked to respond to Communicator tasks as well as recommended tasks). Based on this evidence, we now felt confident that the linking process could proceed.

The Familiarisation stage

As previously stated, the IESOL examination suite was designed to align with the levels of the CEFR. Therefore, familiarisation activities were initially carried out during the examination's development phase. These activities included: sorting the CEFR descriptors, self assessment of language levels and benchmarking samples of candidates' writing to the CEFR levels. Feedback from the activities suggested that even with this degree of familiarisation training, there was still some doubt about the true meaning of the levels, so it was decided to offer familiarisation training throughout the project. Some of the steps taken to increase the effectiveness of the familiarisation training by embedding it into staff development and adapting it to the needs of the organisation included:

- key stakeholders supplied with a copy of the CEFR in order to become familiar with the complete model
- familiarisation training carried out with City & Guilds staff responsible for managing and administering the assessments – this allows the methodology and meta-language associated with the CEFR to permeate throughout the organisation by being constantly discussed, reiterated and embedded.

In addition, familiarisation is a:

- fixed feature of item writer recruitment and development
- precursor to the item writer training sessions
- part of the regular examiner training sessions.

This model of familiarisation can be seen to incorporate three steps:

Communication	Ensuring that everyone involved in the process is speaking the same language by involving everyone in the training.
Documentation	The CEFR references were incorporated into the materials, so there is constant referral back to CEFR levels.
Systematisation	Feedback loops – working to make sure that familiarisation improves over time.

The Specification stage

Before completing the forms, we decided to re-write the test specifications using Weir's (2005) validation frameworks (O'Sullivan had demonstrated that this was feasible in projects such as QALSPELL 2004 and Exaver 2008). The reason for this rewriting of the specifications was to ensure that there was a clearly described theory of validity and validation running right through the project. This approach was vindicated as the project progressed, as it allowed a clear and explicit link to emerge between the different stages of the project.

The complete set of specification forms was initially completed at City & Guilds by the senior members of the IESOL team, reviewed by CLARe staff with a later discussion ensuring a consistent interpretation of what was required. This process was ongoing and iterative, with the specification forms constantly revisited as the project proceeded.

While the Manual (Council of Europe 2003) suggests that it should be possible at this point to make claims based only on the test specification, we feel that such claims are premature as the evidence gathered is based primarily on the developing institution's vision of the test papers. We believe that the claims made at this point are sufficiently strong only to allow for progression to the next stage.

The Standardisation stage

Standard-setting methods

A modified Angoff method was used for the Listening and Reading papers (Cizek and Bunch 2007) as it is appropriate to the type of test and is the most widely used standard-setting method. Judges were asked to first define the least competent learner at B2 (for each skill area), and then to predict how such individuals would respond to each item. To bolster the reliability of these judgements, judges were asked to indicate their level of confidence in each decision. For the Writing paper, a modified Examinee-Paper Selection Method was used.

Training of judges

Since pre-rating familiarisation with tasks and criteria can have a significant and positive impact on subsequent rating (Rethinasamy 2006), it was felt that all judges would benefit from a re-familiarisation activity focusing on level B2 and the two adjoining levels (B1 and C1). This was completed in all cases prior to the standard-setting events themselves.

It also became clear that the judges benefited from their participation in the events, as analysis indicated that they were more confident and more consistent as the project progressed. This suggests that we should also familiarise judges with the standard-setting methods we intend to use.

Standard-setting procedures

In order to demonstrate what we actually did, I will focus briefly on the procedure used for the listening (and reading) events.

Figure 1 offers an overview of the procedure used for the Reading and Writing papers. A draft version of the *minimally acceptable person* (MAP; or least able candidate to be more politically correct) at CEFR B2 was included in the panel members' package, which also included the re-familiarisation tasks, the sample tasks and the evaluation sheets. They were asked to consider this before the standard-setting event as it was the first item on the event's agenda. Following discussion, a final definition was agreed on. It should be noted that there is no *definitive* definition, as different test contexts (different learners, test purposes etc.) will make different demands so each definition may vary slightly. In coming to this definition, the panel members are expected to internalise the critical boundary between those candidates who should be seen as just about at the level and those who have yet to reach the level. Once this has been achieved, the panel members work independently to decide whether the person they have just defined will answer each item correctly (giving a score of 1) or incorrectly (giving a score of 0). We also asked each person to indicate how certain they were of this judgement (1=low to 4=high). A quick multi-faceted Rasch (MFR) analysis of the resulting data suggested a possible cut score (taking the mean *fair average* cut score for each of the panel members). We used MFR as it takes into consideration the harshness and leniency of the judges, and we were also able to use their confidence level as an intervening factor. However, for those who do not have expertise in using MFR, I would recommend that simple mathematical averages be used – these can be calculated in any spreadsheet programme (e.g. Excel). Since we had data from 330 learners who had taken the same test version we based the activity on, we were then able to generate passing and failing numbers based on the initial cut scores. The data from these two exercises then formed the basis of the feedback to the panel and the resulting discussion. The second round of judgements that followed was analysed in the same way and in the discussion that followed the panel agreed on a cut score, believing that further iterations would be unlikely to result in any meaningful change to the recommendation.

In the subsequent linking projects (all of the remaining five examinations in the ESOL series will have been linked to the CEFR by the time this volume has been published), we changed the system slightly, so that instead of asking the panel member to indicate their certainty, we asked them to again indicate whether the typical MAP would answer correctly (again 1) or incorrectly (again 0) and then to imagine 100 MAPs responding to each item. Now they were asked to indicate how many of these would answer each item correctly or incorrectly. In this procedure we used this second probability estimate to calculate the indicative cut score for each individual panel member and then averaged all of the panel members' cut scores to come up with a recommendation.

Figure 1: Overview of the modified Angoff procedure used

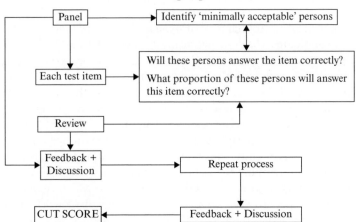

For the writing event, we asked the judges to use the existing Communicator rating scale for B2 to award grades to a set of 14 task performances. These tasks came from two sources (Communicator and the Council of Europe recommended tasks from Cambridge ESOL) and represented three levels (B1, B2 and C1). Judges were asked to use the three core levels of the B2 scale (1=a fail, 2=a pass, 3=a first class pass), while adding a lower level (0=clearly below the level) and a higher level (4=clearly above level). The rationale behind this approach was to allow the judges to consider performances across the entire B2 level. Allowing for decisions beyond the level limits any topping- or bottoming-off effect in the resulting decisions.

Results of standard setting

The standard-setting events indicated that the cut scores for both Listening and Reading (set in relation to the CEFR level B2) and the level of the writing performances reviewed were reached in a reliable and consistent manner, while there was a high level of agreement among the judges (Table 2).

Table 2: Judge agreement and consistency during standard setting

	N	Alpha	ICC	Mean Infit	St. Dev. Infit
Writing	9	.976	.971	1.0	.2
Listening	11	.909	.910	1.0	.2
Reading	11	.850	.848	1.0	.1

A follow-on study will test the validity of the cut scores by comparing the grade decisions made as a result of these with teacher judgements of learner level. A large scale piloting of both teacher and self assessment (based on 'Can Do' statements) has indicated that without training and familiarisation with the CEFR (for teachers) and self assessment (for learners) the exercise is unlikely to offer useful results.

The Empirical Validation stage

Due to limitations of space in this chapter, we must restrict ourselves to an overview of the main evidence gathered.

Brief overview of the validation evidence

Within the broad range of evidence amassed we included Cognitive, Context and Scoring aspects of validity which make up the core of the Weir (2005) frameworks. The evidence was structured in relation to the parameters in each of the above aspects of validity as described by Weir, and was presented as a series of tables, with arguments presented for all parameters. So, for example, when we looked at task purpose across the Listening paper, we were able to show that each task was attempting to assess a different aspect of listening, thus adding to the construct representativeness of the paper. In addition, we asked a group of learners (N=330) to respond to Communicator tasks and also to Council of Europe (CoE) exemplar tasks for level B2 (receptive skills).

Criterion-related evidence for Listening

Table 3 shows the results of a one-way ANOVA for the Listening data. We can see that there is no significant difference between the Communicator tasks and the CoE exemplar tasks, while *post-hoc* analysis confirmed that they were all within 1% of each other in terms of mean score achieved.

Table 3: One-way ANOVA (Listening)

	Sum of Squares	df	Mean Square	F	Sig.
Between Groups	.021	2	.010	.158	.854
Within Groups	64.527	987	.065		
Total	64.548	989			

Criterion-related evidence for Reading

The results from the Reading data were similar to those for Listening. Table 4 shows that there is again no significant difference between the mean scores achieved across the three sets of tasks (one set from the Communicator paper, and two from the CoE). In this case the *post-hoc* analysis also indicated that there was no significant difference across the tasks, indeed the greatest mean difference came to less than 2.5%.

Table 4: One-way ANOVA (Reading)

	Sum of Squares	df	Mean Square	F	Sig.
Between Groups	.088	4	.022	.469	.758
Within Groups	46.597	990	.047		
Total	46.685	994			

We feel that the evidence presented in the above tables, particularly when taken with the rest of the validation evidence contained in the final project report (O'Sullivan and Roberts 2008), allows us to make strong claims of a link between the Communicator Listening and Reading papers and the CEFR.

Scoring-related evidence for Listening and Reading

Table 5 summarises the data collected in support of the Scoring validity claim for Listening and Reading. These figures indicate that the psychometric qualities of the test are satisfactory.

Table 5: Scoring-related evidence for Listening and Reading

Parameter	Listening	Reading
Accuracy of the answer key	Systematically checked on production of task, then again both pre- and post-test administration	
Item performance	Ave. Item Facility=50.86 Ave. Item Disc.=0.36	Ave. Item Facility=48.84 Ave. Item Disc.=0.36
Internal consistency (α)	0.81 (Items=30)	0.77 (Items=30)
Standard error of measurement	1.73 Candidates within 2 points of the cut score will automatically have their scores reviewed	1.94 Candidates within 2 points of the cut score will automatically have their scores reviewed
Marker reliability	OMR is used to capture test scores – expected reliability is 99.98%	

Criterion-related evidence for Writing

As part of the standard-setting procedure, judges were asked to indicate the level of a set of scripts from City & Guilds and Cambridge ESOL (CoE exemplar scripts). The summary chart for the multi-faceted Rasch analysis (Linacre 1989) of the data from this activity indicates that the judges saw the tasks as representing clearly identifiable levels of achievement (Figure 2).

Figure 2: Summary chart for MFR analysis (Writing)

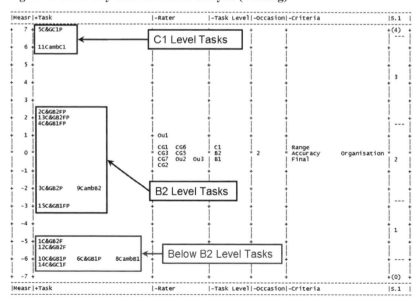

Some of the interesting things to emerge were:

- A strong level of agreement between original scores and those of the judges.
- Some unexpected outcomes, e.g. Item 15C&GB1FP (high B1) was seen by the judges to be at level B2. As it was originally awarded a First Class Pass it may well belong at the higher level.
- The perception of the judges that the First Class Pass performances at B2 were clearly separate from the lower Pass level performances.

Scoring-related evidence for Writing

The information presented in Table 6 indicates that the rating system has been systematically devised with the CEFR in mind. The figures (intra-class correlation coefficient and Cronbach's Alpha) also indicate that the decisions made were both consistent and in agreement.

Table 6: Scoring-related evidence for Writing

Parameter	Writing
Rating Scale	Developed based on the descriptors at level B2. That the scale is working well in that the grades awarded in the test were replicated in the trial, the probability curves from the MFR analysis indicate that the levels are consistent.
Rater Selection	Guidelines mean that only individuals who are experienced and qualified teachers at this level are eligible for selection.
Rater Training	Training is undertaken with the CEFR in mind, and all training decisions are made based on the framework.
Rater Monitoring	Raters are routinely monitored during the year to ensure they are on level. In addition rater agreement and intra-rater reliability are regularly measured.
Rater Agreement	Intra-class correlation coefficient − 0.971 Cronbach Alpha − .976
Rater Consistency	Intra rater reliability is high, as evidenced by the fact that no raters in the project were found to be misfitting.
Rating Conditions	Guidelines are in place to ensure that raters perform their work under set conditions. These are systematically monitored.
Grading and Awarding	Due to the on-demand nature of the test, this is not a feature of the examination that is easily operationalised. Cut scores are regularly monitored to ensure that results are fair.

Reflections on the use of the Manual

Quality assurance of the examination

It became clear to the project team right from the beginning that no linking should take place until there was evidence of the quality of the examination.

It also became clear that asking individuals from within the developing organisation to undertake such a task without the benefit of external expertise would be problematic, as organisational 'insiders' will always have some degree of bias in their judgements due to them having a stake in the outcome of the linking process. The 'external' members made a major contribution to the discussion and final decisions of the review panel.

Specification

It is not easy to visualise the link between the specification forms and the later validation of the examination, due to the fact that there is no explicit theoretical framework driving the linking process suggested in the Manual. As implied above, we felt strongly that any linking project must be seen from the broader perspective of validation. What we really needed to do was develop a validation argument with test *level* as a core element. In order to do this we first required an explicit model of validity and validation. These two concepts are different: the former refers to the theory of what validity *is* while the latter refers to the *practicality of establishing evidence* of validity. One major issue I had with the draft Manual (and now with the final version of the Manual) is that its authors have ignored (or were unaware of) the need for such an underlying model.

We dealt with this issue by re-writing the specifications of the Communicator itself with a view to validation. As mentioned earlier in this chapter, we used Weir's (2005) validation frameworks as a basis for this re-writing, and also as a basis for the presentation of the validity evidence in the final stage of the project as they not only offer a strong theoretical perspective on validity, but also suggest a practical process by which evidence can be gathered. We are not arguing that this is the only way to approach the issue, but we feel strongly that a clearly stated theoretical rationale for the process is vital if we are to expect test developers across Europe and beyond to allocate the considerable resources required of any linking project.

Standard setting

Perhaps the most vital issue to emerge from the standard-setting stage of the linking process was the make-up of the expert panel. While the Manual suggests a group of at least 15 members, we felt it more important to focus on the quality of the members (in terms of their expertise in assessment and in their knowledge of the CEFR levels) rather than on the number. We also felt that the lessons learned from the Critical Review stage of the process suggested that a panel comprised of a number of truly expert 'external' members, would add a great deal of value to any decisions taken during the project as a whole, and would add to the strength of any claims made.

The use of Council of Europe recommended tasks as exemplifications of CEFR level proved very useful, both in the earlier stages of the project when we were critically evaluating the Communicator, and at the standardisation and later validation stages. This was particularly true of the Writing paper, when we were able to compare the judgements made in relation to a number of Cambridge ESOL scripts at levels B1, B2 and C1.

One problem we had was that the level had to be based on a single exemplar. This meant that only one point within the level could be addressed and limited our ability to appreciate the broad range of ability represented. We are hopeful that one of the outcomes of the projects presented in this volume will be the broadening of our knowledge of the B2 and other CEFR levels through the submission of additional exemplars by the various groups involved. One example of how this might be of benefit is in defining the breadth of the level. For example, we saw above that the Communicator B2 level scripts awarded a First Class Pass bunch together, apparently at the upper boundary of the level, while the other B2 level tasks (from Communicator and Cambridge ESOL) bunch together at the lower end of the level. Further research into this phenomenon based on linking projects undertaken across Europe will be needed to confirm (or reject) our interpretation of what is happening.

Empirical validation

It was clear to the project group that the suggestion in the Manual that validation should focus on internal and external evidence of the psychometric qualities of a test being linked to the CEFR is both retrogressive (adapting as it does an outdated understanding of validation) and limiting (in that it does not demand the type of validation evidence expected of a modern test). Our solution was to use a set of established validation frameworks (Weir 2005) to link the specification of the examination to the later validation stage, and to base the validation evidence on the parameters suggested in these frameworks.

We found that using the frameworks allowed us to present a more coherent overview of the validation evidence for the Communicator while still considering the psychometric qualities of the examination. This again suggests to us that any revision of the Manual should carefully consider the theoretical model or models of validation which we should use to support our linking projects.

Limitations and future work

Like any project, this one was not without its limitations. Pressure of time and resources limited the number of participants in the validation project, though the population was sufficiently large to make strong claims of level and quality.

Some readers might feel that the relatively small size of the expert panels will limit their value. We take a very different perspective. We feel that the large panels put in place by some other examination boards for their standard-setting events add little to the quality of their decisions. Our smaller panel of truly expert judges from inside and outside City & Guilds strengthened the claims we were able to make and also means that these claims are more likely to achieve a broader recognition than would be the case had the panel been comprised only of insiders or of a large group of judges whose 'expertise' is questionable.

Impact

For the Communicator examination

We feel that the process of linking the Communicator examination to the CEFR has resulted in systematic and sustainable improvements to the test and to the system that supports the test.

It is clear to us that the process has resulted in a test that is more clearly at level, is sound from internal and external psychometric perspectives, is more replicable and of a higher quality. However, that is not all. The systems that support the examination have also been systematically improved and more explicitly linked to the CEFR.

For City & Guilds

This is just the beginning of the process. The decision has already been made to extend this project to include all examinations in the Spoken ESOL and IESOL suites. Preliminary work has already begun to ensure that the quality of the Communicator can be replicated across the suite. In fact, the whole process has had an impact on the organisation beyond the ESOL division. The expertise gained in participating in this project has strengthened the organisation in relation to its routine use of test item and task analysis (e.g. extending the use of Item Response Theory − IRT), its understanding of test quality and level, and perhaps more importantly to a renewed commitment to embed the lessons learned not only in the ESOL division but across the organisation. This notion of the embedding of quality assurance systems is, we feel, perhaps the greatest single contribution the drive to implement the CEFR and the Manual have had to date. We also feel that the understanding of test level as part of test validation has also grown significantly as a result of projects such as this, and other projects reported in this volume.

For the CEFR linking Manual

The experience we have had in delivering this project suggests an amendment to the linking model; see Figure 3. In this model, Familiarisation is an essential element of all stages of the process, though this familiarisation should extend beyond the CEFR to a familiarisation with the methodology employed at all stages.

Figure 3: Alternative model for linking a test to the CEFR

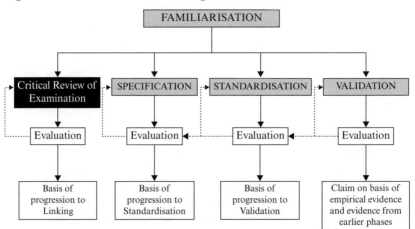

We also feel that the notion of continuous evaluation of progress through-out the linking process should be stressed. Even when the critical review has been completed and any changes that are recommended from this review are in place, we should evaluate the process and the product of the review. It is only when we feel that there is enough evidence to suggest that the test is acceptable in terms of quality and level, that we should contemplate a move to the Specification stage.

Like the Critical Review stage, we suggest that the specification forms should be critically evaluated on completion and only when the linking insti-tution is satisfied that the specification forms are an accurate reflection of the test and its supporting systems should the decision be made to move on to the Standardisation stage. If there are issues found at this stage we should return to the Critical Review stage to identify exactly what the problem or problems might be. In fact, we found that we were re-evaluating the speci-fication forms right to the end of the project. The same process of continu-ous review should be carried out during the Standardisation and Validation stages.

This constant reflection and evaluation means that the process is far from linear. Instead, we should be constantly considering how the findings of the project impact on the test and visa versa. Therefore, by the time we reach the end of the process, we can be quite certain that the test we have attempted to link to the CEFR is not only linked, but that the link is meaningful.

Concluding comments

We are not unhappy with the Manual. If we felt that it was not appropriate we would not have embarked on such a major project in which the methodology adapted was so closely based on the procedures suggested there. While we feel that both the draft and the final version are in need of improvement, we would also like to stress the tremendous value to our two organisations (City & Guilds and CLARe) that this project has brought.

References

Cizek, G J and Bunch, M B (2007) *Standard Setting*, Thousand Oaks, CA: Sage.

Council of Europe (2001) *Common European Framework of Reference for Languages: Learning, teaching, assessment*, Cambridge: Cambridge University Press.

Council of Europe (2003) *Relating Language Examinations to the Common European Framework of Reference for Languages: Learning, teaching, assessment: Preliminary Pilot Manual*, Strasbourg: Council of Europe, Language Policy Division.

Exaver (2008) *Exaver English Examinations Suite*, Universidad Veracruzana (Mexico) and Roehampton University (UK) affordable test development project. Website: www.uv.mx/exaver

Linacre, J M (1989) *Many-facet Rasch measurement*, Chicago: MESA Press.

O'Sullivan, B and Roberts, R (2008) *The Communicator Linking Project: Final Report*, London: City & Guilds.

QALSPELL (2004) *Quality Assurance in Language for Specific Purposes, Estonia Latvia, and Lithuania*, Leonardo da Vinci funded project. Website: www.qalspell.ttu.ee/index.html (accessed 18 July 2008).

Rethinasamy, S (2006) *The effects on rating performance of different training interventions*, unpublished PhD, Roehampton University, London.

Weir, C J (2005) *Language Testing and Validation: an evidence-based approach*, Oxford: Palgrave.

West, R and Reeves, N (2003) *Pathways to Proficiency: the alignment of language proficiency scales for assessing*, Nottingham: DfES Publications. Available online at: www.dfes.gov.uk/readwriteplus/bank/PathwaysToProficiency.pdf (accessed 18 July 2008).

2 Putting the Manual to the test: the TestDaF–CEFR linking project

Gabriele Kecker and Thomas Eckes
TestDaF Institute, Hagen, Germany

Abstract

The TestDaF Institute has taken part in the piloting of the Council of Europe's (2003) Manual based on the methodological steps outlined in the preliminary pilot version: familiarisation, specification, standardisation, and empirical validation. To examine the relation between the TestDaF (Test of German as a Foreign Language) and the Common European Framework of Reference for Languages (CEFR) levels, we conducted a series of studies encompassing all four sections of the test, following each of the four inter-related steps of the Manual approach. In the standardisation phase, we applied the Basket procedure (Kaftandjieva 2009:21) derived from the Angoff method and the benchmarking method as described in the Manual. We looked at inter-rater reliability employing consensus, consistency, and measurement approaches. Regarding empirical validation, the German section of DIALANG served as an external criterion measure for the receptive skills data. For validating the data on productive skills, we collected teacher judgements. Findings have implications for the Manual-based CEFR linking process in general, and for each of the methodological steps outlined in the Manual, in particular.

Introduction

The aim of the Manual *Relating Language Examinations to the Common European Framework of Reference for Languages: Learning, Teaching, Assessment (CEF)* made available by the Council of Europe (CoE) is to provide a sound methodology allowing testing institutions and researchers to link their assessment instruments to the CEFR. Testing agencies like the TestDaF Institute were invited to participate in the piloting process of the preliminary pilot version of the Manual (CoE 2003).

In the following section we will first describe the national context of the examination TestDaF (*Test Deutsch als Fremdsprache* – Test of German as a Foreign Language) and the reasons why the TestDaF Institute participated in the piloting process of the Manual. Then we give a brief overview of the examination content and its rationale. The third section provides an outline of the methodology applied in the linking study, and the fourth section focuses on the procedures followed showing which parts of the Manual were used and where amendments were made. In the last two sections, we present the results, and summarise and discuss our findings as well as the problems encountered in applying the Manual methodology.

Purpose and context of the linking project

The TestDaF Institute was founded in 2001 in order to administer the TestDaF, a high-stakes test officially recognised as a language entry exam for students from abroad. Examinees who have achieved at least TDN 4 in each of the test's four sections (TDN is short for *TestDaF-Niveaustufe*, TestDaF level) are eligible for admission to a German institution of higher education (Eckes, Ellis, Kalnberzina, Pižorn, Springer, Szollás, and Tsagari 2005). The TestDaF is to allow foreign applicants to prove their knowledge of German while still in their home country. The TestDaF Institute was founded to centrally construct and evaluate TestDaF tasks and items and to score TestDaF examinee performance.

During the test development phase, the TestDaF was linked indirectly to the CEFR scales using anchor items of the Association of Language Testers in Europe (ALTE) which had been calibrated previously to the ALTE scales. Due to the fact that the ALTE scales were correlated subsequently with the CEFR scales (Jones 2002), the TestDaF levels TDN 3, 4 and 5 were linked indirectly to the CEFR scales from Lower Vantage Level (B2.1) to Higher Effective Operational Proficiency (C1.2). Although the indirect linkage to the CEFR levels turned out to be an acceptable starting point, the linkage of this high-stakes test required a broader empirical basis and more direct approach. The Council of Europe's Manual and methodological approach to relate language examinations to the CEFR provided a suitable framework to put this project into practice. We decided to apply the methodology of the four inter-related steps (familiarisation, specification, standardisation, empirical validation) outlined in the Manual with regard to the following objectives:

- piloting the four methodological steps as outlined in the Manual (CoE 2003)
- validating the linkage claim of the TestDaF to the CEFR (levels B2 and C1) through an empirical approach; that is, we were interested in the boundaries of the lower (below B2) and upper cut score (above C1)
- linking each of the four TestDaF subtests to the CEFR; that is, two subtests measuring receptive skills (reading, listening) and two subtests measuring productive skills (writing, speaking).

Background to the TestDaF

Since 2001, the TestDaF has been administered worldwide in about 400 test centres in nearly 80 countries. The number of test administrations per year increased from two exams in 2001 to nine exams in 2007 (including three separate exams in the People's Republic of China). Up to the end of 2009, more than 96,000 candidates took this examination, about half of them in Germany. Countries of origin like the People's Republic of China, Russia, Bulgaria, Turkey, Poland and Ukraine represent the main focus of the candidature. Recently, the number of candidates from South Korea and Japan has risen sharply.

Since the TestDaF measures language ability required for beginning study at an institution of higher education in Germany, content and tasks are closely related to academic, scientific, and study-relevant topics.

The TestDaF measures reading, listening, writing, and speaking in separate sections. In the reading and listening sections, examinees have to prove their ability to understand and respond adequately to texts relevant to academic life presented in writing or orally, respectively. Various types of tasks and items are used, including a matching task, multiple-choice questions, and forced-choice items of the type 'yes/no/no relevant information in the text' for reading, and short-answer and true/false questions for listening. The writing section is designed to assess an examinee's ability to produce a coherent and well-structured text on a given topic taken from an academic context including description of statistical data and argumentation. Similarly, the speaking section taps an examinee's ability to communicate appropriately in typical situations of university life; its format is based on the Simulated Oral Proficiency Interview (SOPI; see Kenyon 2000), and the candidates' responses are recorded on tape or CD. For more detailed descriptions of the test format see www.testdaf.de; see also Althaus (2004) and Grotjahn (2004).

Examinee proficiency is represented in terms of TDN levels: TDN 3, TDN 4, or TDN 5. There is no differentiation of language proficiency below TDN 3. An official certificate, issued by the TestDaF Institute, documents an applicant's proficiency level attained in each language skill.

Project design

As already stated, we decided to apply all four methodological steps of the CoE's Manual to each of the four sections of the TestDaF in order to collect sufficient data for the linking process. Relying only on specification is considered as a 'minimum standard' of the linking procedure in the Manual (CoE 2003:29). It is a descriptive approach that provides a content analysis of the test but is not meant to generate the data needed to know whether the candidates' ability is at the intended level of the test. Hence, a standard-setting procedure is called for. Finally, external validation is required to support the conclusions drawn from the previous methodological steps.

Table 1: Timetable of the TestDaF linking project

Methodological steps	Linking procedures
1. Familiarisation	• Work groups of internal staff members 2004/2005 • Experts/judges during standardisation workshops 2005/2006
2. Specification	Work group sessions of internal staff members 2005
3. Standardisation of Judgements	• Preliminary standard-setting workshop for receptive skills 06/2005 (10 judges) • Benchmarking workshop for written production in 02/2006 (14 judges) • Standard-setting workshop for receptive skills 05/2006 (15 judges) • Benchmarking workshop for spoken production 10/2006 (12 judges)
4. Empirical Validation	Examination April 2008 Correlation with external criteria: a) DIALANG b) Teacher judgements of candidates who took the TestDaF

Familiarisation

The Manual stated in several places (CoE 2003:6, 25) that familiarisation with the CEFR and the relevant scales represented a precondition for any linking procedure. This applies for the staff members of the testing institution involved in the linking process as well as for the invited experts or judges of the standardisation procedure. TestDaF staff members were to be trained before the start of the specification and standardisation phases in order to acquire an in-depth knowledge of the CEFR concept and scales and to harmonise their understanding of the underlying proficiency. Experts invited to the standard-setting and benchmarking workshops of the standardisation phase should receive training at the beginning of their workshops or shortly before. The Manual provides a broad range of training material for both groups.

Information about the experts' level of satisfaction with their training in applying the CEFR scales represents an important element of validity evidence in the linking process. An evaluation questionnaire for the experts provides an appropriate instrument to get the desired information (see Hambleton 2001). Data on the experts' consistency and reliability during the standardisation workshops were planned to be collected in the standardisation phase and will provide an additional basis to judge the success of the familiarisation.

Specification of the examination content

According to the Manual approach, the specification of the examination content included two parts: providing evidence of internal validity, and providing evidence of external validity of the examination through a descriptive method. The first part (evidence of internal validity) is a precondition for the whole linking process, since only testing instruments of good quality and equivalent level across different test versions can be linked to a scale (Takala 2007). Internal validation procedures described in the Manual in Chapter 6 on empirical validation, will be treated in this study in 'Specification'. For the analysis of psychometric test quality, classical test theory and item response theory were used (Eckes 2008a). In addition, several qualitative methods were also applied: real-time verbal reports (Arras 2007), task characteristic frameworks, as well as feedback questionnaires for examiners and candidates.

The second part, which focuses on external validity, is the first step of the linking procedure and results in a content analysis of the examination in terms of the CEFR (forms A9 to A22 of the Manual). At the TestDaF Institute, this qualitative approach was adopted and amended by incorporating the CEFR Grids for the analysis of test tasks in the process (see CoE website[1], retrieved 10 July 2008). The grids allowed a more precise analysis of linguistic and cognitive complexity of tasks, items and texts and thus facilitated the classification of difficulty and the linking to the scales. The following procedure was first applied by the project co-ordinator and in a second phase verified by three additional staff members responsible for the test development in the different test sections: (a) selection of the CEFR scales appropriate for the TestDaF, (b) analysis of the test tasks and items with the CEFR Grids, (c) selection of the suitable descriptors in the different CEFR scales, (d) justification of level assignment.

Standardisation of judgements

Concerning standard setting in the receptive skills, the Manual proposed a modification of the Yes/No variant of the Angoff method which had also been used in the DIALANG project (CoE 2003:91) and is known as the Basket procedure (Kaftandjieva 2009:21). Unlike the Yes/No variant of the Angoff method as described, for example, in Impara and Plake (1997) and Cizek (2006), this method does not use the concept of an imaginary borderline person, but of an imaginary proficient person. This has proved to be easier for experts (Alderson 2005:70). Another advantage of the present method is the possibility to integrate feedback data for the experts and consequently have several rounds of judgements and discussion (Cizek and Bunch 2007:84). Additionally, the Angoff method is based on an analytic model of achievement and therefore fits the test format in TestDaF sections of reading and listening, which consists of dichotomously scored items aggregated to a total score per skill (Kane 2001). Short-answer questions are rated using a mark scheme and therefore allow dichotomous scoring as well.

The Basket method was applied to the TestDaF standard-setting procedure for the receptive skills using the following format: judgement training with standardised items in German including individual assessment and discussion, feedback on the outcome of rating, and normative data (item statistics); judgement process with individual assessment of local TestDaF items; no other data was provided. Adjustments of judgements were made when necessary, that is, in case of inconsistency. The decision rule for the cut-score establishment was based on the number of items correctly answered by a person on a specific level. We decided to check the methodological approach in a preliminary workshop (see Table 1) and modified the applied procedures according to our experiences.

In the Manual, the method of benchmarking was described briefly in Chapter 5.6 as a method of standardisation for productive skills. Other methods for the standard setting of constructed response items are discussed by Kaftandjieva (2004) and were applied and described in previous research (e.g., Cizek 2001, 2006, Hambleton and Pitoniak 2006). For reasons of practicability, we decided to pilot the benchmarking approach of the Manual in a modified variant and not to choose, for example, the Contrasting Groups method or the Borderline Group method. The following approach of the Manual benchmarking method was adopted for TestDaF tasks in the productive skills: judgement training in benchmarking with standardised performance samples in German including individual assessment and discussion, feedback on the outcome of rating, and normative data (CEFR level); judgement process with individual assessment of local TestDaF samples; no other data provided, no discussion allowed; adjustments of judgements if necessary.

In contrast to the Manual that suggested a plenary discussion both for training and for actual benchmarking (CoE 2003, Table 5.6, page 81 and Chapter 5.6, page 88), we focused on individual assessments without discussion, since we were interested in independent judgements of the experts on our TestDaF performance samples. This decision was strengthened by the ambition to avoid conflicts of interest for the testing institution, the latter being possibly tempted to influence experts in discussions (Linn 2003:8).

The selection of experts or judges for the standardisation workshops is regarded as a crucial aspect of the standardisation process (Cizek and Bunch 2007, Hambleton and Pitoniak 2006, Kane 2001). We followed two main points which Raymond and Reid (2001:154) considered as a 'common-sense' version of their more extensive guidelines for the selection of experts: (a) they should be familiar with the examinee population and with the subject matter concerned; (b) they should represent all relevant stakeholders. Prior research and practice suggested that a number of 10 to 15 experts per panel represented a sound basis in order to get reliable data for the validation process (Raymond and Reid 2001). This suggestion guided our standard-setting and benchmarking workshops (see Table 1).

Empirical validation

Following the methodological steps outlined in Chapter 6 of the Manual, there are two basic ways to use external criterion measures: (a) correlation of TestDaF results with teacher judgements on the same group of examinees, and (b) correlation of TestDaF results with results of an identical group of examinees taking a similar B2/C1 test (of course, such a test would need to be calibrated to the CEFR).

We decided to apply both methods considering the fact that there was no calibrated German achievement or proficiency test available at that time which had undergone a similar linking procedure as described in the Manual and which entirely covered the four sections of the TestDaF and the relevant CEFR levels B2 and C1. On the other hand, it was not advisable to focus on teacher judgements alone, in the light of limited opportunities for worldwide teacher training and time constraints when requiring judgements from teachers in four different skills.

We selected DIALANG (German version) as a criterion test. DIALANG was developed between 1996 and 2004 with financial support from the European Commission. It was calibrated to the CEFR and had undergone standard-setting procedures (Alderson 2005:6–78). The correlation of a computer-based online test designed for self-assessment purposes with an academic purpose proficiency test like TestDaF certainly had feasibility constraints because it used a different medium and had no time restrictions for candidates working on a task. However, the comparison of the constructs measured in DIALANG and in TestDaF showed that the two receptive skills seemed to be sufficiently similar in their aspects of reading and listening competence. The constructs of the Written Production skill in the two tests overlapped only slightly due to the fact the TestDaF measures text production in a direct performance test (constructed-response task) and DIALANG addresses a more indirect writing competence (selected-response items and short-answer questions). Since DIALANG does not measure Spoken Production, the correlation TestDaF–DIALANG was limited to the receptive skills and had to be complemented by other criteria for the productive skills.

For writing and speaking, judgements of teachers working at licensed test centres of the TestDaF Institute, and preparing future TestDaF candidates for the examination, were employed as criterion measures. The teachers' personal knowledge of the candidates over a longer period of time (at least two weeks) enabled them to assign the assumed level of proficiency to the CEFR scales (Schneider and North 2000). Restricting the sample of candidates to those who could be considered as prototypes of a particular CEFR level (i.e., as the most representative learners at a given level), helped to ensure a sufficiently high reliability of the judgements (Eckes 2010). In our case, this seemed particularly important in the light of lacking training opportunities for teachers abroad, as required by Schneider and North (2000).

Procedures

Familiarisation

Staff members of the TestDaF Institute participated in the familiarisation phase at the end of 2004 and in the beginning of 2005 before the start of the specification and standardisation phases. Familiarisation of the experts involved in the standardisation phase took place during the workshops organised by the TestDaF Institute (Table 1).

In the preliminary workshop the experts had 1.5 hours to familiarise themselves with the CEFR concept and the CEFR scales using exercises and material of the Manual, Chapter 3 (CoE 2003:26–27). At the end of the workshop, they filled in a questionnaire that aimed to evaluate the different phases of the workshop. Based on the obtained data, the following aspects of the familiarisation phase posed some difficulties: (a) lack of time for familiarisation with CEFR and CEFR Grid; (b) too many scales; in particular, those not applied during the actual standard setting (self-assessment grids of DIALANG and European Language Portfolio) should be left out for training.

In response to these results, the following workshops in 2006 were extended to 2.5 days instead of 2 days. The first half day was designated for familiarisation with the CEFR (2 hours 15 minutes) and partly for the application of the different CEFR Grids.

Specification

Internal validity

Data on the TestDaF quality assurance process, in particular concerning the test development process and the item analysis procedures are described in detail elsewhere (Eckes 2008a). In addition, procedures such as the following were set in place for purposes of validating the TestDaF construct: questionnaires for candidates judging the difficulty and appropriateness of the test; DIF analysis related to candidate gender; research on rater types and rater effects (Eckes 2005, 2008b, 2009b); validation studies on retest reliability.

External validity

For the content analysis in terms of the CEFR we used the relevant forms of the Manual corresponding to the test format (forms A9–A22, see CoE 2003), the CEFR overall scales for each skill, and the CEFR scales listed in Table 2, which fit to the construct of the test tasks.

Table 2: CEFR scales used for specification

CEFR scales for receptive skills	CEFR scales for productive skills
Reading Comprehension	Written Production
Reading for Orientation Reading for Information and Argument Identifying Cues and Inferring	Reports and Essays
Listening Comprehension	Spoken Production
Understanding Conversation between Native Speakers Listening as a Member of a Live Audience Note-Taking Identifying Cues and Inferring	Addressing Audiences Sustained Monologue (describing experience)

Problems

The description of the TestDaF tasks in terms of CEFR descriptors faced the following problems:

- not all descriptors of a single selected CEFR scale level fit to the TestDaF task under scrutiny
- several CEFR scales had to be consulted for the assignment of a single TestDaF task (Reading and Listening Comprehension, Written Production)
- certain parts of the descriptors were not applicable or observable, for example, in a Listening Comprehension test: '. . . but may find it difficult to participate effectively in discussion with native speakers who do not modify their language in any way' (CoE 2001:66, scale *Understanding conversation between native speakers*)
- single elements of the TestDaF tasks in Written and Spoken Production were not described in CEFR scales (e.g., to describe statistical data in a graph).

Standardisation of judgements

The standardisation of judgements was organised with external judges or experts in several workshops (Table 1). Each workshop took place over

2.5 days, except the preliminary workshop, where the methodology and the procedures had been tried out. For each workshop, between 10 and 15 participants were invited. The invited experts represented three groups: (a) language teachers at universities or exam centres with more than five years of experience in teaching the target group, (b) TestDaF item writers and/or raters with at least three years of experience, and (c) test developers from our own and other testing institutions.

Judgement procedure for standard setting

The two receptive skills followed the same overall design. Experts were asked to respond to the listening or reading tasks themselves and then to consult the key and check their answers. They received one booklet with items for training (CoE 2005) and a second one for the standard setting of TestDaF items (a complete subtest for listening from *Modellsatz 02*, TestDaF Institute 2005a, live test administered with 1,877 examinees in 2004, Cronbach's Alpha=.81; and a complete subtest for reading, modified sample test *Musterprüfung 1*, TestDaF Institute 2005b, test administered worldwide in 2001 and again 2003 in China with a total of 620 examinees, Cronbach's Alpha=.86).

To estimate item difficulty, the relevant CEFR Grid in German translation was briefly discussed. Then, experts had to assign the items to a CEFR level (six levels and three plus levels) while considering the relevant CEFR scales for reading or listening. They had to answer the following question: 'At what CEFR-level can a test taker already answer the following items correctly?' During training, judges were asked to note their first individual assignment on an extra rating form which was collected to provide them with feedback on their rating (Excel graph) before group discussion. The final decision about the level assignment had to be written down after discussion on the rating form B5 of the Manual. Feedback on item performance was given after the final rating (facility, point-biserial correlation, number of test takers). This procedure guaranteed that any modification of the rating before and after the group discussion became evident. Expert ratings were completed in an anonymous fashion.

Judgement procedure for benchmarking

The judgement procedure during training followed the different steps depicted in the rating form B5 and integrated feedback and discussion: first global impression of the performance, followed by a feedback on the rating in plenary (Excel graph), discussion, followed by analytic rating taking into account the different categories of performance, followed by another discussion and a final rating. Feedback on the performance level and discussion finished the sequence. Decision making for the local performance samples followed the same steps, yet without discussion or feedback.

Problems

Throughout the entire procedure, we observed the following problems that might have influenced the results:

- The use of the CEFR Grid[2] for the analysis of reading and listening tasks and items in English caused time constraints in our preliminary workshop. Therefore, the time schedule of all our subsequent workshops had to be adjusted, and the CEFR Grids translated into German and sent out to the experts before the start of the workshop. Nevertheless, experts found it difficult to come to a judgement about an item level using both the relevant CEFR scale and the CEFR Grid. Not all categories of the grid[3] seemed to be appropriate to guide them to a judgement about the relevant CEFR level. In the standard-setting workshop in 2006, experts were asked instead to consider the CEFR scales first and to consult the grid only optionally.

- The choice of the standardised CoE performance samples available at the CoE website and used for training in Written Production was limited in number (only seven samples) and format (mostly letter format). The selected samples had a high level of correctness, and the experts located some samples at the higher end of the respective CEFR levels (C1 and C2 samples) or even above the intended level (A2 sample). Compared to these samples, local performance samples of the TestDaF exam were likely to be rated exceedingly low. Moreover, it proved to be rather demanding for the experts to compare training samples to TestDaF samples, as the TestDaF task required different cognitive processes ('synthesise information and arguments from a number of sources', B2 on the *Reports and Essays* scale; description of statistical data in a graph).

- The same problem occurred during the workshop for Spoken Production. Here, the standardised training samples were chosen from samples rated by international experts during the 'Seminar to calibrate spoken performance samples to the CEFR' held by the Goethe-Institut in Munich in October 2005 (Bolton, Glaboniat, Lorenz, Perlmann-Balme and Steiner 2008). On the whole, seven samples were selected, showing a good degree of consensus during the seminar and covering the range of six CEFR levels. Only the video sequences of oral production were selected; interaction sequences were only presented in cases of doubt. The videos were not shown in the workshop, only the sound was presented.

- The training samples all consisted of three tasks: a short introduction of the candidate herself, a presentation task, and an interaction task with two candidates, whereas in the TestDaF section of Spoken Production candidates had to deal with seven tasks for production (SOPI). Two

TestDaF tasks called for description and summary of statistical data in a graph and expression of a hypothesis; these language functions were not incorporated in the standardised training samples.

Empirical validation

DIALANG

A representative sample of TestDaF examinees was selected on a voluntary basis: a total of 147 TestDaF examinees participated (54.8% European, 45.2% non-European; 40.4% male, 59.6% female; 87.7% of the examinees were between 17 and 25 years old). Due to technical problems, only data from 133 examinees could be used for reading, and only 143 for listening. Examinees had to take the TestDaF first (April 2008) and subsequently, within a period of two weeks, DIALANG at the same test centre. They received a detailed description of the different steps in DIALANG and had to fill in an assessment form giving details about their self-assessment, the score of the vocabulary placement test, the score of the reading and listening section, and the CEFR level shown by DIALANG as a final result. The examinees' results in the reading and listening section of the TestDaF were compared to their results in these two skills in the DIALANG (see 'Results').

Teacher judgements

Teachers working with TestDaF candidates in preparation courses at TestDaF test centres during a period of at least two weeks were asked to participate in the project. A total of 19 teachers took part and rated between three and 15 candidates each; on average, each teacher rated eight candidates. For writing, the sample consisted of 154 TestDaF examinees; for speaking, 156 examinees participated (58.5% European, 41.5% non-European; 36.5% male, 63.5% female; 71.1% were between 17 and 25 years old).

The teachers received an introduction to the project and to their task and had to assess candidates using the global scales of Written Production and Spoken Production. Before they started the assessment they received a sorting exercise of the scales which they had to do as a kind of training. Within a period of two weeks before the TestDaF exam or two weeks after, they had to select representative TestDaF candidates (prototype candidates) of their preparation course for the level B1 or B2 or C1 in each skill considered and allocate them to the above-mentioned scales. Participants showing proficiency below B1 were not likely to join the course as they were generally advised not to take the test. The candidates' results in the two productive skills of the TestDaF were compared to the CEFR levels awarded to them by the teachers.

Problems

Examinees who took the DIALANG test faced technical problems. The reading section of the test did not show all distractors of the multiple-choice items on the screen. Apparently, these problems occurred, because certain software systems did not fit entirely to the DIALANG system. About eight items were affected by these problems (items 3, 16, 17, 18, 19, 21, 22, 23). In these cases, the candidates could not respond to the items correctly and therefore could not reach a result representing their actual proficiency level. The scores of 14 candidates were biased by this effect and were not considered further. Possibly, the results of other candidates were similarly affected, but they failed to report any problems. One candidate reported on a breakdown of the program after having worked on item 19.

Results

Overview

In this section, we mainly focus on standardisation and empirical valida-tion. Results of the specification phase are dealt with only briefly. Results of the familiarisation phase are reported in the section about standardisation (reliability). Data from an evaluation questionnaire distributed during the standardisation workshops indicated that the familiarisation with the CEFR could be considered successful: 57% of the experts judged the introduction to the CEFR as very successful, 43% as successful; 46% considered the CEFR scales as very important for classifying candidate performances, 46% as important, and 8% as partially important.

Specification

On the whole, the assignment of the four TestDaF sections to the levels B2 and C1 of the relevant CEFR scales was confirmed. Nevertheless, in apply-ing the CEFR scales to the TestDaF tasks, we detected a tendency towards level B1+ in listening and reading, and towards C2 in reading. In writing and speaking, the descriptors of the levels B2 and C1 of the scales fit to the tasks, but parts of the TestDaF construct (describing data in a graph) could not be related to any scale.

Standardisation

Overview of data analysis

According to the Manual (CoE 2003), the standardisation phase involves (a) implementing a common understanding of the CEFR levels, and (b) confirming that such a common understanding has been achieved.

Therefore, to examine the degree to which our judges were on common ground when rating TestDaF items and performance samples in terms of CEFR levels, we performed various analyses providing evidence on inter-rater reliability. In each TestDaF section, we used three different approaches to estimate the reliability of judgements: the consensus, the consistency, and the measurement approach (see, for a detailed comparison of these approaches, Stemler and Tsai 2008).

The consensus approach to inter-rater reliability aims at assessing the extent to which independent raters provided exactly the same rating of a particular person or object. In contrast, the consistency approach to inter-rater reliability focuses on the relative ordering or ranking of the persons or objects rated.

Given that consensus and consistency approaches each refer to distinct aspects of inter-rater reliability, it is important not to rest one's conclusions on a single index alone. In our reliability analysis, we computed three consensus and consistency indices each.

The consensus indices used were: (a) exact agreement index, (b) rater agreement index (RAI; Burry-Stock, Shaw, Laurie and Chissom 1996), (c) within-group agreement index (r_{wg}; James, Demaree and Wolf 1984). The consistency indices used were: (a) mean Pearson correlation coefficient (mean Pearson-r), (b) Kendall's W (coefficient of concordance), (c) Cronbach's Alpha.

The third approach to inter-rater reliability, the measurement approach, is markedly different from the first two approaches. The measurement approach expands the basic Rasch model to include the additional facet of judges, beyond the facets of examinees and items. This approach rests on the *many-facet Rasch measurement model* (*MFRM* or *facets model*; Linacre 1989; Linacre and Wright 2002; see also Eckes 2009a).

In our application of the facets model, we employed the computer program FACETS (Version 3.61; Linacre 2006). However, we used this model in the standard-setting and benchmarking stages (final ratings) only. The reason for this was that the goal of the training stages (i.e., reaching perfect consensus among the judges through multiple rating-and-discussion rounds) runs counter to the assumptions of the many-facet Rasch model, which construes the judges as independent experts rating items on an individual basis (Linacre 1998).

Judgements of reading items

Table 3 shows the consensus and consistency indices for judgements of reading items in the two phases of the training stage (i.e., before and after group discussion), as well as in the standard-setting stage.

Several conclusions can be drawn: (1) Reaching exact agreement on judging the reading items along the CEFR scale was extremely difficult, if not impossible; even after discussion of disagreements in the training stage, we

Table 3: Inter-rater reliability indices for ratings of reading items in training and standard-setting stages

Inter-rater reliability	Training		Standard setting
	Before discussion	**After discussion**	
Consensus indices			
Exact agreement	.38	.47	.40
Rater agreement index (RAI)	.91	.93	.92
Within-group agreement index (r_{wg})	.88	.93	.91
Consistency indices			
Pearson-r (mean)	.90	.94	.67
Kendall's W	.84	.90	.70
Cronbach's Alpha	.99	.99	.96

*Note: Pearson-*r *values ranged from .77 to 1.0 (before discussion), from .84 to .99 (after discussion), and from .26 to .95 (standard setting).*

observed only 47% exact agreements. (2) Yet, most disagreements were due to differences by only a few scale points, as the other two consensus indices demonstrate; that is, both the RAI and the r_{wg} document a high level of agreement before discussion of first-round ratings commenced, and agreement was even higher after discussion. (3) There was more variability of judgements in the standard-setting stage than in the training sessions; as evidenced by the relatively low values of mean Pearson-r and Kendall's W, the final ordering of the items along the 9-point CEFR scale seemed to be somewhat inconsistent among judges. (4) Overall, judges reached a sufficiently high level of reliability before the start of the standard-setting stage.

Based on final judgements of reading items provided in the standard-setting session, we conducted a FACETS analysis. This analysis revealed that three judges performed inconsistently. We eliminated these judges from further analysis.

Next, we computed cut scores according to the procedure outlined in the Manual (2003:91). That is, we (a) counted, for each of the 12 judges separately, the number of reading items up to each level, (b) averaged these counts over judges, and (c) rounded averages down. Table 4 presents the results of this cut-score computation for the relevant CEFR levels from B1+ up to C1.

The cut scores empirically derived through the process of standard setting are in fairly close agreement with the cut scores operationally used beforehand with this particular TestDaF examination (with this exam, at least 15 points were required for TDN 3, at least 21 points for TDN 4, and at least 26 points for TDN 5). As can be seen, though, the range of the relevant cut scores shown in Table 4 is five points larger than the range of the operationally used cut scores.

Table 4: Setting cut scores on the TestDaF reading section

CEFR level	TDN level	M	SD	Cut Score
B1+	–	5.67	3.11	5
B2	3	13.33	3.53	13
B2+	4	21.50	2.58	21
C1	5	29.42	0.67	29

Note: Number of raters=12.

Judgements of listening items

Table 5 shows the reliability indices for judgements of listening items in the two phases of the training stage (i.e., before and after group discussion), as well as in the standard-setting stage.

Table 5: Inter-rater reliability indices for ratings of listening items in training and standard-setting stages

Inter-rater reliability	Training		Standard setting
	Before discussion	After discussion	
Consensus indices			
Exact agreement	.37	.46	.37
Rater agreement index (RAI)	.90	.93	.92
Within-group agreement index (r_{wg})	.84	.93	.90
Consistency indices			
Pearson-r (mean)	.81	.90	.80
Kendall's W	.80	.88	.82
Cronbach's Alpha	.98	.99	.98

Note: Pearson-r values ranged from .41 to .98 (before discussion), from .78 to .98 (after discussion), and from .63 to .93 (standard setting).

The consensus and consistency values observed for the judgements of listening items reveal much the same pattern as the values observed for the judgements of reading items: fairly low exact agreement, yet sufficiently high agreement as shown by the other indices, particularly after discussion. In the standard-setting stage, judges accomplished the task of rating the listening items along the 9-point CEFR scale in a more consistent way than they did when rating the reading items.

The FACETS analysis of the final judgements in the standard-setting stage showed that one judge performed inconsistently. This judge was eliminated from further analysis.

We computed cut scores for the set of listening items in the same way as we did for the set of reading items. Table 6 presents the results of this cut-score computation for the relevant CEFR levels from B1+ up to C1.

Table 6: Setting cut scores on the TestDaF listening section

CEFR level	TDN level	M	SD	Cut Score
B1+	–	7.20	2.73	7
B2	3	12.40	3.60	12
B2+	4	16.20	3.26	16
C1	5	23.53	1.46	23

Note: Number of raters=14.

The agreement between the empirically derived cut scores and the cut scores that were operationally used beforehand with this particular TestDaF examination is even somewhat higher than for the reading items (with this exam, at least 12 points were required for TDN 3, at least 17 points for TDN 4, and at least 21 points for TDN 5). Still, the range of the relevant cut scores shown in Table 6 is two points larger than the range of the operationally used cut scores.

Judgements of written production samples

The samples of written production considered were the standardised (CoE) samples used in the training stage and the local (TestDaF) samples used in the benchmarking stage. We analysed the final ratings only, which were provided after group discussion in the training stage, and individually (i.e., without discussion) in the benchmarking stage. Table 7 shows the consensus and consistency indices for the judgements of written production samples in the training stage (i.e., after group discussion) and in the benchmarking stage.

Table 7: Inter-rater reliability indices for ratings of written production samples in training and benchmarking stages

Inter-rater reliability	Training	Benchmarking
Consensus indices		
Exact agreement	.63	.30
Rater agreement index (RAI)	.95	.89
Within-group agreement index (r_{wg})	.97	.83
Consistency indices		
Pearson-r (mean)	.98	.81
Kendall's W	.97	.81
Cronbach's Alpha	.99	.98

Note: Pearson-r values ranged from .95 to 1.0 (training) and from .50 to .96 (benchmarking).

The results can be summarised as follows: (1) Consensus and consistency indices confirmed that, at the end of the training stage, our judges had reached a very high level of inter-rater reliability; nearly two out of three judgements were exact agreements. (2) Since the aim of the training was to push the judges as close as possible toward the correct rating, that is, to the CoE-calibrated level, we are safe to conclude that the training stage was successful. (3) At the end of the benchmarking stage, the level of inter-rater reliability was still satisfactorily high; yet, we observed exact agreements in only 30% of the judgements.

Using the final judgements of TestDaF performance samples provided in the benchmarking session as input, we conducted a FACETS analysis. This analysis also allowed us to examine the degree of congruence between the samples' pre-assigned TestDaF level on the one hand and the CEFR level as assigned by the judges on the other.

Figure 1: Variable map from the FACETS analysis of judgements of nine written production samples (WPS). The horizontal dashed lines in the Scale column indicate the category threshold measures. Scale categories 1–9 refer to CEFR levels A1–C2 (including plus levels).

Logit	Sample	Judge	Scale
	High	*Severe*	
			(9)
5			
	WPS_5		
4			8
3	WPS_9		
	WPS_6		

2			
	WPS_2 WPS_8	A5	7

1		A3	
		H1	6
	WPS_1	A4 H3 H5 T2	-----
0		A1	
	WPS_4	H4 T3	5
		A2 A7	-----
−1		T1 T4	
			4
	WPS_7		
−2	WPS_3		-----
			3

−3			(1)
	Low	*Lenient*	

Table 8: Inter-rater reliability indices for ratings of spoken production samples in training and benchmarking stages

Inter-rater reliability	Training	Benchmarking
Consensus indices		
Exact agreement	.75	.32
Rater agreement index (RAI)	.97	.87
Within-group agreement index (r_{wg})	.98	.76
Consistency indices		
Pearson-r (mean)	.98	.84
Kendall's W	.98	.87
Cronbach's Alpha	.99	.98

*Note: Pearson-*r *values ranged from .93 to 1.0 (training) and from .59 to .98 (benchmarking).*

All judges performed consistently in terms of judge fit statistics. The variable map representing the calibrations of the nine TestDaF samples, the 14 judges, and the 9-point rating scale is displayed in Figure 1.

Overall, the ordering of the TestDaF samples along the logit scale was in good agreement with the TestDaF level assignments, and also with the intended CEFR levels. That is, Sample 3 had the pre-assigned TestDaF level below TDN 3 (calibrated to be placed somewhat below the threshold between CEFR levels A2+ and B1), Samples 7 and 4 were at TDN 3 (placed at B1 and B1+, respectively), Samples 1 and 8 were at TDN 4 (placed at B2 and B2+, respectively), and Samples 2 (placed at B2+), 6, 9 and 5 were at TDN 5 (all placed at C1).

However, two samples were placed too low on the logit scale: Sample 7 (a whole level) and Sample 2 (half a level). More detailed analysis based on the criterion-related ratings (analytical ratings) revealed that these two samples received particularly low ratings on the accuracy criterion. Importantly, the training samples were all consistently high on accuracy, yet accuracy is a criterion to which little weight is attached in the context of TestDaF examinations (it is considered only an implicit criterion in TestDaF; see also Eckes 2008b). Thus, the marked difference in the relevance of the accuracy criterion in training vs. local samples, along with our judges' reference to this criterion in the benchmarking stage, may account for the misplacement of Samples 2 and 7.

Judgements of spoken production samples

As before, we analysed the final ratings of samples of spoken production only. These ratings were provided after group discussion in the training stage (CoE samples), and individually (i.e., without discussion) in the benchmarking stage (TestDaF samples). Table 8 shows the consensus and consistency indices for the judgements of spoken production samples in the training stage (i.e., after group discussion) and in the benchmarking stage.

Overall, the findings attest to a high level of inter-rater reliability. As compared to the previous analysis regarding written production samples, the training of spoken performance samples was even more successful in communicating to judges a common understanding of the CEFR levels. Even the exact agreement index shows that three out of four judgements were identical. Considering the benchmarking stage, exact agreement goes down to only 32%, but the other indices still demonstrate that judges agree with each other to a considerable extent.

The FACETS analysis revealed that four judges performed inconsistently in terms of judge fit statistics. We eliminated these judges from further study. The variable map representing the calibrations of the nine TestDaF samples, the remaining eight judges, and the 9-point rating scale is displayed in Figure 2.

The ordering of the TestDaF samples along the logit scale was in good agreement with most of the pre-assigned TestDaF levels. That is, Samples 7, 3, and 8 were at TDN 3, Samples 4, 9, and 1 were at TDN 4, Samples 2, 6, and 5 were at TDN 5.

However, Samples 7 and 3 were placed much too low on the scale, as judged by the CEFR levels. These two samples should have been placed at CEFR scale category 6 (corresponding to B2) or at least at category 5 (corresponding to B1+). Thus, according to this analysis, at the low end of the TestDaF scale the link of the speaking section to the CEFR seems to be fairly weak.

Empirical validation

Overview of data analysis

According to the Manual (CoE 2003), the empirical validation phase comprises (a) internal validation, that is, establishing the quality of the examination in its own terms, and (b) external validation, that is, independently corroborating the standards set in the examination by studying relationships with other assessments. Procedures concerning internal validation have been treated in the section about procedures followed in specification.

In this section, we briefly describe the results of two studies concerned with the external validation of the TestDaF. The first study addresses the receptive skills and relates the TestDaF levels that examinees achieved in the reading and listening sections of a recent TestDaF examination to the same examinees' CEFR levels achieved in the German version of DIALANG. Examinees' TestDaF levels were determined using the cut scores relevant for that particular examination.

The second study addresses the productive skills and relates the TestDaF levels that examinees achieved in the writing and speaking sections of that TestDaF examination to the same examinees' CEFR levels awarded to them by their teachers.

Figure 2: Variable map from the FACETS analysis of judgements of nine spoken production samples (SPS). The horizontal dashed lines in the Scale column indicate the category threshold measures. Scale categories 1 – 9 refer to CEFR levels A1–C2 (including plus levels).

Logit	Sample	Judge	Scale
	High	*Severe*	
			(9)
10	SPS_5		
9			
8			
			8
7			
	SPS_6		
6			
5	SPS_2		-----
4			7
3			

2	SPS_1	H3	
		A4	
1		A1 H2	
		H4	6
0	SPS_9		

−1	SPS_4 SPS_8	H1	5
−2		T2	-----
			4
−3		T3	

−4			3
	SPS_3		-----
−5			
	SPS_7		2
−6			
−7			

−8			(1)
	Low	*Lenient*	

Our focus is on the resulting cross-classification frequencies computed for each skill separately. Note that the Manual uses the term 'decision table' to refer to these cross-classifications. In addition, we report on the correlations between the respective level assignments, using Pearson-*r*, Spearman's rho, and Kendall's tau-b. In contrast to Pearson-r, both Spearman's rho and Kendall's tau-b only require ordinal-level data. Moreover, Kendall's tau-b takes tied ranks into account (tied ranks are frequently encountered when the number of ordinal categories is small, as with CEFR and TestDaF levels, respectively).

Receptive skills: TestDaF vs. DIALANG

The TestDaF–DIALANG cross-classification frequencies for reading are presented in Table 9.

Table 9: TestDaF–DIALANG cross-classification of proficiency levels for reading

DIALANG levels	TDN levels				Total
	below TDN 3	TDN 3	TDN 4	TDN 5	
A1	2	2	0	0	4
A2	11	18	16	2	47
B1	7	9	23	13	52
B2	1	2	14	12	29
C1	0	0	0	1	1
Total	21	31	53	28	133

If it can be assumed that DIALANG reliably assesses reading proficiency at CEFR levels A1 through C2, and TestDaF reliably assesses reading proficiency at TDN 3 through TDN 5, which by design translates into CEFR levels B2 to C1, then examinees should fall within one of the six cells covering level combinations B2/C1 by TDN 3/TDN 5. Obviously, this is not the case. In fact, most examinees are placed in cells other than those where they should be placed. For example, 18 examinees achieved TDN 3 in the TestDaF, but A2 in the DIALANG test. Only 37 out of 133 examinees (or 27.8%) fell within the predicted level combinations. Twenty of them belong to the level below TDN 3.

Not surprisingly, the correlation coefficients were fairly low, though statistically significant: Pearson-r = .48 (p < .001), Spearman's rho = .49 (p < .001), and Kendall's tau-b = .43 (p < .001).

For listening, the TestDaF–DIALANG cross-classification frequencies are presented in Table 10.

As compared to reading, the congruence between TestDaF and DIALANG level assignments for listening was much higher: 72 out of 143 examinees (or 50.3%) fell within the predicted level combinations. Fourteen of them belong to the level below TDN 3.

Accordingly, the correlation coefficients increased: Pearson-r = .59 (p < .001), Spearman's rho = .60 (p < .001), and Kendall's tau-b = .52 (p < .001).

Table 10: TestDaF–DIALANG cross-classification of proficiency levels for listening

DIALANG levels	TDN levels				Total
	below TDN 3	TDN 3	TDN 4	TDN 5	
A2	10	9	4	0	23
B1	4	20	13	5	42
B2	5	5	17	10	37
C1	0	2	16	20	38
C2	0	0	1	2	3
Total	19	36	51	37	143

Productive skills: TestDaF vs. teacher judgements

When comparing examinees' TestDaF writing proficiency levels to the CEFR levels provided by their teachers, we obtained the cross-classification frequencies shown in Table 11.

Table 11: TestDaF–teacher cross-classification of proficiency levels for writing

Teacher judgement	TDN levels				Total
	below TDN 3	TDN 3	TDN 4	TDN 5	
B1	8	13	9	0	30
B2	1	23	36	6	66
C1	0	8	33	15	56
C2	0	0	2	0	2
Total	9	44	80	21	154

TestDaF levels and teacher-assigned CEFR levels were as predicted in 115 out of 154 examinees (or 74.7%). The correlation coefficients were as follows: Pearson-r = .49 ($p < .001$), Spearman's rho = .48 ($p < .001$), and Kendall's tau-b = .43 ($p < .001$).

Regarding examinees' level of speaking proficiency, we obtained the cross-classification frequencies shown in Table 12.

TestDaF levels and teacher-assigned CEFR levels were as predicted in 113 out of 156 examinees (or 72.4%). The correlation coefficients were as follows: Pearson-r = .42 ($p < .001$), Spearman's rho = .43 ($p < .001$), and Kendall's tau-b = .39 ($p < .001$).

The assignment of one examinee to level A2 (TDN 4 in the TestDaF) was commented on by the relevant teacher using the assessment sheet. The teacher noted grammatical mistakes slightly impeding understanding, well-developed speaking competence and simple vocabulary. These notes revealed a certain degree of inconsistent understanding of A2 performance.

Table 12: TestDaF–teacher cross-classification of proficiency levels for speaking

Teacher judgement	TDN levels				Total
	below TDN 3	TDN 3	TDN 4	TDN 5	
A2	0	0	1	0	1
B1	2	14	11	1	28
B2	1	25	35	9	70
C1	0	6	29	22	57
Total	3	45	76	32	156

Reflections on the use of the draft Manual

Problems and solutions

We identified two aspects, which seem to have a strong impact on the results of our linking project: (a) the material used as reference material for external validity, standardisation, and external validation, (b) the Manual's methodological 4-step approach. In the following, we discuss each of these two aspects.

(a) Reference material. Using the CEFR scales as reference points for the linkage of test tasks revealed two problems. Firstly, there was a problem inherent in the methodology: CEFR performance descriptions do not include the notion of task or task fulfilment and do not describe cognitive processes in detail (Alderson, Figueras, Kuijper, Nold, Takala and Tardieu 2006:12–13). In particular, in productive skills, the examination result generally depends on the language proficiency shown in relation to the task fulfilment and not on the linguistic realisation alone. We tried to cope with this problem using the CEFR Grids for the analysis of tasks and items and to take into consideration the task difficulty in the final judgement of the standardisation procedure.

Secondly, the scales applied did not always cover the examination content completely (see Written Production and Spoken Production), or caused problems in application because they were not coherent. At one scale level, content features were used as descriptors (text type, topic) and at another level of the same scale, linguistic features prevailed (standard dialect, clear articulation). The only solution here was to consult several scales, although this did not always lead to satisfactory results, as, for example, in reading task 1. The difficulties encountered when selecting descriptors of different scales for the assignment of the tasks to CEFR levels may have led to the inconsistencies detected in their judgements (see Table 3, 'Results').

Furthermore, the standardised CoE material used for standardisation consisted of item and performance samples, which turned out to be not sufficient for the required purpose. This was, obviously, due to the fact that the CoE Manual project was at its starting point. Performance samples in German with a broader range of task format and level of accuracy for the different CEFR levels are clearly called for.

Finally, using DIALANG as an external criterion measure to validate the claim of link between the TestDaF and the CEFR through an indirect approach turned out to be difficult due to technical constraints described above. Similar problems had already occurred in a different validation context (i.e., the onDaF–DIALANG validation study; Eckes 2010). The correlation index of the TestDaF–DIALANG comparison was rather low, in particular for Reading Comprehension (Pearson-r=.48). The above-mentioned onDaF–DIALANG study depicted even lower values (.24) for Reading Comprehension (Eckes 2010). Unfortunately, item statistics of the German items used in DIALANG to examine potential problems at the item level were not available.

(b) The Manual. Based on our findings it seems safe to conclude that the 4-step methodology of the Manual provided a sound approach for the intended purpose. Problems that occurred were to some extent due to the fact that the CEFR was not the perfect tool required for the linkage but needed amendments in the form of CEFR Grids or item samples (Alderson et al 2006). Thus, we think that the Manual's Chapter 5 on standardisation is in need of a more precise definition of benchmarking. The Manual described the benchmarking process for different purposes, that is, (a) for the selection of benchmarks to be used as reference material in assessment, and (b) for the evaluation of performance tasks employed in local exams (CoE 2003:71). This inconsistency may lead to some misunderstanding among users when applying the Manual approach.

How reliable and generalisable are the results?

Concerning the receptive skills, results of the specification phase (tendency of TDN level 3 in the receptive skills towards B1+ and of TDN 5 in reading towards C2) were confirmed by results of the standard-setting phase, except for the tendency towards C2 for reading. However, results of the external validation with DIALANG did not provide further confirmation in this direction but were partially (reading) impeded by technical problems. As for listening, no particularly strong correlation was found.

Regarding the productive skills, the results of benchmarking did not confirm results of the content analysis. Experts assigned some TestDaF performance samples of TDN 3 (assumed B2) to the level B1+, or in a few cases even lower, which was not in line with results of the previous content analysis conducted in the specification phase. As stated before, this may be due to some extent to the limited choice of standardised performance samples, which served as a reference point for the standard. Moreover, the high level of accuracy in these samples certainly played a role. External validation of the productive skills using teacher judgements as an external criterion measure produced results that were more satisfactory. For writing, 74.7% of the assigned CEFR levels corresponded to the predicted TestDaF levels, and for speaking, the level of agreement was as high as 72.4 %. The sample of candidates was representative for the TestDaF candidature in terms of age, country of origin, and gender.

Altogether, our application of the Manual methodology produced reliable results, although parts of it did not contribute to validating the linkage claim and need further investigation (particularly, external validation of the receptive skills and standardisation of the productive skills). Evidence on the generalisability of the results, as recommended by Cizek and Bunch (2007), was difficult to obtain. Moreover, due to financial limitations, the application of multiple methods or replication of the same method with another panel of experts, as recommended by Kaftandjieva (2004), was not feasible (Linn 2003:9). Apart from that, multiple methods or different panel groups often do not produce similar results (Jaeger 1989, Kane 2001:75). Hence, deciding on the 'true' cut-off remains an intricate problem.

Another point in the Manual that needs clarification concerns the role of modelling the rating behaviour of judges or panellists by means of a many-facet Rasch measurement approach (Linacre 1989, Linacre and Wright 2002). In various places (Section 1.4.2, Section 5.6), the Manual recommends using this Rasch modelling approach to identify inconsistent behaviour of the judges and to adjust ratings for judge severity or leniency. At the same time, the Manual recommends to enforce 'discussion of spread and iteration until suitable agreement is reached' (CoE 2003:8). Yet, forcing judges to reach 'reliable consensus' is bound to create some degree of dependence among judges. This could lead to violating the IRT assumption of local independence (see, e.g., Henning 1989, Yen and Fitzpatrick 2006). That is, judges are to behave like 'scoring machines', rather than to act as individual experts. It is important to note that the many-facet Rasch model construes judges as independent experts (Linacre 1998, 2006). Therefore, we used this model only in the standard-setting or benchmarking sessions, where we did not include any discussion. We instead encouraged our judges to provide ratings on an individual basis. Using the Rasch-Kappa index proposed by Linacre (2006), we actually confirmed that the extent of rater dependence was negligibly small in the standard-setting and benchmarking sessions, respectively, but unduly high in the training sessions.

Concluding remarks

In light of the results and problems discussed above, we think that our study highlights the need to probe more deeply into the TestDaF–CEFR linkage. For example, we observed a tendency of reading and listening items, belonging to part one in the relevant TestDaF sections, towards level B1+, although this deviation represented only half a level below the targeted level of B2. It seems advisable either to replicate the standard-setting procedure applying a different method or to look for some other external criterion measure.

Another part of our research that possibly needs further scrutiny concerns the benchmarking of the productive skills, which suffered from two problems: (a) the narrow range of standardised German performance samples available used for experts' training, and (b) a relatively limited number of samples used for training and benchmarking. Meanwhile, more performance samples in German have been made available for Written Production on the CoE website (two TestDaF samples, which reached a good degree of consensus in our standardisation phase were added), and some others for Spoken Production have been published (Bolton et al 2008). Here again, a replication of the standard-setting procedure using an additional method like, for example, the Body of Work method is conceivable.

Finally, the findings of our study may lead into yet another direction, the rethinking of our test format and TestDaF level description including the rating criteria.

Acknowledgements

We would like to thank our colleagues at the TestDaF Institute for many stimulating discussions on various issues concerning the TestDaF–CEFR linking project. Special thanks go to Sonja Zimmermann for her commitment in organising and documenting the TestDaF standardisation workshops.

Notes

1. <www.coe.int/T/DG4/Portfolio/?L=E&M=/main_pages/illustrationse.html)>
2. Grid 4, the final grid, retrieved in 2005 from <www.ling.lancs.ac.uk/cefgrid>. See Alderson, J C, Figueras, N, Kuijper, H, Nold, G, Takala, S and Tardieu, C (2004) *The development of specifications for item development and classification within the Common European Framework of Reference for Languages: Learning, teaching, assessment: Reading and listening,* final report of the Dutch DEF Construct Project.
3. The following categories of the grid which proved to be significant to estimate item difficulty were used: (a) for listening: 'nature of content', 'vocabulary', 'grammar', 'text speed', 'number of participants', 'accent/standard', 'clarity of articulation', 'how often played', and 'operations', (b) for reading: 'nature of content', 'text length', 'vocabulary', 'grammar', and 'operations'.

References

Alderson, J C (2005) *Diagnosing foreign language proficiency: The interface between learning and assessment,* London: Continuum.

Alderson, J C, Figueras, N, Kuijper, H, Nold, G, Takala, S and Tardieu, C (2004) *The development of specifications for item development and classification within the Common European Framework of Reference for Languages: Learning, teaching, assessment: Reading and Listening,* final report of the Dutch DEF Construct Project.

Alderson, J C, Figueras, N, Kuijper, H, Nold, G, Takala, S and Tardieu, C (2006) Analysing tests of reading and listening in relation to the common European framework of reference: The experience of the Dutch CEFR construct project, *Language Assessment Quarterly* 3 (1), 3–30.

Althaus, H-J (2004) Der TestDaF, in DAAD (Ed.) *Die internationale Hochschule: Ein Handbuch für Politik und Praxis*, Bielefeld: Bertelsmann, Vol. 8, 80–87.

Arras, U (2007) *Wie beurteilen wir Leistung in der Fremdsprache? Strategien und Prozesse bei der Beurteilung schriftlicher Leistungen in der Fremdsprache am Beispiel der Prüfung Test Deutsch als Fremdsprache (TestDaF)*, Tübingen: Narr.

Bolton, S, Glaboniat, M, Lorenz, H, Perlmann-Balme, M and Steiner, S (2008) *Mündlich: Mündliche Produktion und Interaktion Deutsch: Illustration der Niveaustufen des Gemeinsamen europäischen Referenzrahmens*, Berlin: Langenscheidt.

Burry-Stock, J A, Shaw, D G, Laurie, C and Chissom, B S (1996) Rater agreement indexes for performance assessment, *Educational and Psychological Measurement* 56, 251–262.

Cizek, G J (2001) *Setting performance standards, concepts, methods, perspectives*, Mahwah, NJ: Erlbaum.

Cizek, G J (2006) Standard setting, in Downing, S M and Haladyna, T M (Eds) *Handbook of test development*, Mahwah, NJ: Erlbaum, 225–258.

Cizek, G J and Bunch, M B (2007) *Standard setting: A guide to establishing and evaluating performance standards on tests*, Thousand Oaks, CA: Sage.

Council of Europe (2001) *Common European Framework of Reference for Languages: Learning, teaching, assessment*, Cambridge: Cambridge University Press.

Council of Europe (2003) *Relating language examinations to the Common European Framework of Reference for Languages: Learning, teaching, assessment (CEF). Manual. Preliminary pilot version,* Strasbourg: Language Policy Division.

Council of Europe (2005) *Relating language examinations to the Common European Framework of Reference for Languages: Learning, teaching, assessment (CEFR). Reading and listening items and tasks: Pilot samples illustrating the common reference levels in English, French, German, Italian and Spanish*, Strasbourg: Language Policy Division.

Eckes, T (2005) Examining rater effects in TestDaF writing and speaking performance assessments: A many-facet Rasch analysis, *Language Assessment Quarterly* 2, 197–221.

Eckes, T (2008a) Assuring the quality of TestDaF examinations: A psychometric modeling approach, in Taylor, L and Weir, C J (Eds) *Multilingualism and assessment*, Cambridge: UCLES/Cambridge University Press, 157–178.

Eckes, T (2008b) Rater types in writing performance assessments: A classification approach to rater variability, *Language Testing* 25, 155–185.

Eckes, T (2009a) Many-facet Rasch measurement, in Takala, S (Ed.), *Reference supplement to the manual for relating language examinations to the Common European Framework of Reference for Languages: Learning, teaching, assessment* (Section H), Strasbourg, France: Council of Europe/Language Policy Division.

Eckes, T (2009b) On common ground? How raters perceive scoring criteria in oral proficiency testing, in Brown, A and Hill, K (Eds) *Tasks and criteria in performance assessment: Proceedings of the 28th Language Testing Research Colloquium*, Frankfurt, Germany: Lang, 43–73.

Eckes, T (2010) Der Online-Einstufungstest Deutsch als Fremdsprache (onDaF): Theoretische Grundlagen, Konstruktion und Validierung [The online-placement test of German as a foreign language (onDaF): Theoretical foundations, construction, and validation], in Grotjahn, R (Ed.) *Der C-Test: Beiträge aus der aktuellen Forschung/The C-test: Contributions from current research*, Frankfurt, Germany: Lang, 125–192.

Eckes, T, Ellis, M, Kalnberzina, V, Pižorn, K, Springer, C, Szollás, K and Tsagari, C (2005) Progress and problems in reforming public language examinations in Europe: Cameos from the Baltic States, Greece, Hungary, Poland, Slovenia, France, and Germany, *Language Testing* 22, 355–377.

Grotjahn, R (2004) TestDaF: Theoretical basis and empirical research, in Milanovic, M and Weir, C J (Eds) *European language testing in a global context: Proceedings of the ALTE Barcelona Conference July,* Cambridge: UCLES/Cambridge University Press, 189–203.

Hambleton, R (2001) Setting performance standards on educational assessments and criteria for evaluating the process, in Cizek, G J (Ed.) *Setting performance standards*, Mahwah, NJ: Erlbaum, 89–116.

Hambleton, R and Pitoniak, M (2006) Setting performance standards, in Brennan, R (Ed.) *Educational Measurement* (4th ed.), Westport: American Council on Education/Praeger, 433–470.

Henning, G (1989) Meanings and implications of the principle of local independence, *Language Testing* 6, 95–108.

Impara, J C and Plake, B S (1997) Standard-setting: An alternative approach, *Journal of Educational Measurement* 34, 353–366.

Jaeger, R M (1989) Certification of student competence, in Linn, R L (Ed.) *Educational measurement* (3rd ed.), Washington, DC: American Council on Education, 485–511.

James, L R, Demaree, R G and Wolf, G (1984) Estimating within-group inter-rater reliability with and without response bias, *Journal of Applied Psychology* 69, 85–98.

Jones, N (2002) Relating the ALTE Framework to the Common European Framework of Reference, in Alderson, J C (Ed.) *Common European Framework of Reference for Languages: Learning, teaching, assessment – Case studies*, Strasbourg: Council of Europe, 167–183.

Kaftandjieva, F (2004) Standard Setting, in *Reference supplement to the preliminary pilot version of the manual for relating language examinations to the common European framework*, section B, Strasbourg: Language Policy Division.

Kaftandjieva, F (2009) Basket procedure: The bread basket or the basket case of standard setting methods? in Figueras, N and Noijons, J (Eds), *Linking to the CEFR levels: Research Perspectives*, Arnhem: Cito/EALTA, 21–34.

Kane, M (2001) So much remains the same: conceptions and status of validation in setting standards, in Cizek, G J (Ed.) *Setting performance standards*, Mahwah, NJ: Erlbaum, 53−88.

Kenyon, D M (2000) Tape-mediated oral proficiency testing: Considerations in developing Simulated Oral Proficiency Interviews (SOPIs), in Bolton, S (Ed.) *TESTDAF: Grundlagen für die Entwicklung eines neuen Sprachtests. Beiträge aus einem Expertenseminar*, Köln: VUB Gilde, 87−106.

Linacre, J M (1989) *Many-facet Rasch measurement*, Chicago: MESA Press.

Linacre, J M (1998) Rating, judges and fairness, *Rasch Measurement Transactions* 12, 630−631.

Linacre, J M (2006) *A user's guide to FACETS: Rasch-model computer programs* [Software manual], Chicago: Winsteps.com.

Linacre, J M and Wright, B D (2002) Construction of measures from many-facet data, *Journal of Applied Measurement* 3, 484−509.

Linn, R L (2003) Performance Standards: Utility for different uses of assessments, *Education Policy Analysis Archives* 11 (31).

Raymond, M and Reid, J (2001) Who made thee a judge? Selecting and Training Participants for Standard Setting, in Cizek, G J (Ed.) *Setting performance standards*, Mahwah, NJ: Erlbaum, 117−158.

Schneider, G and North, B (2000) *Fremdsprachen können – was heißt das?*, Chur, Switzerland: Rüegger.

Stemler, S E and Tsai, J (2008) Best practices in inter-rater reliability: Three common approaches, in Osborne, J W (Ed.) *Best practices in quantitative methods*, Los Angeles, CA: Sage, 29−49.

Takala, S (2007) Relating language examinations to the Common European Framework, in Beck, B and Klieme, E (Eds) *Sprachliche Kompetenzen*, Weinheim: Beltz, 306−313.

TestDaF-Institut (2005a) *Modellsatz 02*, www.testdaf.de

TestDaF-Institut (2005b) *Musterprüfung 1*, Ismaning: Hueber.

Yen, W M and Fitzpatrick, A R (2006) Item response theory, in Brennan, R L (Ed.) *Educational measurement* (4th ed.), Westport, CT: American Council on Education/Praeger, 111−153.

3 Maintaining alignment to the CEFR: the FCE case study

Hanan Khalifa, Angela ffrench and Angeliki Salamoura

University of Cambridge ESOL Examinations, UK

Abstract

In this paper, we focus on the relationship between the Common European Framework of Reference for Languages (CEFR) and a well-established examination which pre-dates it, the First Certificate in English (FCE). We provide reflections from piloting the Manual procedures, in particular Familiarisation and Specification, as a means of: (a) maintaining the FCE/CEFR alignment, and (b) weaving Manual-prescribed procedures into Cambridge ESOL practices. This discussion will demonstrate how the Manual activities can be constructively used and extended, not only to build a linking argument, but also, and more importantly, to maintain it.

Introduction

This case study investigates the use of the Manual in relation to an examination which pre-dates the CEFR, the First Certificate in English (www.CambridgeESOL.org/exams/general-english/fce.html).

Both the CEFR and Cambridge ESOL examinations, of which FCE is part, have shared purposes: provision of a learning ladder and proficiency framework. The CEFR sets learning objectives as being 'a comprehensive, transparent and coherent framework for language learning, teaching and assessment' (Council of Europe 2001:9) and the examinations assess the outcomes through defining levels of proficiency which allow learners' progress to be measured at each stage of learning. North, one of the CEFR authors, acknowledges that 'the process of defining these [CEFR] levels started in 1913 with the Cambridge Proficiency Exam (CPE) that defines a practical mastery of the language as a non-native speaker. This level has become C2. In 1939, Cambridge introduced the First Certificate (FCE), which is still seen as the first level of proficiency of interest for office work, now associated with B2' (2008:31).

Subsequent developments resulted in three more examinations being introduced into the Cambridge suite, KET (A2), PET (B1) and CAE (C1), and it is against this context of evolution, and Cambridge ESOL's practice of providing a validity argument for its examinations based on a socio-cognitive approach towards test development, that we started investigating and reflecting on the use of the Manual.

For both the Familiarisation and Standardisation aspects of the study, we highlight the procedures as defined by the Manual, outline how we implemented the procedures, offer alternatives (which are better suited to the FCE context) to some of the activities suggested by the Manual in the form of modifications or extensions to the processes suggested by the Manual, present results from the various activities, and finally reflect on the process.

We consider the extent to which the pilot version of the Manual meets the requirements of a manual. We explore how effective the Manual and non Manual prescribed Familiarisation and Training activities are in enhancing participants' knowledge of the CEFR and in training them to rate performances and tasks using the CEFR scales. We consider how useful the time management tables provided by the Manual are. We highlight practical issues not adequately covered in the Manual. And we offer suggestions for improvement.

In providing reflections from piloting the Familiarisation and Standardisation procedures of the Manual, we demonstrate how the Manual activities can be integrated into the FCE test cycle. Standardisation of judgements and Empirical Validation (the other two stages in the CEFR linking process as suggested by the Manual) are ongoing processes for Cambridge ESOL and are discussed in a number of other publications (e.g. Jones 2000, 2001, 2002; Khalifa and ffrench 2008; Taylor and Jones 2006).

The project

Here we discuss the piloting of the Manual Familiarisation and Specification procedures in relation to FCE, as well as the design and implementation of a number of activities that further extend some of the activities suggested by the Manual which are better suited to the FCE context. We subsequently provide reflections on this piloting and finally discuss the integration of these procedures/activities in the FCE test cycle (see Saville 2003 for a detailed presentation of the test cycle of Cambridge ESOL examinations).

Familiarisation procedures

The Manual perceives the Familiarisation procedure as 'a selection of activities designed to ensure that participants in the linking process have a detailed knowledge of the CEF' and considers it an 'indispensable starting point' before a linking exercise can be carried out effectively (Council of Europe 2003a:1).

Implementation of Familiarisation procedures

Cambridge ESOL implemented a number of Manual prescribed and non Manual prescribed Familiarisation activities in a face-to-face workshop with internal and external staff responsible for FCE test construction, marking, analysis and grading. The workshop included a variety of activities relevant to the FCE context. The non Manual prescribed activities were designed by Cambridge ESOL to complement the Manual activities and ensure full coverage of the needs and purposes of the workshop. The aim of the workshop was to enable reflections on:

- how effective the Manual activities are in familiarising participants with the CEFR
- how the activities can be complemented to reflect the FCE context more appropriately (see the non Manual prescribed activities in Table 1)
- how effective they are as a means of maintaining the FCE–CEFR alignment
- how best they can be incorporated in the FCE test cycle.

The full-day workshop brought together a total of 14 FCE subject managers, subject officers, validation officers, item-writer chairs, Professional Support Leaders, and Principal Examiners. All participants had extensive experience in developing and validating tests. The event also included pre- and post-workshop activities, all of which are shown in Table 1 below. The majority of the tasks dealt with the CEFR B2 level – the FCE exam level – and its adjacent B1 and C1 levels. The focus on the B2 level and comparisons with the B1 and C1 levels was a feature introduced to aid understanding of the characteristics of this level and its differences from the adjoining levels.

Before the workshop, participants carried out preparation tasks, such as background reading, to update their knowledge of the CEFR and its associated projects, such as the European Language Portfolio and how the CEFR has affected the development of Cambridge ESOL examinations. They also reflected on how the use of the CEFR has affected their own work on Cambridge ESOL examinations, e.g. in terms of item writing, scale construction, marking productive skills, etc. Other pre-workshop tasks aimed at ensuring common understanding of the CEFR global scale and a selection of B1 to C1 language use descriptors related to the four language skills: listening, speaking, reading and writing. A descriptor-classification exercise was used to achieve this aim. A further task involved using the CEFR global scale to self-assess own ability in a second language.

The face-to-face workshop itself started with an introductory focus on the origins, aims and nature of the CEFR, its relevance for language assessment

Table 1: The FCE–CEFR workshop programme

The FCE–CEFR workshop programme

Pre-workshop activities: Introduction to the topics and activities of the face-to-face workshop

Manual Prescribed	Non Manual Prescribed
• Descriptor-sorting activity (activity d, p. 27), sorting out mixed up descriptors from a variety of CEFR scales into B1–C1 levels • Self-assessment of foreign language ability using CEFR (activity c, p. 26)	• Background reading: Taylor, L and Jones, N (2006:1–5) • Juxtaposing the target B2 level with its adjacent B1 and C1 levels in all descriptor-sorting and rating activities throughout the workshop

Face-to-face workshop

Manual Prescribed	Non Manual Prescribed
• Descriptor-sorting activity (activity d, p. 27) • Rating activity (pp. 74–84), rating of spoken and written performances as well as reading and listening tasks across B1–C1 levels	Presentations on the origins, aims and nature of the CEFR

Post-workshop activities: Consolidation of knowledge gained and feedback on workshop effectiveness

Manual Prescribed	Non Manual Prescribed
Descriptor-sorting activity (activity d, p. 27)	Workshop Feedback Questionnaire

and its implications for participants as professional language testers working with Cambridge ESOL (see Appendix 1 for the day's programme). The workshop then moved on to a descriptor-sorting activity where participants classified language use descriptors into CEFR levels, building on one of the pre-workshop tasks. The workshop ended by training participants in applying skill-specific CEFR B1 to C1 level scales to CEFR-calibrated spoken and written performances, as well as CEFR-calibrated reading and listening tasks (rating activity in Table 1). The CEFR-calibrated materials used were those published by the Council of Europe (2003b, 2003c, 2005). This rating activity is, strictly speaking, part of the Training of the Standardisation phase suggested by the Manual rather than the Familiarisation phase. However, we will discuss it together with the Familiarisation activities in this paper since, like the Familiarisation tasks, it is one of the introductory/background activities that precede the actual linking procedures and ensure that participants are familiar with CEFR and the CEFR linking processes. It differs from the Familiarisation tasks in that in addition to familiarisation with certain CEFR scales, it also offers training in using these scales to rate exam tasks and learner performances.

As follow-up to the workshop, participants carried out a range of tasks designed to evaluate the effectiveness of the Familiarisation and Training activities and materials in the CEFR Manual. For example, participants were asked to revisit their earlier classification of descriptors into CEFR levels, building on the knowledge gained and the discussion that took place at the workshop. A comparison of the results from the pre- and post-workshop descriptor-sorting tasks was carried out to check the effect of the workshop descriptor-sorting on familiarising participants with the CEFR scales used in these tasks.

Results obtained

How effective were the Manual and non Manual prescribed Familiarisation and Training activities in enhancing participants' knowledge of the CEFR and in training them to rate performances and tasks using the CEFR scales? To answer this question, we collected both qualitative data (participant feedback on workshop activities) and quantitative data (statistical analyses of descriptor-sorting and rating data).

Qualitative data

In the post-workshop tasks, participants were asked to evaluate the effectiveness of the activities used before and during the workshop in terms of familiarising participants with the CEFR. Figure 1 summarises the replies to the Workshop Feedback Questionnaire. Overall, the participants found the workshop activities effective. Figure 1 shows that juxtaposing the B2 level with its adjacent B1 and C1 levels was judged to be the most effective feature of the workshop. This was followed by a self-assessment activity, background reading, and a descriptor-sorting activity. A number of queries were raised in relation to classifying the CEFR descriptors into levels. Participants, for example, commented on ambiguities in the CEFR descriptor terminology

Figure 1: Participant feedback on the effectiveness of the workshop activities

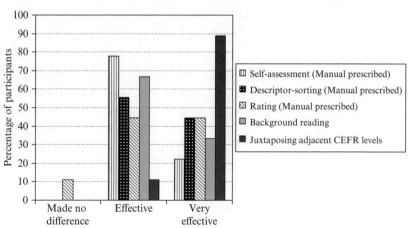

84

(e.g. from the Speaking descriptors: ' "can narrate a story", what kind of story, simple, complex, of medium complexity?', 'what is the meaning of "style"?', etc.) and on difficulties in relating the CEFR classification to real-life experience (e.g. from the Listening descriptors: ' "only extreme noise" affecting our ability to understand is classified as B2, whereas *extreme noise* affects everyone's ability to understand at whatever level').

Quantitative data

Figure 2 presents the mean percentage of rater responses matching the target CEFR level in the pre- and post-workshop descriptor-sorting sessions and shows how many descriptors were placed at the correct CEFR level. Exact agreement in all sessions is satisfactory as it has an average of 77% and never fell below 66%. Although there is some variation across the four skills, on average raw scores improved or stayed the same from the pre-workshop exercises to the post-workshop ones.

Figure 2: Mean percentage of rater responses matching target CEFR level in the pre- and post-workshop descriptor-sorting activities

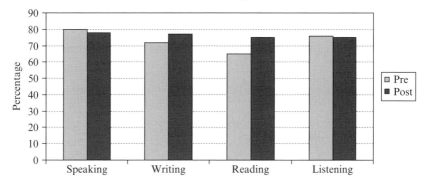

Improvement varies but this may be due to the high level of previous familiarity and experience of participants with the CEFR. The majority of our participants (58%) claimed (in a pre-workshop questionnaire) that they were fairly familiar with the framework before the workshop. As a result, they scored at least 66% in the pre-workshop sessions where they had been instructed to classify the descriptors based on their *own* background knowledge and experience with the framework. The previous high familiarity of participants with the CEFR, reflected in the quantitative results here, may also explain why participants did not judge Background Reading as one of the most effective activities in terms of CEFR familiarisation (see Figure 1).

It is worth distinguishing here two different scenarios with respect to the Familiarisation impact. In the first scenario, trainees have little prior awareness of the CEFR and there is, therefore, the possibility of a significant impact of the Familiarisation tasks. In the alternative scenario, trainees already have quite a high level of CEFR awareness and, as a result, there is little leeway for a significant impact of the Familiarisation activities. Our evidence shows that in this study the second scenario holds. Although participants had never received any formal CEFR Familiarisation training before, our pre-workshop estimation was that they would be familiar with the CEFR to varying degrees, as all of them were very experienced FCE item writers and examiners. Moreover, they were not only experienced at the FCE level but across the Cambridge ESOL levels and knew where exactly the FCE exam fits in the language ladder. This estimation was confirmed by their responses in a pre-workshop questionnaire which showed that the majority of them (58%) thought they were fairly familiar with the CEFR. To test the hypothesis that it is the prior high familiarity with the CEFR that prevented a high impact of Familiarisation, one needs to compare the impact of Familiarisation activities between the current group of participants, who are a representative sample of the Cambridge ESOL network of item writers and examiners, and a group of CEFR novices.

Table 2 presents a summary of intra-rater (Spearman) correlations for each of the four skill-specific scales of the descriptor-sorting activity. As Table 2 shows, intra-rater reliability is satisfactory across all four scales, meaning that the raters were sufficiently consistent with themselves.

Table 2: Intra-rater reliability in the pre- and post-workshop descriptor-sorting activities

Scales	Raters	Intra-rater reliability		
		Mean	Min	Max
Speaking	9	0.90	0.79	1
Writing	9	0.85	0.63	0.98
Reading	9	0.90	0.66	1
Listening	9	0.94	0.71	1

Average values of inter-rater reliability are shown in Table 3. With the exception of some minimum correlations which are significant at $p \leq 0.047$, all other Spearman correlations in this table are significant at $p \leq 0.01$. These inter-rater reliability values together with the high Alpha values indicate a high agreement among raters on sorting the descriptors from the lowest (B1) to the highest level (C1). It is also encouraging that the mean and minimum correlations are better in the post-workshop sessions across all four sets of descriptors – except for Listening. One factor contributing to the Listening result may be the participants' prior familiarity with the CEFR (see discussion above) which could have led to regression in this case. An additional factor could be the ambiguities encountered in interpreting the Listening descriptors. From the participants' feedback, it appears that they found the Listening descriptors more vague than others. As one participant put it: 'Paradoxically, I found the CEFR descriptors most problematic in relation to my own paper (Listening), especially in trying to untangle some of the key words, e.g. "abstract, complex, extended, field of specialisation" – terms we have assiduously avoided using in many cases!'

Table 3: Inter-rater reliability in the pre- and post-workshop descriptor-sorting activities

Scales	Raters	Inter-rater reliability			Alpha
		Mean	Min	Max	
Speaking Pre	9	0.83**	0.62**	0.95**	0.97
Speaking Post	8	0.82**	0.71**	0.93**	0.97
Writing Pre	10	0.76**	0.56*	0.92**	0.96
Writing Post	8	0.79**	0.55*	0.95**	0.96
Reading Pre	10	0.89**	0.58*	1**	0.97
Reading Post	8	0.92**	0.76**	1**	0.98
Listening Pre	10	0.95**	0.78**	1**	0.99
Listening Post	8	0.79**	0.59*	0.97**	0.96

$** p \leq 0.01; * p \leq 0.05$

Table 4 summarises the participants' correct scores in the rating activity across the four skills. The scores in Speaking (7/9 – 78%) and Writing (14/14 – 100%) show a robust, common understanding of the CEFR B1–C1 levels by raters. The scores in Reading (9/15 – 60%) and Listening (7/13 – 54%) are satisfactory but somewhat lower.

Table 4: Number and proportion of rater responses matching target CEFR level in the rating activity

Skill	N	N matching responses		Total correct: Incorrect
		single level (e.g. B2)	over 2 levels (e.g. B2/C1)	
Speaking (performances)	9	2	5	7 : 2
Writing (performances)	14	9	5	14 : 0
Reading (tasks)	15	8	1	9 : 6
Listening (tasks)	13	7	0	7 : 6

Reflections on Familiarisation procedures

The Manual prescribed activities appear to be effective in terms of familiarising participants in the linking process with the CEFR. However, the type and amount of Familiarisation activities need to be considered depending on the extent of participants' familiarity with the CEFR (see our discussion of this issue in the previous section). In the contexts where participants are not yet familiar with it, it may be appropriate for them to start with some scaffolding activities, such as background reading on the origin, aims and aspirations of the CEFR. Their awareness should also be raised to the existence of the CEFR toolkit of resources. In contexts where participants (such as the group in this study) are quite familiar with CEFR, activities like the one Cambridge ESOL introduced which focus on carefully examining adjacent levels and identifying criterial differences between these levels may prove to be beneficial in understanding the CEFR levels/descriptors/scales. The familiarisation activity would further benefit from clearer descriptor terminology, perhaps through the use of a glossary. This would enhance a common understanding of the CEFR content, e.g. on a simple–complex continuum.

The Familiarisation workshop also raised a number of practical issues which were not adequately covered in the pilot version of the Manual. A number of participants, for instance, voiced their wish for a discussion about the practical applications of the CEFR to their work (beyond the one-off linking exercise). Such a discussion could also facilitate the integration of the Manual procedures in an exam's test cycle (see our discussion below). The fact that the Manual and the CEFR are so rich with scales and tables that accompany each linking activity raises the question of selection criteria; for example, is a global/overall scale better than an analytic/specific scale for a particular task? How does one do the selection? Moreover, the running of Familiarisation and Training activities required a substantial number of (human and technical) resources, including three people to organise and run the workshop, computer equipment to play materials, recording of sessions for backup purposes etc. All these are issues which need careful planning and thought.

The quantitative data show a mixed picture regarding CEFR Familiarisation and Training. In the descriptor-sorting activity, the intra-rater reliability was highly acceptable for all skills (Table 2). The inter-rater reliability and percentage of matching responses (Table 3 and Figure 2) improved or showed no significant difference from the pre- to the post-workshop task for all skills except listening where inter-rater reliability declined. These results were largely linked to the participants' pre-existing high level of CEFR awareness. Another potential source of variance in the descriptor-sorting task may also be the way of descriptor presentation, e.g. classifying more than one individual descriptor per level, as in the descriptor-sorting activity of this study, versus classifying one set of descriptors per level. These are issues that remain to be explored in future research.

The rating activity showed a receptive vs. productive skills effect (Table 4) with high rating scores in Speaking (7/9 – 78%) and Writing (14/14 – 100%) and somewhat lower scores in Reading (9/15 – 60%) and Listening (7/13 – 54%). This effect may simply reflect the different nature of the productive vs. receptive skills; productive performance is more readily observed, described and measured than receptive performance. In this case, however, the effect may have been accentuated by the fact that there is less coverage of the receptive skills in the Manual (Table 4.3, p. 53) than of Speaking and Writing (Table 4.4, p. 58; Table 4.5, p. 60; Table 5.4, p. 78; Table 5.5, p. 79; Table 5.8, p. 82). The lower scores in Reading and Listening could also be attributed to difficulties in relating the CEFR-calibrated receptive tasks (Council of Europe 2005) to the CEFR descriptors as evidenced in participants' reflective comments on the activity: '*We found some of the [Reading] texts and items rather confusing and couldn't see how they were deemed to fit in certain levels.*' Another factor in the Listening tasks may have also been the quality of some of the materials used in the exercise which were drawn from the Council of Europe's pool of materials illustrating the CEFR levels: '*I think my responses to text/level were affected by the unconvincing delivery of some of the actors and the apparent weak construction of the task.*' By contrast, feedback from the rating of the calibrated spoken and written performances did not reveal such a difficulty: '*Overall, though, we felt reassured that FCE/B2/CEFR descriptors did not conflict with one another, but actually bore each other out.*'

The results reported above should be interpreted with caution though as there were only two raters per any given skill in the rating activity and only eight people who participated fully in the Familiarisation activity (due to practical constraints of setting up the workshop).

In terms of timing the activities, how useful were the time management tables provided by the Manual? Let us look at the example: Table 3.1– Time Management for Familiarisation Activities (Council of Europe 2003a:28). We felt that the 30 minutes proposed for a brief presentation of the CEFR by the co-ordinator are not adequate unless participants are already fairly familiar with the Framework (cf. Table 5 for a comparison). We used a 45-minute session for introducing the CEFR and we received positive feedback from the participants about this timing. The timings suggested for the self-assessment activity (Introductory activity: 45 minutes) and the descriptor-sorting activity (Qualitative activity: 1 hour 45 minutes) were adequate but they depend on the context of use of these activities. For example, we ran the self-assessment as a pre-workshop self-access activity, which could not include discussion, and we allowed 30 minutes for this. Similarly, we ran four parallel sessions of descriptor-sorting – one for each skill – allowing 40 minutes for each session.

Table 5: Comparison of time management for Familiarisation activities between the Manual proposal and our practice

	Time management for Familiarisation activities	
	Manual proposal (based on Table 3.1:28)	**Our practice**
• *Brief presentation of CEF by the co-ordinator*	30'	45'
• *Introductory activity (a–c) and discussion*	45'	30' *
• *Qualitative activity (d–f) including group work*	60'	4 parallel sessions (one for each skill) x 40'
• *Discussion*	30'	30'
• *Concluding*	15'	15'

* Only 30' were allowed for the self-assessment activity because it was administered as a pre-workshop self-access activity and therefore did not include a discussion.

For Cambridge ESOL, Familiarisation with the CEFR is seen as part of consolidating and building on existing knowledge as well as an awareness-raising activity especially for staff and networks just entering the organisation. As a direct consequence of the FCE–CEFR workshop, four self-access CEFR Induction Worksheets were designed as CEFR 'familiarisation tools' for use as part of Cambridge ESOL's staff training and induction programme. The worksheets focus on different aspects of the CEFR and the relationship between Cambridge ESOL examinations and the CEFR (Table 6).

Table 6: Topic and focus of the Cambridge ESOL CEFR Induction Worksheets

Topic \ Focus	Theoretical	Practical
CEFR	Induction Worksheet 1	Induction Worksheet 3
ESOL exams and CEFR	Induction Worksheet 2	Induction Worksheet 4

The first worksheet provides a general introduction to the CEFR. The second discusses the relationship of the Cambridge ESOL exams and the CEFR. The third includes two hands-on activities both based on the Manual Familiarisation tasks (Chapter 3): self-assessment in a foreign language using the CEFR and descriptor-sorting. Finally, the fourth worksheet asks participants to compare and contrast one Cambridge ESOL assessment scale with an equivalent one from the CEFR. (See Appendix 2 for a sample page from the first worksheet.) Cambridge ESOL staff are required to complete at least two of the four worksheets, the selection being guided by their work focus and needs.

The current Cambridge ESOL process for recruiting, inducting, training, co-ordinating, monitoring and evaluating (RITCME) item writers and examiners includes explicit reference to the CEFR where appropriate.

Specification procedures

According to the Manual, *Specification* involves 'mapping the coverage of the examination in relation to the categories of the CEFR' (Council of Europe 2003a:6). It aims to build a linking claim of how an exam relates to the CEFR via a thorough description of the exam content, implemented by filling in the Specification Forms A1–A23 provided by the Manual in Chapter 4 (Council of Europe 2003a:34–63).

Implementation of Specification procedures

To complete this phase, Cambridge ESOL commissioned an external consultant who is familiar with both the FCE exam and the CEFR being currently a Principal Examiner and item writer for FCE. Other roles have helped the consultant develop a thorough knowledge of the CEFR (e.g. presenter on the topic of FCE–CEFR link within the Cambridge ESOL network, inspector of EAQUALS schools including their work on mapping their class levels to the CEFR). The consultant worked individually and with a number of internal staff (from the Assessment and Operations and the Research and Validation divisions of Cambridge ESOL) in order to fill in Forms A1–A23 and to map the construct of the FCE to the CEFR. This process involved:

- Reading thoroughly Chapter 4 of the Manual on Specification, as well as Chapters 1 and 2 to obtain introductory and background information.
- Consulting all the CEFR scales suggested in the Specification forms, a variety of FCE related documents, including the FCE test specifications (FCE Handbook) and task specifications (Item Writer Guidelines), as well as *Vantage* (Van Ek and Trim 2001).
- Completing relevant forms. Forms A15–18 and A22 were not completed as the FCE exam does not explicitly test integrated or mediation skills. The content of the forms was also discussed and agreed on by the FCE subject manager and subject officers.
- Providing a written report on the process (Daldry 2006).

Results obtained

The FCE was classified as B2 level across all four skills. Overall, the procedures suggested and the forms completed were found useful in mapping the FCE construct to the CEFR. Here we provide an example of the B2 justification compiled for each skill for the FCE exam.

Speaking

Table 7: The B2 (and B2+) descriptors from the CEFR scale 'Overall Spoken Interaction' (Council of Europe 2001:74)

Overall Spoken Interaction
B2   *Can use the language fluently, accurately and effectively on a wide range of general, academic, vocational or leisure topics, marking clearly the relationships between ideas. Can communicate spontaneously with good grammatical control without much sign of having to restrict what he/she wants to say, adopting a level of formality appropriate to the circumstances.* *Can interact with a degree of fluency and spontaneity that makes regular interaction, and sustained relationships with native speakers quite possible without imposing strain on either party. Can highlight the personal significance of events and experiences, account for and sustain views clearly by providing relevant explanations and arguments.*

In the FCE Speaking test candidates are required to express their views on a wide range of topics and to organise what they say ('Do you have a favourite newspaper or magazine?', 'Why do you like it?'). The candidate is required to provide reasons and explanations. There is no preparation time given in Parts 1, 3 and 4 and the candidates are required to answer spontaneously. They have to handle different levels of formality, one with the Interlocutor (likely to be older and not viewed as a peer) and another with the second candidate, likely to be a peer ('Let's go for that, OK?', 'What about you?' etc.).

Writing

Table 8: The B2 descriptors from the CEFR scales 'Overall Written Interaction' and 'Correspondence' (Council of Europe 2001:83)

Overall Written Interaction
B2   *Can express news and views effectively in writing, and relate to those of others.*

Correspondence
B2   *Can write letters conveying degrees of emotion and highlighting the personal significance of events and experiences and commenting on the correspondent's news and views.*

The Part 1 letter/email of the FCE exam requires candidates to reply to the input text and deal with the questions and comments raised (in the form of prompts) and in an appropriate style. The prompts steer candidates towards using a range of functions in their reply (agreeing, disagreeing, suggesting, recommending, apologising etc.). The CEFR scale Notes, Messages and Forms (Council of Europe 2001:84) is not relevant to the FCE Writing paper because the sample required (minimum 120 words) makes this text-type inappropriate. It is clearly very likely, however, that a candidate who can write extensively at the level can also produce shorter texts.

Reading

Table 9: The B2 descriptor from the CEFR scale 'Overall Reading Comprehension' (Council of Europe 2001:69)

Overall Reading Comprehension
B2 *Can read with a large degree of independence, adapting style and speed of reading to different texts and purposes, and using appropriate reference sources selectively. Has a broad active reading vocabulary, but may experience some difficulty with low frequency items.*

Independence

An FCE candidate has to utilise strategies for dealing with unfamiliar words and phrases; has to be able to deal with a wide range of topics and approaches. FCE Reading does not test the use of reference sources.

Broad active reading vocabulary

FCE Reading texts cover a wide range of topics. An FCE candidate needs a lexical range of at least that outlined in *Vantage* level (Van Ek and Trim 2001:114–139) with the obvious addition of lexical items relating to fast-changing areas (technology, for example) and some idiom. Low frequency items do occur but the FCE candidate can employ strategies to ignore the word or phrase (redundant) or guess its meaning if it is deemed important to the task. In the FCE Sample Reading paper Part 1, 'ivy' might cause difficulty but, together with the paraphrase in the question, the candidate can work out its meaning from the context (*grew untidily over . . . climbing up to . . .*). Other low frequency lexical items at this level (e.g. '*dispersed*', '*clattering*') play no role in the key to questions and an FCE candidate has acquired strategies to enable them to decide 'whether closer study is worthwhile'.

Adapting style and speed of reading

FCE Reading Part 1 tests detailed reading of a long text and requires deduction. FCE Reading Part 2 tests detailed reading of a shorter, more factual text. FCE Reading Part 3 tests the scanning of four short texts to locate specific information (within the time limit of the Reading paper).

Listening

FCE Listening tasks test whether candidates can identify the main points of longer texts. It is, therefore, likely that the candidates would be able to follow the essentials (but not necessarily the details) of lectures etc.

Table 10: The B2 descriptor from the CEFR scale 'Listening as a member of a live audience' (Council of Europe 2001:67)

Listening as a member of a live audience
B2 *Can follow the essentials of lectures, talks and reports and other forms of academic/ professional presentation which are propositionally and linguistically complex.*

Table 11: The B2 descriptor from the CEFR scale 'Listening to announcements and instructions' (Council of Europe 2001:67)

Listening to announcements and instructions
B2 *Can understand announcements and messages on concrete and abstract topics spoken in standard dialect at normal speed.*

FCE Listening Part 1 tests whether candidates can understand a range of short texts (e.g. from radio documentaries and features, instructions, lectures, news, public announcements, discussions, interviews, radio plays, etc.) with a variety of focuses (e.g. gist, detail, purpose, attitude, opinion, topic, situation, agreement etc.) delivered in a variety of accents.

FCE's graphical CEFR profile

Figure 3 presents a graphic representation of the relationship of FCE to the levels of the CEFR as it emerged from the descriptions provided in Forms A8–A23. Figure 3 presents a uniform B2 profile across all components of FCE. This reflects FCE's test construction specifications which target one CEFR level: B2. FCE is constructed so as to exhibit a narrow range of item and task difficulty in order to test learner ability at B2 level as accurately as possible. This, however, does not mean that FCE has a completely flat CEFR profile. For example, around 10% of the items in the Listening paper (three items out of 30) will be either at B1.2 or B2.2 level but overall all Listening items will average B2 level, not B1.2 or B2.2.

Finally, FCE is neither intended nor designed to cover all forms of language functions described in the CEFR, e.g. spoken or written mediation. The length and components of the FCE exam are determined by the test takers' characteristics and needs (see p. 35 of the Manual). For instance, the FCE candidature varies widely in terms of first language, making first language mediation tasks impractical.

Reflections on Specification procedures

Reflections here will focus on two aspects: the practical use of the forms and how information sought by the forms can be embedded within an examination board practice.

Figure 3: Graphic profile of the relationship of FCE to CEFR levels (Form A23, p. 63 of the Manual). The term Language Competence in the graph entails linguistic, socio-linguistic, pragmatic and strategic competence

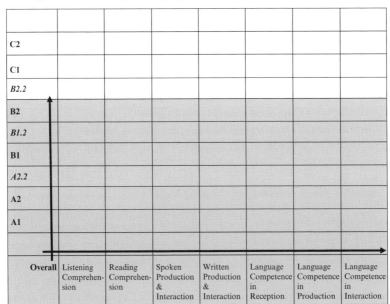

A manual by definition should be *concise* (whatever its length) and *practical* with the process explained logically step by step. Its *terminology must be consistent and unambiguous*, concepts should be defined, *information* should be easily distinguishable from *instructions*, and outcomes should be clearly specified. Above all, the target user must be considered at all times (Daldry 2006). We will consider below the extent to which the pilot version of the Manual meets these criteria and suggest ways in which it could be improved.

Concerning conciseness and practicality, in its current form the Manual provides an overload of background information. This often obscures the practical steps of gathering this background information which may be available to end users in a variety of documentation, e.g. in handbooks for teachers, candidate leaflets, or information provided on websites. Secondly, it is written in frequently dense prose with little attempt to guide the user by the use of layout conventions (e.g. bulleted lists, consistent and prominent numbering).

The practicality and conciseness could be improved as follows:

- By separating, with a simple referencing system, instructions which will form its main text from information sections which can be located in separate appendices. Lists of tables and forms should also be accessed in this way.

- The steps in the process should be bulleted and expressed using imperatives. Examples are needed for each step.
- The level of detail required on each form should be indicated. Currently, Form A6, for example, refers to feedback on the exam but does not indicate whether this is formal, informal, statistical or anecdotal.
- Forms, scales and tables should not be split over pages.
- Thought may be given to fixing the electronic forms so that lines do not move when words are typed on them. Similarly, thought may be given to facilitating the use of lozenges electronically.
- Certain sections or parts of sections may not be applicable to a particular examination. The introduction of a 'not applicable' category would provide that indication. For instance, for papers with OMR marking most of the questions on Form A3 are not relevant, but currently there is no way of showing this.

Terminology is another area where the Manual would benefit immensely from addressing issues arising. For example, what is the difference between a 'communicative task' and a 'communicative activity'? What is the difference between a 'content category' and a 'communication theme'? The references pointing to the CEFR are not helpful in these cases and may result in unhelpful repetition on the forms and/or confusing assumptions. A definition of terms or glossary would lead to greater clarification. Similarly, brief illustrative examples would be useful in avoiding overlap of information. Thought may be given to standardising the use of terminology (e.g. Form A3: rating grid/rating scale; performance in test/test performance; aspect of task/aspect of test performance; marker/rater). Cross referencing to Vantage level when working with a B2 level examination is essential. However, due to a lack of shared terminology, this process may prove to be time-consuming.

An issue that needs clarification is the target audience of the Specification forms which influences the style and, possibly, the level of detail disclosed. For example, is the user of the Manual to assume any shared knowledge of the examination being analysed or should there be extensive referencing to item-types and detail of content? Although sometimes the information required is factual, at other times the required information might not currently be in the public domain, for example details of grading (Forms A3–A4) or data analysis (Forms A5–A6). The forms also appear to record much information that overlaps with itself. The idea behind the graphical profile of Form A23 is clear but thought must be given as to how this form can be expanded to include all columns necessary for an examination testing four skills, such as FCE.

We will now move on to discuss how the information required by the

Manual can be embedded within an examination board practice. The Manual Specification forms aim at providing:

(i) a general and detailed description of the examination content with regard to issues of test development, marking, grading, data analysis, results reporting and rationale for decisions (Forms A1−A7)

(ii) mapping of the examination content onto the CEFR (Forms A8− A23) along individual and integrated skills as well as the language competence required by the examination.

Cambridge ESOL already makes available the information outlined in (i) in relation to FCE via internal documents, such as item writer guidelines, routine test production documentation, standard operational procedures for exam production, and grading manuals, as well as via publicly available documents, including the FCE Handbook and annual reports on FCE performance which can be accessed through the Cambridge ESOL website. These documents describe the objectives and the content of the FCE and explain how they are implemented.

Mapping an exam onto the CEFR, as envisaged in the Manual, corresponds to the planning and design phases of the FCE, and in general Cambridge ESOL's test development model (for a detailed description of the model see Saville 2003). In these phases, test specifications are produced linking needs to requirements of test usefulness and to frameworks of reference such as the CEFR. Decisions are made with regard to item types, text features, range of topics etc. Task design and scale construction take place which include explicit CEFR reference. This is documented in research publications (e.g. Khalifa and ffrench 2008 on the comparison of the CEFR and the FCE Speaking scales; Galaczi and ffrench 2007 on the revised Speaking assessment scales for Main Suite and BEC), examiner instruction booklets and item writer guidelines, and is fed back to examiners and item writers via training and co-ordination sessions.

The move towards further clarifying how the FCE (and the other Main Suite examinations) define and operationalise reading, listening, speaking and writing constructs in terms of, among other things, the CEFR is currently being documented in this UCLES/Cambridge University Press series *Studies in Language Testing* (e.g. Shaw and Weir 2007, Khalifa and Weir 2009). One of the key questions addressed, for example in the volume *Examining Writing* (Shaw and Weir 2007) is 'what are the criterial differences in terms of contextual parameters when assessing writing at the different CEFR levels?'. Further explicit reference to the CEFR is being introduced into the FCE processes over time where this serves to complement or clarify, for example when the FCE is revised and updated.

Conclusion

This paper has provided reflections on the piloting of the Manual Familiarisation and Specification procedures with an examination which already has an established connection with the CEFR, the FCE. More importantly, it has also shown how the Manual procedures can be complemented with non Manual activities which are in line with the aims of the Manual but more appropriate to an examination's context (here the FCE context) and how best they can be incorporated in FCE test development and validation processes as a means of maintaining the FCE−CEFR alignment. Ways of *maintaining* an exam−CEFR linkage, once a linking argument has been built, are not discussed in any detail in the current form of the Manual and we would welcome a more thorough treatment of this issue in the revised version.

We hope that this study has demonstrated that there are a number of ways of constructively using and complementing the Manual activities not only to build a linking argument but also to maintain it. As the regulatory function of the CEFR gathers pace, there is a risk that the Manual will become more prescriptive, which would be to the detriment of language testing and users of the results. We believe that the strength of the Manual lies, above all, in offering valid but also flexible linking procedures to ensure its ecological validity and a significant contribution to the field of language assessment.

References

Council of Europe (2001) *Common European Framework of Reference for Languages: Learning, teaching, assessment*, Cambridge: Cambridge University Press.

Council of Europe (2003a) *Relating language examinations to the Common European Framework of Reference for Languages: Learning, teaching, assessment: Manual, Preliminary Pilot Version*, Strasbourg: Council of Europe.

Council of Europe (2003b) *Samples of oral production illustrating, for English, the levels of the Common European Framework of Reference for Languages*, University of Cambridge ESOL Examinations DVD.

Council of Europe (2003c) *Samples of oral production illustrating, for English, the levels of the Common European Framework of Reference for Languages*, Eurocentres CD-ROM.

Council of Europe (2005) *Relating language examinations to the Common European Framework of Reference for Languages: learning, teaching, assessment (CEFR). Reading and Listening Items and Tasks: Pilot Samples illustrating the common reference levels in English, French, German, Italian and Spanish*, CD-ROM.

Daldry, H (2006) *Feedback on the use of the Preliminary Pilot version of the COE Manual in mapping the Cambridge ESOL FCE examination onto the CEFR*, Cambridge ESOL internal report.

Galaczi, E and ffrench, A (2007) Developing revised assessment scales for Main Suite and BEC Speaking tests, *Research Notes* 30, 28−31.

Jones, N (2000) Background to the validation of the ALTE 'Can-do' project and the revised Common European Framework, *Research Notes* 2, 11−13.

Jones, N (2001) The ALTE Can Do Project and the role of measurement in constructing a proficiency framework, *Research Notes* 5, 5–8.

Jones, N (2002) Relating the ALTE Framework to the Common European Framework of Reference, in Council of Europe, *Common European Framework of Reference for Languages: Learning, Teaching, Assessment. Case Studies*, Strasbourg: Council of Europe Publishing, 167–183.

Khalifa, H and ffrench, A (2008) *Aligning Cambridge ESOL exams and the CEFR: Issues and practices*, paper presented at the 34th Annual Conference of the International Association for Educational Assessment, Cambridge, UK, September 2008.

Khalifa, H and Weir, C (2009) *Examining Reading: Research and practice in assessing second language reading*, Cambridge: UCLES/Cambridge University Press.

North, B (2008) The CEFR levels and descriptor scales, in Taylor, L and Weir, C J (2008) *Multilingualism and Assessment: Achieving transparency, assuring quality, sustaining diversity. Proceedings of the ALTE Berlin Conference, May 2005*, Cambridge: UCLES/Cambridge University Press.

Saville, N (2003) The process of test development and revision within UCLES EFL, in Weir, C and Milanovic, M (Eds) *Continuity and innovation: revising the Cambridge Proficiency in English Examination 1913−2002*, Cambridge: UCLES/Cambridge University Press, 57−120.

Shaw, S and Weir, C (2007) *Examining Writing: Research and practice in assessing second language writing*, Cambridge: UCLES/Cambridge University Press.

Taylor, L and Jones, N (2006) Cambridge ESOL exams and the Common European Framework of Reference (CEFR), *Research Notes* 24, 1−5.

Van Ek, J and Trim, J (2001) *Vantage*, Cambridge: Cambridge University Press.

Appendices

Appendix 1: Workshop Programme

Programme of the CEFR Familiarisation and Training workshop, Cambridge, Friday 16 November 2007

9.30–10.00	Coffee and refreshments
10.00–10.15	Welcome and Introduction

CEFR Familiarisation

10.15–11.00	The origins, aims and nature of the CEFR The CEFR and Cambridge ESOL exams Using the CEFR to describe language exams
11.00–11.30	Coffee break
11.30–12.10	How the CEFR scales work: (i) Speaking, (ii) Writing, (iii) Reading & (iv) Listening (Descriptor-sorting) – four parallel sessions, one for each skill
12.10–13.00	Group discussion
13.00–14.00	Lunch break

CEFR Training

14.00–15.30	Using the CEFR to assess sample (Speaking and Writing) performances and (Reading and Listening) tasks (Rating activities) – four parallel sessions, one for each skill
15.30–16.45	Group discussion
16.45–17.00	Closing remarks

Appendix 2: A sample page from a Cambridge ESOL CEFR Induction Worksheet

Topic: The Common European Framework of Reference (CEFR)

Time req'd: 45–50 mins approx (accessing, reading, answering inc.)

Materials (all needed):
1. Council of Europe's (CoE) website on the CEFR
2. CEFR, 2001, Council of Europe
3. CoE's Publications List website
4. Materials illustrating the CEFR levels

Where to find materials:
1. http://www.coe.int/t/dg4/linguistic/CADRE_EN.asp
2. http://www.coe.int/t/dg4/linguistic/Source/Framework EN.pdf
   or the CEFR hard copy ('blue book') in the ESOL library: Council of Europe (2001) *Common European Framework of Reference for Languages: Learning, teaching, assessment*, Cambridge: Cambridge University Press
3. http://www.coe.int/t/dg4/linguistic/Publications_EN.asp
4. http://www.coe.int/T/DG4/Portfolio/?L=E&M=/main_p ages/illustrationse.html

induction worksheet

CODE:

The Common European Framework of Reference for Languages (CEFR)

Name ....

Unit ....

Location ....

CEFR: Its aims, uses and nature

Please consult the CoE's website on the CEFR [No 1 in the Materials list above] and answer the following questions.

1. In your own words what is the CEFR and what are its main aims?
    ....
    ....

2. To whom and why may the CEFR be of interest?
    ....
    ....

3. How many language versions of the CEFR currently exist?
    ....
    ....

Now please read pp. 1–2, 5–8 of the CEFR [2 in the Materials list], and answer the following questions.

4. Name two practical uses of the CEFR.
    ....
    ....

5. Why is the CEFR of interest for an assessment board such as Cambridge ESOL?
    ....
    ....

4 Benchmarking a high-stakes proficiency exam: the COPE linking project

Elif Kantarcıoğlu, Carole Thomas and John O'Dwyer
Bilkent University, Ankara, Turkey

Barry O'Sullivan
Roehampton University, London, UK

Abstract

Bilkent University School of English Language is linking its proficiency examination, the Certificate of Proficiency in English (COPE) examination, to the Common European Framework of Reference for Languages (CEFR). In order to achieve this, a project framework was designed which closely follows the guidelines set out in the preliminary draft of a Manual for *Relating language examinations to the Common European Framework of Reference for Languages* (Council of Europe 2003). This report presents the case study and the initial findings from the familiarisation, specification, standardisation and empirical validation stages of the project and includes reflections on the use of the Manual.

Purpose and context of the project

Background

Bilkent University, Ankara, Turkey, teaches in the medium of English. Students enrolled in the university who do not meet the required proficiency level of English to start their degree courses take English courses at the School of English Language (BUSEL). BUSEL produces and administers Bilkent's proficiency exam, the Certificate of Proficiency in English (COPE). Taken each year by approximately 3,000 students, the COPE is a high-stakes exam which determines whether students have the English language proficiency required for degree courses.

Goals

The 'COPE linking project', initiated in July 2006, aimed to link the exam to the CEFR at B2 level, thus strengthening the validity claim of the exam and meeting one of the principal aims of the CEFR, viz. to 'facilitate the mutual recognition of qualifications gained in different learning contexts and accordingly (will) aid European mobility' (Council of Europe 2001:1).

Relevance to national policy

The linking project supports political initiatives in Turkey, namely participation in negotiations to join the European Union, and the 1999 Bologna Declaration, which aims to facilitate mobility of students in the context of higher education. Turkey aligns itself strongly with European educational norms and practice. For example, schools are adopting the European Language Portfolio (ELP) and becoming more versed with the principles embodied in the CEFR initiative.

The COPE examination

The COPE exam, first set in 1990, was originally a general English language proficiency test. Since its inception, the exam has been modified and developed in line with practices in the field of proficiency testing. In particular, it has moved away from an emphasis on discrete point testing of grammar and vocabulary to a skills-based approach, approximating more the real life conditions the candidates will be exposed to. Major revisions took place between 1997 and 1998, followed by a further 2-year revision process between 2002 and 2004. The second period incorporated the use of the Rasch measurement model based on Item Response Theory (IRT) (Baker 1997, Hambleton, Swaminathan and Rogers 1991), and the extended Rasch model for dichotomous data by Linacre (1989). IRT is now used for anchoring, post test analysis and item banking, addressing a key concern of Alderson's (see Council of Europe 2003:66): 'if each time a new form of examination is produced, it varies according to content and difficulty, it is very difficult to compare the examination to the CEFR since the examination does not present a stable standard.' Minor modifications in 2005 based on Weir's Validation Framework (2005) led to a more fully developed set of test specifications and it was now felt that the exam had reached a stage whereby it would be meaningful and appropriate to link it to an external benchmark such as the CEFR.

The COPE consists of four papers: reading, writing, listening and language – a speaking exam has been developed to reflect CEFR level B2 and is awaiting implementation. The linking study focuses on the work that has been carried out to date on writing, reading and listening, details for which are provided in Appendix 1.

Reliability and validity evidence

Weir's framework views validity as a unitary concept and evidence of the validity of an exam must be gathered at all stages from initial development to post test analysis. Based on Weir's framework, the COPE has considered evidence of validity throughout the whole linking process. The test specifications reflect the BUSEL preparatory school syllabus with its skills based construct and tests are written to reflect these. New items are normally trialled and tests are composed of new and banked items, which serve as anchor items to place each version of the test onto a common scale. Detailed invigilation instructions are produced in booklet form to ensure uniformity of administration and special needs candidates are catered for as required by university and national regulations. A rigorous standardisation of raters is carried out and double marking is standard procedure. Standard setting is based on both Classical Test Theory and Item Response Theory analysis, that is carried out prior to setting the cut score. In order to ensure that all candidates have been fairly treated, borderline remarking is carried out whereby all candidates who fall short of the cut score by 10 points have their papers re-marked.

Project design

Scope

The COPE linking project closely followed the methodology described in the preliminary draft of a Manual for relating examinations to the CEFR (Council of Europe 2003) (henceforth referred to as 'the Manual') and all four interrelated stages – Familiarisation, Specification, Standardisation and Empirical Validation – were undertaken.

Participants

The make-up of the panel of judges and the quality of the judgements made are determining factors in the success of a linking project. The Manual advocates a group composed of a minimum of 10 people to act as judges throughout the linking process. The COPE linking project group was formed from 15 members of BUSEL, five of whom had some familiarity with the CEFR, and included representatives from all parties in the school from senior managers to teachers. The project was developed and led by two of the group members who were closely involved in the development and production of COPE. The project leaders led the familiarisation, specification and standardisation sessions and also participated in the activities and acted as judges in standard setting. External experts were brought in at different stages in order to have an outsider perspective and to guard against institutional bias.

Familiarisation stage (Chapter 3 of the Manual)

The familiarisation stage followed the activities suggested in the Manual, supplemented by a number of in-house prepared materials, including short tests, referred to as quizzes. The nature of the group and its relative inexperience in using the CEFR led to the decision to extend the familiarisation activities over a period of eight months.

An important element of the familiarisation stage is the empirical validation of the judges. Table 1 presents an analysis of the principal tasks used in the familiarisation stage, providing evidence on both the consistency of the judges while working with the CEFR descriptors and their level of familiarity with the CEFR framework. Data was gathered and analysed through Cronbach Alpha, Intraclass correlation coefficient (ICC) and Pearson correlations as well as FACETS, based on the many-facet Rasch model (Linacre 1989) enabling the comparison of the facets involved in the familiarisation activities, viz. the descriptors in the scales and the judges' performance. Scores from Alpha, ICC and Pearson correlation indices presented in Table 1 show that the judges performed successfully in the familiarisation tasks. However, FACETS outcomes are difficult to interpret. In terms of the fit statistics, the mean infit values are within the acceptable range as an infit of between 0.4 and 1.2 for raters' performance is considered reasonable by Linacre and Wright (1994). In order to accurately interpret the reliability, on the other hand, it is crucial to indicate here that the Rasch reliability index is:

> . . . a rather misleading term as it is *not* an indication of the extent of agreement between raters (the traditional meaning of reliability indices between raters) but the extent to which they really differ in their level of severity. High reliability indices in this table indicate real differences between raters, not in their overall ranking of candidates, but in the actual levels of scores assigned to them (McNamara 1996:140).

Therefore, the reliability index needs to be low for raters, that is, judges in our context (Linacre 2007:149). Here, however, this is not the case and it contradicts the raw data where the judges seem to have misplaced only one or two descriptors. A possible conclusion is that the raw data was almost perfect and slight drifts became big deviations in the analysis. This is also reflected in the reliability indices. In order to ensure reliability, monitoring and training of the judges continued throughout the specification and standardisation stages.

Table 1: Agreement and consistency of judges – familiarisation activities

	Global	Read.	Listen.	Writ.	Qz 1	Qz 2
Alpha	.9935	.9970	.9974	.9977	.9734	.9695
ICC	.9935	.9970	.9974	.9977	.9734	.9695
Pear. Corr.	1.000	1.000	.9977	1.000	.7950	.7950
Mean Infit	.70	.76	.85	.62	.83	.92
Reliability	1.00	1.00	1.00	1.00	.43	.51

Specification stage (Chapter 4 of the Manual)

Phase 1 of the specification stage required a general description of the exam, using Forms A1–A8 which are provided in the Manual. These were filled in by the project leaders as not all the details required were known by the other project members. In phase 2, the detailed description of content in relation to the CEFR, and the descriptive sections of the specification forms that were relevant for the COPE exam (A9, A10, A14, A19, A21) were also filled in by the project leaders but no CEFR levels were assigned. It was decided that for reliability purposes, the CEFR level for each paper would be assigned by the CEFR project group members during the specification session.

During the specification session, forms A9 (listening comprehension), A10 (reading comprehension) and A14 (written production) were looked at by the group. Terminology was discussed to ensure a shared understanding of the CEFR's 'action-oriented approach' to language learning (Council of Europe 2001:9). Once this had been agreed, the assigning of the level for each skill was carried out by looking at the COPE, the test specifications and the CEFR descriptors. This was undertaken individually, followed by whole group discussion until a level consensus was reached. The group showed a 100% agreement on the level of listening comprehension and written production, and a 90% agreement for reading comprehension. Time constraints, and the perceived complexity of the forms for aspects of communicative language competence, led to the decision for group members to fill in the forms in their own time. This turned out to be a complex task and as a result, the forms were returned to individual group members several times before final agreement could be reached.

The results of the specification stage are summarised in Appendix 2, using a graphical profile. They support the initial assumption that the COPE exam is generally at B2 level. The listening paper falls into the higher end of the B2 scale, particularly with reference to the scale for listening to audio media and recordings, whereby candidates have to be able to identify speakers' viewpoints and attitudes as well as information content (B2+). The slightly higher profile for linguistic and strategic competence in reception compared to production is not unexpected given that students are in a non-English speaking environment. For example, they have a broad lexical repertoire and can understand idiomatic expressions and colloquialisms (C1) but are unable to reproduce this high level of linguistic competence for written production. In the socio-linguistic band, found to be relevant only for the listening paper, students were placed lower due to the fact that they can recognise salient politeness conventions (B1 level) but are unable to keep up with fast and colloquial discussions (B2 level).

Standardisation stage (Chapter 5 of the Manual)

Standard setting methods

The Examinee-Paper Selection Method was used for the standard setting of the writing paper as it is considered to be the most suitable for polytomously scored performance tasks and because standard-setting decisions are based on actual examinee papers (Hambleton, Jaeger, Plake and Mills 2000). Both the original Angoff, also known as the Footnote method, and the Yes/No method, an Angoff-based method modified by Impara and Plake (Cizek and Bunch 2007), were employed for the reading and listening paper standard setting. The two Angoff-based methods were chosen as they are not only the most widely used and most thoroughly researched standard-setting methods but are 'well suited for tests comprising multiple choice format items' (Cizek and Bunch 2007:82). The use of two distinct methods allowed for potentially different cut scores and comparison of these, which contributed to the reliability of the established cut score.

Training of judges

The judges underwent an extensive familiarisation stage before being called upon to act as judges, and the degree of the judges' internalisation of the CEFR was monitored until it became clear that they were ready to move on to standardisation. Prior to standard setting, the judges were further trained by using the CEFR calibrated samples provided by the Council of Europe.

Table 2 presents data regarding agreement and consistency among the judges in the training stages of each standard-setting panel. The types of indices provided in this table demonstrate that the writing and reading

Table 2: Agreement and consistency among judges – standard setting

	Writing	Reading	Listening
Alpha	.8499	.9791	.9011
ICC	.8015	.9773	.8989
Pear. Corr.	.373	.782	.456
Mean Infit	.76	1.00	.93
Reliability	.00	.00	.67

training sessions were clearly successful with very high alpha, ICC and Rasch reliability values with the exception of the listening paper. Further training was carried out until the group reached consensus on the levels allocated for the calibrated samples.

Standard-setting procedures

Although different standard-setting methods were used for productive and receptive skills, the procedures followed were similar and cyclical, as illustrated in Figure 1. Judges were first asked to analyse the performance samples or items individually and answer the standard-setting question relevant to the method used as described above. Individual judgements were then entered onto an Excel sheet and the collated results shared with the judges. The information consisted of mean ratings for each sample or item, standard deviation indices, and the ratings of each judge. This was followed by a group discussion of the aggregated results where raters had a chance to justify their ratings. After the discussion, in order to inform the decision making process for round 2, the judges were given live test data showing how these same items performed under exam conditions. In addition to the procedures followed in Figure 1, at the end of each round judges were asked to indicate their confidence level in their judgements for each of the performance samples/items

Figure 1: General procedures followed in the standard-setting sessions for all skills

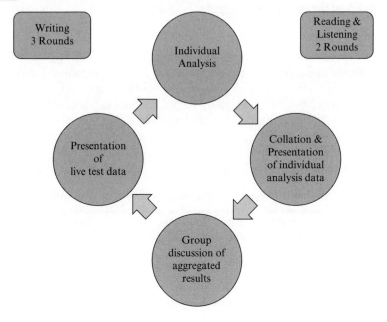

(Hambleton and Plake 1995) so that extra information could be collected regarding the reliability of the standard-setting process.

Results of standard setting

The consistency of the judges was demonstrated using Cronbach Alpha and the Pearson correlation. The agreement was demonstrated using intraclass correlation coefficient (ICC), which shows to what extent the average rater agreed with all others. Kaftandjieva (Council of Europe 2004:23) points out that correlational analyses are not appropriate for standard-setting purposes as 'it is possible to have a perfect correlation of ± 1.00 between two judges with zero-agreement between them about the levels to which descriptors, items, examinees or their performances belong'. Therefore, consistency and agreement among judges are also reported using multi-faceted Rasch (MFR) analysis, which looks at a score based on a number of facets. In this case, the facets involved are the samples, judges and the CEFR scales. Lord's 1983 suggestion that Rasch is the most appropriate IRT model for small data sets supports the decision to use MFR (in Baker 1993:204). The data in Tables 3, 4, 5 and 6 shows that the standard-setting sessions were successful. Table 3 presents information about the agreement and consistency of the judges. Alpha and ICC were clearly acceptable in all the standard-setting sessions.

Table 3: Agreement and consistency of the judges

	N	Alpha	ICC	Pear. Corr.	Mean Infit	Reliability	Av. Confid. Level
Writing	11	.9963	.9704	.946	.47	.00	3.40
Reading – Yes/No	10	.7901	.7920	.313	1.02	.32	3.44
Reading – Angoff	10	.9223	.9217	.286	.94	.87	3.22
Listening – Yes/No	11	.9347	.9347	.566	.97	.31	3.41
Listening – Angoff	11	.8946	.8946	.459	.96	.81	3.33

Empirical validation stage (Chapter 6 of the Manual)

The empirical validation stage has been ongoing and therefore, limited evidence regarding the internal and external validity of June 2008 COPE is presented here. The first type of evidence comes from the live exam itself. Table 4 presents the descriptive statistics for the reading and listening papers from the live running of the exam. It can be seen that the mean for the reading paper is slightly below the cut score established at the standard-setting, which is 21, and that of the listening paper is almost the same as the standard setting decision, which is 16. Both papers have acceptable difficulty and point biserial values with moderate reliability. The population for the June administration is truncated as the candidates tend to be from the BUSEL programme. This would account for the relatively low reliability values reported here (the average reliability values for COPE over the past four years are 0.79 for reading and 0.78 for listening).

Table 4: Descriptive statistics for reading and listening

N: 948	READING PAPER (out of 35)	LISTENING PAPER (out of 30)
Mean	18.652	15.858
Variance	20.721	14.981
St. Dev.	4.552	3.871
Skew	−0.061	0.087
Kurtosis	0.155	0.156
Min	3	0
Max	32	28
Median	19	16
Alpha	0.667	0.603
SEM	2.629	2.437
Mean P	0.533	0.529
Mean Item-tot	0.283	0.282
Mean Biserial	0.375	0.375

The second type of evidence is based on teacher judgements. As a preliminary study, two months before the exam was administered, three members of the project group were asked to assess a small sample of students and assign CEFR levels in skills and language competence. This sample was too small to make solid statistical statements about the cut score but it does allow for moderate approximations. The results were promising, as shown in Table 5. This small scale study shows a 70.83% agreement (17 students out of 24) between the classifications based on the test performance interpreted using the estimated cut score from the standard-setting stage of the project and on the criterion, which is the teacher assessment of student ability.

Table 5: COPE–CEFR standard-setting decision table

Test (Item Bank)

		Below B2	B2	Above B2	Total
Criterion (teachers)	Below B2	9	2		11
	B2	5	8		13
	Above B2			0	0
	Total	14	10	0	24

The third type of evidence provided is a result of the correlations between judges' estimates of reading and listening item difficulty established in the standard-setting sessions and the actual difficulty values of those items from the June administration. Table 6 indicates that there were acceptable correlations between the judges' estimates and the true difficulty values of the items.

Table 6: Correlations between judge estimates and item difficulty values

Correlations	Yes/No Method	Angoff Method
Judge estimates and item difficulty for listening	0.56	0.63
Judge estimates and item difficulty for reading	0.51	0.49

Reflections on the use of the draft Manual

Issues encountered

Setting up the CEFR project group

The Manual stipulates that the CEFR project group should be composed of people who have experience in different fields such as syllabus design, test specification writing, assessing productive skills, language testing, item writing, standard setting and the co-ordination and training of groups of teachers and examiners (p. 66). Forming a team which meets such criteria would present a challenge to any organisation. The Manual seeks to encourage networking, both local and international, in the linking process. However, international networking, which involves bringing people into the institution, has proved time consuming and costly, even in a context with good international connections. Local networking has been challenging due to the difficulty of finding people in the Turkish university sector who have worked with the CEFR. It would appear that the Manual is somewhat unrealistic in terms of the availability of expertise within any regular educational organisation. The solution in our context was to form an internal group of 15 experts who underwent an 8-month CEFR training period prior to commencing the project.

Familiarisation

The success of any linking project depends on how reliable the judgements are. The data from the familiarisation activities indicated that the judges were quite familiar with the CEFR and shared a common understanding of the CEFR as an educational policy. In particular, they had a clear notion of what the B2 level entails. To reach the level of familiarisation required to proceed to the specification and standardisation stages was a lengthy process and the proposed schedule in the Manual is unhelpful, particularly when the group is relatively inexperienced in terms of the CEFR. Although the familiarisation activities suggested were useful, it was found to be far more meaningful and the CEFR levels were more clearly understood when they were applied in context, that is when familiarisation moved on to working directly with the COPE itself and with the Council of Europe recommended exemplar tasks (Council of Europe 2005). In our experience, real familiarisation comes with the standardisation. This was particularly evident with the reading paper, the standard setting for which had to be carried out over five sessions, with the end result being a shared understanding of the B2 level in particular.

Specification

All members of the group were involved in the specification stage and this was successful in terms of completing the forms for reading, listening and writing. However, before the forms could be filled in, lengthy discussion was held in order to clarify terms such as the difference between a task and an activity. Although the Manual does not actually stipulate that these forms should be filled in by the whole group, it was, nevertheless felt to be a valuable training exercise and was more reliable as the specification forms were looked at from multiple perspectives and not only from a testing point of view. A significant problem was felt to be with the forms of communicative language competence which had to be sent out to the participants twice. It soon became clear that individual judgement outside of a formal session could not be relied upon as it was difficult to get agreement without whole group discussion. The time constraints hindered the process and it was not always possible to rely on work being done outside of the session. The issue was only resolved by holding a further specification session to complete the forms. Despite the initial problems, however, this was a very beneficial exercise to carry out, allowing as it does, for a very thorough inspection of the exam in question. As a result of specification, minor modifications were made to the COPE test specifications.

Standard setting

The procedure outlined in the Manual presents a rather linear process. However, in our experience, this was far from being the case, epitomised by our repeated efforts to set a cut score for the reading paper as mentioned in the previous section.

There was also the issue of using more than one standard-setting method. This decision was taken due to our lack of experience with standard-setting methods and the need to find the most suitable method for our specific context. The initial standard-setting session for the reading paper involved the use of three different methods (Basket, Angoff and Yes/No) and this proved to be too much for many of the judges, requiring as it does a different mind-set each time a different method is employed. Based on this experience, the subsequent standard-setting sessions for both reading and listening employed only two methods. It was decided that the Basket method should not be used as it was not based on the definition of the least able B2 candidate used by the other two methods, and is not suitable where a single level and cut score are required. Of the two methods employed, the use of the Angoff method caused difficulty for some of the judges who found it hard to make decisions based on the question 'what is the probability of the least able B2 candidate getting this question correct?'. The Angoff ratings also proved to be less reliable in terms of the FACETS reliability indices presented in Table 3. Therefore, it would appear to be more reliable, at least in our experience, to base the cut scores of dichotomously scored receptive papers on the Yes/No method results.

As is advocated in the Manual, a number of CEFR calibrated writing scripts were chosen for the purpose of training the judges. Three samples were taken from Cambridge ESOL and one sample from IELTS. Although the Cambridge ESOL samples are benchmarked to the CEFR, they are difficult to relate to the academic context, in particular the short letter format. Thus an IELTS sample was included based on the claims in a guide which suggests a link between scores on the IELTS Writing paper and the CEFR descriptors (Taylor 2004). The reading and listening samples were less problematic and the group made use of DIALANG, Cambridge ESOL and the Finnish Matriculation samples (Council of Europe 2005). The Finnish matriculation samples were found to be particularly useful and appropriate for our context as they have items at different levels for one text, similar to the COPE reading and listening papers which have an item range for a single text from B1 to C1 level.

Empirical validation

The empirical validation stage of a linking study, as presented in the Manual, has two main parts; internal validation and external validation. Empirical validation is seen as confirming the claims formulated through the Specification and Standardisation stages (p. 100) and comes at the end of this linear process of linking. However, it was our experience that every stage of the linking process is a learning experience which requires going back to previous stages and making modifications. Therefore, the entire linking project should be recognised as being a cyclical process. Standardisation in particular is a stage where participants get a chance to work with concrete samples reflecting CEFR levels with written justifications which help them understand, for instance, the key features of B2 level items, tasks or text levels. Such an activity helps participants deepen their familiarity with the levels and this new understanding of the levels may conflict with the premature understanding they may have demonstrated at the specification stage. Therefore the participants may feel the need to make modifications to the specification forms – something which actually occurred in this project, particularly in relation to the writing paper.

The cyclical nature of the linking process also comes into play while collecting evidence regarding the validity of the linking claim. This suggests that validation should not be left to the end of the process. Part of the evidence on the validity of the claim results from the data accumulated on the quality of each of the stages in the linking process. Starting from the familiarisation stage, data needs to be gathered so as to provide evidence on how well each stage was carried out. In fact, we would argue that the linking procedure itself is a key element of validation in which evidence of level and quality are seen as contributing significantly to the validation argument.

Limitations and future work

One limitation to the study undertaken was the limited number of COPE writing samples that were chosen. Two days of discussion and training only allowed the group to look at five scripts. This may be too small a sample to make any strong claim that a band 3 COPE paper (out of 5) is equivalent to B2. This will be remedied in the near future where the intention is to look at a much broader range of samples and to determine what COPE bands 3, 4 and 5 mean in terms of the CEFR.

While the initial work with teacher judgements was beneficial as a preliminary study, we feel that a much larger sample would provide us with more stable and reliable data with which to confirm the cut score. In fact, this work has already begun, with an expanded study scheduled for January 2009. Also in the future, we intend to use the benefits of the linking project to improve institutional familiarity with the target level. This in itself will, we believe, increase the validity claims of courses that are delivered to achieve the B2 standard.

Impact

The COPE linking project has had an impact on the exam and the institution. In particular, following the linking process has allowed for minor modifactions to the production and delivery of the COPE. In terms of the writing paper, minor changes have been made to the prompts provided. As for the reading and listening papers, the detailed analysis of the relationship between text and questions has provided a deeper insight into item writing and what differentiates a question aimed at B2 level candidates from that aimed at B1 or C1 level. This has now been incorporated into the test specifications for item writers.

In terms of its benefit to the institution, one of the most positive aspects has been on the awareness raising of a group of 15 key members of the school who are now very familiar with the B2 level. This group of people will be used to disseminate the CEFR throughout the school and to train teachers who are working at the Pre Faculty level to ensure that teachers and students have a shared understanding of exit level required in BUSEL. There are plans to align the exams at lower levels in BUSEL and to plan full scale linking projects at B1 and A2 levels.

Concluding comments

The project reported on here has already had a major impact on the COPE examination and on BUSEL. The level of the examination is now far clearer than previously understood while the quality of the papers has also improved due to the increased professionalisation of the writing and delivery process. The impact on the institution is, to date, unclear. However, anecdotal evidence suggests that there have been improvements to the way in which assessment is viewed within the school and, perhaps more importantly, the project has contributed significantly to our conceptualisation of the B2 learner.

Any linking project is a major undertaking, and it has been our experience that the real benefit to an institution undertaking such a project is the embedding of the culture of quality and standards into the institution itself, an integral element of organisational learning (O'Dwyer 2008).

References

Alderson, J C (2002) *Relating Language Examinations to the Common European Framework: The Hungarian experience*, unpublished manuscript, in Council of Europe (2003) *Relating Language Examinations to the Common European Framework of Reference for Languages: Learning, teaching, assessment: Preliminary Pilot Manual*, Strasbourg: Council of Europe, Language Policy Division.

Baker, F B (1993) Sensitivity to the linear logistic test model to misspecification of the weight matrix, *Applied Psychological Measurement* 17, London: Sage Publications, 201.

Baker, R (1997) *Classical test theory and item response theory in test analysis: Extracts from an investigation of the Rasch model in its application to foreign language proficiency testing* (Language testing update. Special Report No 2), Lancaster: Lancaster University.

Cizek, G J and Bunch, M B (2007) *Standard Setting*, Thousand Oaks, CA: Sage.

Council of Europe (2001) *Common European Framework of Reference for Languages: Learning, teaching, assessment*, Cambridge: Cambridge University Press.

Council of Europe (2003) *Relating Language Examinations to the Common European Framework of Reference for Languages: Learning, teaching, assessment: Preliminary Pilot Manual*, Strasbourg: Council of Europe, Language Policy Division.

Council of Europe (2004) *Reference Supplement to the Preliminary Pilot Version of the Manual for Relating Language Examinations to the Common European Framework of Reference for Languages: Learning, teaching, assessment*, Strasbourg: Council of Europe, Language Policy Division.

Council of Europe (2005) CD-ROM to accompany the Manual for *Relating Language Examinations to the Common European Framework of Reference for Languages: Learning, teaching, assessment*, Council of Europe, Language Policy Division.

Hambleton, R K and Plake, B S (1995) Using an Extended Angoff procedure to set standards on complex performance assessments, *Applied Measurement in Education* 8 (1), 41–55.

Hambleton, R K, Swaminathan, H and Rogers, H J (1991) *Fundamentals of Item Response Theory*, London: Sage Publications.

Hambleton, R K, Jaeger, R M, Plake, B S and Mills, C (2000) Setting performance standards on complex educational assessments, *Applied Psychological Measurement* 24, 355–366.

Linacre, J M (1989) *Many-facet Rasch measurement*, Chicago: MESA Press.

Linacre, J M (2007) FACETS Rasch measurement computer program, Chicago: winsteps.com.

Linacre, J M and Wright, B D (1994) Reasonable mean-square fit values, *Rasch Measurement Transactions* 8 (3), 370.

McNamara, T (1996) Measuring Second Language Performance, New York: Addison Wesley Longman.

O'Dwyer, J (2008) *Formative Evaluation for Organisational Learning*, Frankfurt: Peter Lang.

Taylor, L (2004) IELTS, Cambridge ESOL examinations and the Common European Framework, *Research Notes* 18, 2–3.

Weir, C J (2005) *Language Testing and Validation: an evidence-based approach*, Oxford: Palgrave.

APPENDIX 1

Table 1: Writing paper

Aim	To test the ability to produce an extended piece of meaningful and appropriate discourse in response to a given prompt.
Objectives tested	Comprehension of a given prompt. Production of accurate, fluent, appropriate and coherent prose. Clear organisation and prioritisation of ideas. Justification of a viewpoint through the provision of supporting detail and examples.
Duration	60 minutes.
Word limit	350 words.
Task	A choice of two topics – a written prompt of approximately five lines.
Criteria	Scale of 5 – Holistic criteria with a focus on content, organisation, grammar and vocabulary. Band 3 is considered as the pass grade.
Marking procedures	Standardisation sessions take place before each exam marking. Double marking is done. In cases of discrepancies the first and the second raters are asked to discuss the grades together and reach a decision. If agreement cannot be reached the moderator is consulted and makes the final decision. Borderline remarking is also carried out and any candidate who fails to meet the overall cut-off score for the exam has their writing paper re-marked.
Training and monitoring raters	A core group of 18 people make up the COPE writing marking team. They were initially chosen based on prior rating experience and were trained over a period of time. After each marking session, IRT analysis is carried out to monitor rater performance. FACETS Rater reliability coefficient: .92 (June 2007) and .97 (September 2007).

Table 2: Reading paper

Aim	To test the ability to comprehend and interpret directly stated and/or inferred information from a reading text.
Objectives tested	Reading carefully for global and local comprehension. Propositional inferencing.
Duration	1 hour 15 minutes.
Tasks	Six reading texts with a total of 35 questions.
Criteria	1 point for each correct answer.
Marking procedures	Machine scored as all responses are multiple choice.

Table 3: Listening paper

Aim	To test the ability to comprehend and interpret directly stated and/or inferred information from a reading text.
Objectives tested	Listening carefully for global and local comprehension.
Duration	55 minutes.
Tasks	Two listening texts (lecture style) with a total of 30 questions.
Criteria	1 point for each correct answer.
Marking procedures	Machine scored as all responses are multiple choice.

APPENDIX 2

Graphic profile of the relationship of the COPE examination to CEFR levels

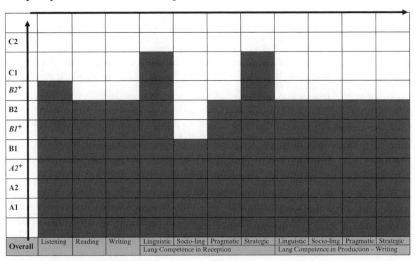

5 Mapping the Advanced Level Certificate in English (ALCE) examination onto the CEFR

Nigel Downey and Charalambos Kollias
Hellenic American Union and Hellenic American
University, Athens, Greece

Abstract

This document describes the procedures conducted by the Hellenic American Union and the Hellenic American University to map the Advanced Level Certificate in English (ALCE) to the Common European Framework of Reference for Languages (CEFR), in accordance with the preliminary draft of a Manual for relating language examinations to the CEFR. The linking project was carried out following thorough familiarisation with the descriptions of the levels as set out in the CEFR and with the linking procedures set out in the Preliminary Pilot Version (Council of Europe 2003). The result of the claim by specification and standard setting suggests that the ALCE examination is targeted at the C1 level of the CEFR.

Case study report

Background, purpose and context of the linking project

The Advanced Level Certificate in English (ALCE) is a high-stakes standardised examination designed for candidates who require certification of their competency in English as a foreign language at an advanced proficiency level and is administered in Greece, Turkey and the Balkans. The examination is divided into four parts: a Listening Section of 40 multiple-choice items; a Grammar, Vocabulary and Reading (GVR) Section, comprising 40 multiple-choice grammar items, 40 multiple-choice vocabulary items and 20 multiple-choice reading items; one task from the Writing Section; and a Speaking Section lasting approximately 15 minutes. Each of the four sections has a separate cut-off score, and receives equal weighting in the final scoring. The overall pass/fail grade is awarded through aggregate scoring of the IRT weighted scores for the Listening and GVR Sections with the scores from the

Writing and Speaking Sections, and allows candidates a narrow fail in one section, provided their overall score is above the combined overall cut-off score.

Candidates who are successful in the ALCE examination obtain a certificate which documents their level of English for educational, occupational, public or personal purposes. For example, the ALCE certificate can be used as proof of language competence when applying to universities and colleges in Europe and further abroad, and it is recognised by the Greek Supreme Council for Civil Personnel Selection (ΑΣΕΠ) at the level of 'very good knowledge' (πολύ καλή γνώση), and can therefore be used as language certification for obtaining employment and promotion in both the public and private sectors in Greece.

The linking project was begun in order to assess the ALCE examination in terms of the levels defined by the CEFR. The ALCE examination was designed to bridge the gap between examinations claimed respectively to be at B2 and C2 level and had been extensively revised in the light of the CEFR scales and descriptors. It was therefore necessary to investigate whether the revised ALCE examination could be linked to the C1 level.

Design of the linking project and the instruments used

The project involved familiarisation with the CEFR and the descriptors of the levels, followed by a detailed analysis of the specifications of the ALCE examination in order to determine its correlation with the levels of the CEFR. This was then followed by the Standardisation Phase. These phases are explained below.

The linking project was carried out by a committee of 10 members, comprising eight item writers and two co-ordinators working for the Hellenic American University on the ALCE examination. Nine of the project members were holders of an MA in TEFL and all were teachers of EFL and teacher trainers, in addition to being testing specialists. Seven of the members had a native English speaker background and three were non-native speakers. Throughout the linking process, the committee was advised by consultants from Cito, the Netherlands.

The project was divided into four phases, as proposed in the Preliminary Pilot Version of the *Manual for Relating Language Examinations to the CEF* (Council of Europe 2003, henceforth: the Manual): Phase 1: Familiarisation; Phase 2: Specification; Phase 3: Standardisation; and Phase 4: Empirical validation. The fourth phase is planned for future research, and therefore this report will discuss the execution and results of the first three phases only.

Phase 1: Familiarisation

As suggested by the Manual (p. 6), an in-depth familiarisation with the content and levels of the CEFR was carried out before proceeding with further phases. The familiarisation involved a number of stages. These stages were carried out during a series of group sessions led by consultants from Cito, the Netherlands:

1. Project members studied copies of the Common European Framework and the Preliminary Pilot Version of the Manual prior to commencing the group sessions.
2. Project members carried out a group discussion on the aims, objectives and content of the CEFR, and its relevance to language teaching and testing.
3. The global scales defining the six levels were discussed and a jumbled list of the descriptors was then sorted and allotted to each level. A further discussion of the levels in the light of this process was then carried out.
4. A jumbled list of the overall descriptors for each of the sections – listening, reading, spoken interaction, spoken production and writing – was given to project members and was in turn sorted according to level and the results discussed.
5. Project members discussed the illustrative subscales for each of these sections, noting which subscales were most relevant to the content of the ALCE examination.
6. Finally, project members also sorted and discussed descriptors from the DIALANG scales.

Phase 2: Specification

The Specification Phase involved the project members mapping the ALCE examination in relation to the categories and levels of the CEFR.

Firstly, a full Manual for the ALCE examination was produced, which described the format, content and rationale of all sections of the examination in detail. Using information gained during this process, a content analysis of the ALCE examination was then carried out in order to complete Forms 1–23 of the Preliminary Pilot Manual. This process involved examining each component of the ALCE examination in terms of which domain candidates are expected to show ability in; which communicative themes, tasks, activities, strategies, text-types and tasks candidates are expected to handle; and at which level on the CEFR scales each component should be situated.

From this data, a table was compiled showing a graphic profile of the relationship between the ALCE examination and the CEFR levels (Figure 1). The final impression after carrying out the Specification Phase was that the ALCE examination should be mapped to the C1 level. This is consistent with its design and rationale as a high-stakes examination at advanced proficiency

Figure 1: Form A23: Graphic profile of relationship of ALCE examination to CEFR levels

	Overall	Listening	Reading	Social Conversation	Information Exchange	Notes, Messages and Forms	Socio-linguistic	Pragmatic	Linguistic
C2									
C1									
B2.2									
B2									
B1.2									
B1									
A2.2									
A2									
A1									

level. It should be noted that extensive revisions to the ALCE examination had been carried out prior to the linking project, which entailed detailed familiarisation with the CEFR in general and the C1 level in particular, in order to ensure that the tasks, content and rationale were appropriate for an examination aiming at this level.

Phase 3: Standardisation

The procedures for the standard setting of the ALCE examination follow those set out in the Manual and in the *Reference Supplement to the Preliminary Pilot Version of the Manual for Relating Language Examinations to the Common European Framework of Reference for Languages* (Council of Europe 2004).

The procedures used were as follows:

- the selection of the most appropriate and effective method of standard setting for each section of the ALCE examination
- the selection of a large number of judges, based on their qualifications and experience of language teaching and testing

- the training of the judges on the appropriate criteria, as defined in the CEFR and the *Manual for the Advanced Level Certificate in English* (Hellenic American University, 2005)
- the establishment by the judges of cut-off scores for each section
- data analysis of the judges' cut-off scores.

Since the Listening Section and Grammar, Vocabulary and Reading Section of the ALCE examination are machine scored, the standard setting for these two sections followed precisely the same procedures. However, as the Speaking Section and the Writing Section are scored by individual raters, the standard setting for each was performed separately.

The standard setting was carried out on the items used in the January 2006 ALCE examination in successive meetings during January and February 2006. Standard setting was carried out on the Writing Section and Speaking Section in June 2006.

Listening Section and Grammar, Vocabulary and Reading (GVR) Section

Standard setting for the Listening Section and Grammar, Vocabulary and Reading (GVR) Section of the ALCE examination was carried out using the modified Angoff method (Taube 1997). This method was chosen due to its appropriateness for a multiple-choice format and its efficiency of use.

In carrying out this method, carefully selected judges first took part in a thorough familiarisation and training session before assessing each section. They were then asked to examine each item and assess the percentage of candidates minimally acceptable at the level that would be likely to choose the correct answer choice for this item. The judges' decisions were collated and a cut-off score for each section set. The number of judges suggested by the literature for carrying out the modified Angoff standard setting should be 'at least 10 and ideally 15 to 20 judges' (Brandon 2004:68). Thus, for greater precision in setting the cut-off score estimates, 20 judges were used for the standard setting of the Listening and the GVR Sections.

The judges used were selected for their qualifications and experience of teaching English as a Foreign Language and of testing in this field. Ten of the judges had prior experience of standard-setting procedures, of whom nine also had experience of item writing for high-stakes tests. All the judges were practising teachers at the time of the standard setting and all had experience as Oral Examiners for a variety of tests at a variety of levels.

Each of the judges was asked to complete a Background Information Form. The Form records a summary of their educational and teaching experience, as well as any experience they may have had with the ALCE examination, for inclusion in the documentation of the standard setting. In addition, a Curriculum Vitae of each judge was also kept on file. In order to familiarise the judges with the CEFR and the CEFR scales, the judges were first introduced to the rationale and context of the CEFR. The next part of the judges' training involved familiarisation with the 'Can Do' statements of the CEFR. Before each section of the ALCE examination, the judges were required to examine the 'Can Do' statements for that section, both the overall descriptors and those more specific, in order to rank them according to the six scales of the CEFR. The participants carried out this task individually and then compared their rankings in pairs and groups.

A detailed discussion of the rankings followed, with participants justifying their decisions and receiving feedback on the order as defined in the CEFR. All present were able to reach a consensus on the ranking without difficulty and developed their awareness of what defines each level as described by the CEFR. Participants were then directed to focus on the descriptors for the C1 level – the level which the ALCE examination is aimed at. This level was discussed in detail and contrasted with the C2 level above and the B2 level below in order to clarify exactly what C1 means in terms of the CEFR. For the Grammar and Vocabulary Sections, the DIALANG scales were also used as a reference point as there are no CEFR detailed descriptors for discrete grammar and vocabulary items.

Having established the criteria for the level, the judges were then trained in the criteria for making a decision on actual test items according to the modified Angoff method. They were asked to examine each of the test items in terms of the percentage of candidates minimally acceptable at the level that would be likely to choose the correct answer choice.

Familiarisation was carried out for Listening, Grammar, Vocabulary and Reading in turn. After each familiarisation activity, the judges examined the items relating to that particular language area. For the Listening Section, the recording was played with a longer pause after each item to allow the judges sufficient time to record their decision. Forms were given to the judges to record their decisions for each of the language areas and the same procedures were followed for each. They first recorded their individual decision and were then given the key to each item. The opportunity to discuss their findings in pairs and groups then followed, after which they once again recorded their decision, based on the discussion. The judges were then given empirical statistics on how candidates performed on the items, followed by a plenary discussion, and then they recorded their final decision. In this way, each judge recorded three impression marks for each of the items.

The judges' decisions were collated and merged to give the overall cut-off scores for each section. The judges' estimates of each round were entered into an Excel database and descriptive statistics were calculated. The median, average and standard deviation for each rater were calculated, as well as the minimum and maximum score given. The cut-off score for the ALCE examination was calculated on data from the final empirical round. In order to investigate the precision of the cut-off scores, the formula for the Standard

Table 1: Precision of cut-off score estimations

	Listening Section	Grammar, Vocabulary and Reading Section
Standard Deviation of cut-off score (SDc)	3.99	3.73
Standard Error in the test (SEM)	2.88	4.60
Standard Error of cut-off score (SEc)	0.89	0.83
Internal validity check	0.31	0.18

Error of the cut score (SEc) was calculated as a validity check (Council of Europe 2004:21–22). The results are shown in Table 1 above.

An average rating for each item was produced from the figures given and the average of these ratings was calculated to give the cut-off score. The internal validity check revealed that the SEc for the Listening Section and the Grammar, Vocabulary and Reading Section were .31 and .18 of the SEM respectively. Cohen, Kane and Crooks (1999:364) claim that SEc should be at least less than .5 of the SEM to ensure minimum impact on the misclassification rates. Thus, the SEc of both sections 'can be considered as relatively small and acceptable' (Council of Europe 2004:22).

Writing Section: benchmarking and standard setting

The Writing Section of the ALCE examination comprises one writing task, chosen from two options. The first option is an essay arguing a point of view, while the second is a report. Each report or essay is initially graded by two raters, independently of one another. These ratings are collated and where there is a significant difference between the two ratings for a candidate's writing, it is then graded by a third rater. Each rater is given a Rater Code, allowing for intra-rater and inter-rater reliability analysis.

The standard setting for the ALCE Writing Section took place in June 2006 and was carried out by 14 judges. The judges were selected for their knowledge and experience of teaching English at this level and their knowledge of testing procedures. Many of the judges also participated in other sections of the standard-setting procedures. The training of the judges was carried out in a similar manner to that of the Listening and GVR Sections. Having examined, sorted and discussed the relevant descriptors from the CEFR, the judges were given the rating descriptors for the ALCE examination. These were discussed and key features distinguishing the scoring criteria were emphasised.

The judges examined a total of 30 written scripts (15 essays and 15 reports) from the June 2006 administration. The written scripts had been selected by two members of the linking project committee and were chosen as they exhibited a range of writing ability. They were marked by the judges and then the marks were discussed until a consensus was reached for each piece of writing.

The benchmarked essays and reports formed the basis for rater training for the Writing Section of the June ALCE examination. During the benchmarking procedure, it was agreed by all judges that the descriptors for a Pass in the Writing Section of the ALCE examination correspond to the level set out by the descriptors from the CEFR at C1 level.

Speaking Section: benchmarking and standard setting

The Speaking Test of the ALCE examination is rated by one rater who acts concurrently as interlocutor and rater and examines one candidate at a time. All raters are given a rater code and also record which Examination Form is used for each candidate. This allows for inter-rater and intra-rater analysis to check inter-rater and intra-rater reliability. Six to eight Forms are used at each administration of the ALCE examination.

Judges were trained in the CEFR speaking scales and the ALCE scoring criteria, and then watched videos of nine candidates being examined on materials from the June 2006 examination. After individual and collective discussion, a grade was assigned to each candidate to provide a standard for raters. The judges were selected for their knowledge and experience of teaching English at this level and their knowledge of testing procedures. Many of the judges also participated in other sections of the standard-setting procedures.

The training of the judges was carried out in a similar manner to that of the Listening, GVR and Writing Sections. Having examined, sorted and discussed the relevant descriptors from the CEFR, the judges were given the rating descriptors for the ALCE examination. These were discussed and key features distinguishing the scoring criteria were emphasised. The judges examined videos of nine candidates being examined on materials from the June 2006 administration. These were rated by the judges and their ratings discussed until a consensus was reached for each candidate. The benchmarked videos formed the basis for rater training for the Speaking Section of the following ALCE examination. During the benchmarking procedure, it was agreed by all judges that the descriptors for a Pass in the Speaking Section of the ALCE examination correspond to the level set out by the descriptors from the CEFR at C1 level.

Phase 4: Empirical validation

Phase 4 is planned for future research.

Reflections on the use of the draft Manual

Through the Claim by Specification and Standard Setting, the ALCE examination is judged to be aiming at the C1 level of the CEFR in all parts of the test. However, there were some difficulties encountered in using the CEFR during the linking process. In the Familiarisation Phase there was a sense on the part of the participants that the C1 level of the CEFR was defined as requiring a level of language competence higher than that expected by the project members. Although the members were familiar with a range of examinations from a variety of bodies which were claimed to be at specific levels of the CEFR, a detailed analysis of the descriptors showed that members had to redefine their own sense of what is appropriate at C1 level.

More specifically, the emphasis on understanding extended texts on *abstract, complex, unfamiliar* topics, as required by the scales for both reading and listening, was seen by the participants as placing more demands on the test taker than those of a number of examinations claiming to be at C1. There was a concern that even native speakers might find such texts challenging, and also concern relating to the cognitive load placed on the test taker and how this might result in a test score that does not necessarily reflect language ability alone, but also cognitive ability.

Also during this phase, project members were concerned that the apparent restriction at this level to content which is unfamiliar or abstract implies that the level is more appropriate for the educational or occupational domains, while omitting reference to complex language use in other domains. For example, members pointed out that employers may require staff with exceptionally high language ability in contexts other than those of the educational or occupational domains, but that such contexts appear under the heading B2 or even B1 and thus would be tested only at those levels.

Linked to this was an impression that there was insufficient guidance in the CEFR in terms of level of language difficulty, although it was understood that language difficulty and context are closely related. For example, complex formal listening or reading texts are likely to display more syntactical and grammatical complexity and include more context-specific lexical items, factors which are likely to make texts inaccessible to test takers with insufficient language ability. However, project members felt that this was not an automatic guide to language ability and in particular makes no distinction between the C1 and C2 levels.

Because it is 'language neutral', the CEFR does not provide scales for tests that include discrete grammar and vocabulary items. To compensate during the Standardisation Phase, the judges were given the DIALANG scales to use for their evaluation of these items (Alderson, Figueras, Kuijper, Nold, Takala and Tardieu 2006). However, the DIALANG grammar scales mostly focus on form, whereas in the ALCE Grammar Section, the primary focus is on meaning.

A suggested modification to any future standard setting carried out on the ALCE examination is to hold parallel sessions with at least 10 judges in each group and then statistically compare group cut-off scores. In this way research into whether the person conducting the standard-setting has any impact on the judge's scores could also be carried out. Furthermore, it may be preferable to use a different variation of the Angoff method, in particular the Yes/No method or Borderline method proposed by Impara and Plake (cited in Cizek and Bunch 2007:88–89), as this method does not require judges to enter a probability score, but to state whether the borderline candidate would get the item correct. This method is cognitively simplistic and reduces the probability estimate that judges need to form into a dichotomous one (Cizek, Bunch and Koons 2004:42). The continued use of three rounds would allow the judges to get feedback on their estimates before a final cut-off score is calculated and thus increase judges' confidence and satisfaction of their final cut-off score.

It should be noted that all ALCE examinations are linked to one another through Item Response Theory (IRT), thus, a smaller scale second standard setting for the Listening and GVR Sections was carried out on the June 2006 ALCE examination.

Conclusion

The linking project has had an impact on the literature that is disseminated to the public, due to the creation of an ALCE Manual. The Manual contains the aim of and rationale for each section or subsection of the test, sample items, test specifications for publishers, and descriptors for the Writing and Speaking Sections. As a consequence, prospective candidates and teachers have achieved a better insight into the test and are aware of the level the ALCE examination is aimed at. This may have contributed to an increased pass rate for the ALCE examination over the last two years.

The linking project was also an invaluable tool for test developers to assess to what extent the ALCE examination reflects the C1 level. Although it was understood that the CEFR is intended as a reference for a wide variety of purposes and languages, the Project did, however, also highlight many difficulties of using the CEFR in examining language tests in terms of level. For example, an adequate distinction between the C1 and C2 levels is lacking, particularly as many descriptors for C2 say 'as C1'. Additionally, there is the question of whether the C1 level applies only to specific domains, rather than language ability across all the domains. Finally, there is the concern that C1 level implies a certain ability at a cognitive level, with the result that many native speakers would find themselves languishing at B2 level, and yet fully in possession of competent language skills that would be the envy of many a non-native speaker judged to be at a 'higher' level.

References

Alderson, J C, Figueras, N, Kuijper, H, Nold, G, Takala, S and Tardieu, C (2006) Analysing Tests of Reading and Listening in Relation to the Common European Framework of Reference: The Experience of The Dutch CEFR Construct Project, *Language Assessment Quarterly: An International Journal* 3 (1), 3−30.

Brandon, P R (2004) Conclusions about Frequently Studied Modified Angoff Standard-Setting Topics, *Applied Measurement in Education* 17 (1), 59−88.

Cizek, G and Bunch, M (2007) *Standard Setting: A Guide to Establishing and Evaluating Performance on Tests*, Thousand Oaks, CA: SAGE.

Cizek, G, Bunch M and Koons, H (2004) Setting Performance Standards: Contemporary Methods, *Educational Measurement: Issues and Practices* 23 (4), 31–50.

Cohen, A S, Kane, M T and Crooks, T J (1999) A generalized examinee-centered method for setting standards on achievement test, *Applied Measurement in Education* 12 (4), 343–366.

Council of Europe (2003) *Relating Language Examinations to the Common European Framework of Reference for Languages: Learning, Teaching, Assessment (CEF). Manual. Pilot Preliminary Version* <www.coe.int/T/DG4/Portfolio/documents/Manual%20for%20relating%20Language%20Examinations%20ot%20the%20CEF.pdf> accessed 20 July 2008.

Council of Europe (2004) *Reference Supplement to the Preliminary Pilot Version of the Manual for Relating Language Examinations to the Common European Framework of Reference for Languages: Learning, Teaching, Assessment (CEF)* <www.coe.int/T/DG4/Portfolio/documents/CEF%20reference%20supplement%20version%203.pdf> accessed 20 July 2008.

Hellenic American University (2005) *Manual for the Advanced Level Certificate in English* <www.hau.gov/resources/orfeas/alce/alce_manual.pdf>

Taube, KT (1997) The incorporation of empirical item difficulty data in the Angoff standard setting procedure, *Evaluation and Health Profession* 20, 479–498.

Section Two
Linking a suite of exams to the CEFR

6 Relating language examinations to the CEFR: ECL as a case study

Gábor Szabó
ECL Examinations, University of Pécs, Hungary

Abstract

This paper intends to provide an overview of how the European Consortium for the Certificate of Attainment in Modern Languages (ECL) examination system implemented a project aimed at aligning ECL exam levels with the levels of the Common European Framework of Reference for Languages (CEFR). First, background information on ECL and the linking project will be presented, followed by a description of the various stages of the project. Next, the design and instruments used will be discussed, along with information on procedures and results. Evidence will be provided for the claimed alignment with CEFR levels both in terms of qualitative as well as quantitative analyses. Finally, a discussion of potential problems and practical difficulties experienced in the linking process will also be presented, with special regard to empirical validation and to aligning examinations in less commonly taught languages. Reference will also be made to ECL's special position in the context of the Hungarian system of national accreditation of foreign language examinations.

ECL as a case study

Background

ECL as an international language examination system was originally launched in 1992. Back then the purpose was the development of a standardised language examination system for the languages of the European Union. Since its beginnings, ECL has grown into a language testing system of 11 languages, including non-EU languages such as Serbian or Russian. Originally, ECL was launched as a 4-level system, where the levels were not directly linked to the CEFR, as it did not exist at the time. The exams in all languages are built upon the same principles. The four skills are tested in communicative ways, through tasks modelling authentic situations of language use. Each skill is tested in a separate paper, and in order to pass, test takers must pass each paper. Candidates, approximately 80% of whom are under 30 years of age, include test takers from 11 European and two American countries.

The publication of the *Common European Framework of Reference for Languages: Learning, Teaching, Assessment* (Council of Europe 2001) marked a turning point in the life of European language teaching and language assessment. With the common reference levels the need arose to determine how existing examinations' levels relate to the CEFR levels. Moreover, it became a factor of primary importance to go beyond mere claims concerning the relationship between examination levels and CEFR levels. It was this situation that prompted ECL to launch a linking project whose purpose was to examine ECL levels' relationship to the CEFR as well as to implement modifications – if need be – to guarantee a match.

Soon after the launch of the project another circumstance arose that resulted in more pressure to speed up the linking process. ECL's administrative and logistical headquarters are in Pécs, Hungary, and ECL is one of the nationally accredited language examinations in Hungary. A governmental decree issued soon after the project was launched required all nationally accredited language examination systems to align their accredited levels with the CEFR levels. While ECL started work on linking before the issue of the decree, the time frame had to be revised in accordance with the legal requirements. In practice, this meant that certain phases of the linking process had to be completed sooner than originally planned.

Also, owing to the Hungarian context, the focus of the linking project was slightly changed in order to give priority to the languages with a nationally accredited status in Hungary (English, German and Hungarian as a foreign language) along with the three levels the Hungarian system of accreditation would acknowledge: B1, B2 and C1. Accordingly, the case study presented in this paper will also focus on these languages and levels.

Project design and instruments used

Since ECL was an already existing examination, the linking process was designed around first analysing ECL as related to the CEFR, and then around potentially modifying any aspects of the actual exam that would be found problematic.

In order to accomplish this, a lot of emphasis was given to making use of the preliminary pilot version of *Relating language examinations to the Common European Framework of Reference for Languages: Learning, Teaching, Assessment* (Council of Europe 2003), the document commonly referred to as the Manual. What this meant in practice was that the design of the project was based on the structure suggested by the Manual (Chapters 3 to 6).

Accordingly, the first stage was to be familiarisation, the second specification, the third standardisation, and finally, the fourth empirical validation.

At this point, however, an important observation needs to be made. Though the present project is technically finished in terms of linking the examinations to the CEFR, the actual linking of the exam papers themselves must obviously be a continuous process performed routinely by the examination provider. As new tasks are constructed, they must go through the process described below as part of the usual procedure. This effectively means that it is only the linking of exam specifications that can truly be called 'completed'; the exam papers themselves need ongoing linking.

As suggested by the Manual, familiarisation was conducted at different phases of the project for different participants. In other words, the different phases of the project requiring different kinds of expertise and experience necessitated different occasions for familiarisation training sessions.

Since ECL's test specifications are the same across languages, the specification stage only involved a core team of experts, whose task was to review and potentially revise the exam specifications. Standardisation was performed in separate sessions for different languages and different skills. The participants formed stable groups whose cohesion increased over time.

The empirical validation stage proved to be the most problematic, as will be discussed later. It comprised ECL tasks as well as criterion tasks, with several hundred test takers involved in the data collection. Unfortunately, empirical validation in this sense was only possible in English and German, as will be discussed later in more detail.

Participants included a wide range of professionals with different kinds of expertise, including ECL's test development team, item writers, assessors and oral examiners, as well as non-ECL affiliated testing experts, examiners and language teachers. The make-up of the participants was to guarantee, on the one hand, a wide range of professional expertise and, on the other hand, a balance of 'insider' and 'outsider' views and opinions, aimed at providing a more comprehensive approach to the problems encountered.

The time-line of the project, as was mentioned earlier, was heavily influenced by the legal environment in Hungary. As a result, though the project was launched in 2004, even the empirical validation stage was expected to have been completed by early 2007. Indeed, this was the main reason for restricting the focus of the project.

The tests utilised in the course of the project came from a variety of sources, depending on the field of application. First, for obvious reasons, ECL's own materials need to be mentioned. This group included tasks in all three languages involved in the linking process. In reading and listening complete tasks were used where empirical data was already available concerning the quality of the items. In writing and speaking both tasks and actual performances were used.

Another source of materials used was the Council of Europe Manual Project. One goal of the project was to disseminate performance samples for productive skills in order to facilitate the CEFR linking related standardisation processes of various examination systems. Thus, video recordings of oral performances provided by the Manual Project were used accordingly in the ECL linking project as well in setting CEFR-based standards for oral performances. This, however, was not possible in the case of all the languages involved.

The Manual Project also provided tasks to assist the empirical validation of tests measuring receptive skills. These tasks and their levels of difficulty were to be used as representations of various CEFR levels, so that local tests could be linked to the CEFR empirically via the tests provided. While these tasks in English and German proved to be helpful in the ECL linking process, they were not without problems, as will be discussed later. Also, in the third language involved in this particular project (Hungarian) such tasks were not available, which was clearly a disadvantage.

Concerning the quality of the materials used, a somewhat awkward situation emerged. ECL tasks used in the process had been analysed statistically beforehand in order to guarantee quality. Accordingly, tasks with reliability figures below 0.8 were not used in the linking process, and item level statistics in terms of facility values and discrimination indices were also taken into consideration. Thus, tasks in which item discrimination indices were below 0.3 were, again, not included in the linking process. As ECL tasks are produced regularly in a way that includes various means of quality control, the reliability and validity of the tasks to be included in the linking process were judged to be appropriate.

On the other hand, ECL had very little specific information on the tasks provided by the Manual Project. While it was assumed – since they were presented as criterion tasks offering points of reference – that they were sufficiently reliable and valid, the actual figures were not available, and, as will be discussed later, occasional concerns did emerge in the course of empirical validation.

Procedures and results

In accordance with the above, the initial stage of the project was familiarisation. First, as was mentioned earlier, it was necessary for a core team of experts to go through familiarisation. They were to review ECL specifications later. This stage of familiarisation happened largely on the basis of discussions of CEFR levels in the light of various scales as well as on rearranging jumbled level descriptors. Since the core team was relatively small (comprising three members), and because core team members were to be involved in later familiarisation sessions, discussions took place in a small circle and also included practical points concerning how CEFR-related training could be implemented.

At a later stage, familiarisation sessions were held for various groups of experts involved in the linking process. As ECL tests in every language are produced by the relevant consortium member institution in the target language countries, familiarisation sessions were not held centrally for all item writers. Instead, a centrally organised familiarisation session was held for representatives of partner institutions for all languages, which was followed by local sessions in the respective countries. Besides, separate familiarisation sessions were held for the experts involved in the standardisation process as well. In the course of these sessions a variety of activities described in Chapter 3 of the Manual were utilised quite successfully. Among other tasks, the discussions of the participants' own levels based on the self-assessment scales, or rearranging various jumbled scale descriptors along with discussing the content of descriptors proved to be interesting and worthwhile activities for the participants. Familiarity with CEFR levels was also monitored through tests on CEFR level descriptors, which included the identification or the rearrangement of different descriptors of various CEFR scales.

Stage two of the linking project was specification. As was mentioned above, ECL specifications were reviewed by a small group of core team members. This was made possible by the fact that ECL, even from its very birth was inspired by notions and approaches that later became manifest in CEFR levels. Indeed, the 1993 version of the ECL spoken proficiency scale is listed in Appendix B of the CEFR as a source for the development of CEFR scales (see CEFR 2001:224). The consequence of this relatedness was that major modifications in ECL level descriptions were not deemed necessary. This, of course, does not mean that the specification process had no impact on ECL specifications. In fact, relying on the forms provided in Chapter 4 of the Manual it was possible to conduct a detailed analysis of ECL specifications, and the degree of conformity with CEFR levels could be established. This was done by describing the existing specifications in the light of the questions included in the forms, which was followed by discussions of how much ECL specifications could be claimed to be linked to the CEFR. As a result, minor modifications did occur, and the analysis proved that the specification process was, indeed, inevitable. It has to be noted, however, that using the forms provided in the Manual did prove to be problematic sometimes. The categories provided were not always transparent, and overlaps were also observed. For instance, the various aspects of communicative language competence seemed to be difficult to distinguish in terms of interaction versus production. While the systematic nature of the forms was apparent, often the results appeared to be repetitive and yielding little extra information. Overall, though, the core team found the procedures and methods described in the Manual useful and effective, and – as a result of this stage of the linking process – ECL specifications can now be considered to be in harmony with the CEFR as presented in Table 1. It should be noted here that the original level labels (A, B, C, D) have now been changed in order to avoid any potential confusion.

Table 1: Relationship between ECL levels and CEFR levels

ECL levels	CEFR levels
	C2
C1	C1
B2	B2
B1	B1
A2	A2
	A1

While ECL specifications – as was mentioned above – are common across languages, standardisation, obviously, had to be carried out separately for the languages involved. First, in each language a team of judges was selected and trained through familiarisation exercises. Then, listening and reading tasks produced according to ECL specifications were considered by the judges. Their job for each item in each task was to determine what CEFR level a candidate would need to be at to be able to respond to that item correctly. This way fairly detailed information was collected on both the relative difficulty of the items as well as on their relationship to the CEFR. The information thus gathered was quantified and analysed, as a result of which item and task levels were determined and inter-judge reliability figures were calculated.

In the case of productive skills the procedures were slightly different in that before the actual standardisation judges received training with the help of standardised performance samples made available by the Manual Project. Unfortunately, the number of such samples was relatively low, and in some cases (e.g. for Hungarian as a foreign language) they were missing completely. In such cases local performance samples were used from the very beginning.

In the cases where standardised performance samples were available, judges were first trained through these samples making it possible for them to internalise the characteristics of the performances illustrating various CEFR levels. It was only after this that local performance samples were considered. Judges had to decide what CEFR levels those performances matched. Once again, the data was quantified and analysed, inter-judge correlation figures were computed and the CEFR levels of performances were determined. Wherever it was possible, the level of agreement between decisions based on CEFR ratings and ECL scales was also examined, and generally relatively high agreement was found (Kappa~0.8).

In the course of empirical validation, one needs to make a clear difference between the internal and external dimension. Concerning internal validation, ECL has long been applying various classical and IRT-based procedures for internal validation purposes. Owing to the number of candidates, classical test theory has been more dominant, but concerning larger numbers of candidates in some of the most popular exams, Rasch analyses have also been performed. In the light of the empirical results as well as on the basis of the qualitative dimension of validation, ECL tests have been found valid internally. In the course of this process, statistical results on the tests' reliability, standard error of measurement as well as general descriptive statistics were overviewed, along with item facility values, discrimination indices and IRT-based item difficulty logit values and fit statistics. As for qualitative analyses, test content and format were compared to test specifications.

External validation, on the other hand, has largely been restricted by the availability of tasks considered to represent CEFR levels. While the Manual Project has made some such tasks available, there have been two kinds of problems with them. First, they were often made up of a relatively small number of items, which made it rather difficult to rely on the empirical data. A task of only three items, for instance, was quite difficult to use as a point of reference. Second, over time a number of people have questioned whether those tasks have, indeed, been proven to represent one CEFR level or another. Unfortunately, relatively few of the tasks were accompanied by the kind of evidence that was deemed satisfactory.

Apart from the problems above, once again, there were some cases where no tests or tasks were available to serve as a point of reference. In these cases external empirical validation has not been conducted yet. It should be noted, however, that weaker forms of external validation, such as relying on teacher judgments, could have been used, but the degree of certainty that could have been gained this way was not considered high enough.

Despite these problems, empirical validation has been performed on a number of tasks. In the case of English and German reading and listening tests at CEFR levels B2 and C1, empirical validation took place with the help of IRT in the following way. Tests were constructed where one task was a validated one provided by the Manual Project, while the other was an ECL task. The tests were then administered to sufficiently large populations (300 to 600 depending on language and level) and the results were analysed. In the course of the analysis the item difficulty logits were estimated. Next, a T-test was conducted to see whether there is any difference between the difficulty of the validated task items and the ECL task items. The results demonstrated that in all cases the differences were minor, indeed, statistically not significant, and the spread of item difficulties was nearly the same as well. An example of the graphical representation of this relationship is shown in Figure 1.

Figure 1: Relationship of item difficulty between a reference task and an ECL task in English B2 reading

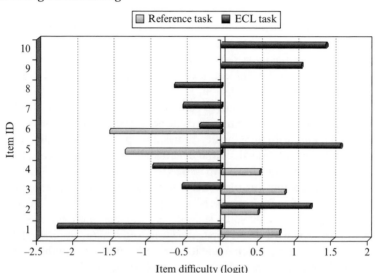

Item difficulty (logit)

Reflections on the linking project

In this section an overview of the experiences concerning the project will be presented. First, some of the difficulties will be enumerated with suggested solutions to the problems. Next, further work will be outlined, which will be followed by assessing the impact of the project.

Difficulties encountered

As has already been mentioned, participants encountered a variety of difficulties in the course of the project. Here these problems will be presented in relationship to the relevant stages in the linking process.

Concerning the familiarisation stage, it has to be noted that in various familiarisation sessions some common themes arose. It had to be acknowledged, for instance, that the CEFR itself is far from being perfect. Many participants commented on the problem of the lack of certain descriptors, and also on some technically existing but clearly unrealistic ones (e.g. C2 listening). Also, occasional inconsistencies were detected in global and specific scales. For instance, the C2 level descriptor in the overall reading comprehension scale contains no restrictions whatever, while both in the *Reading for Correspondence* scale and the *Reading Instructions* scale C2 is defined 'as C1', even though the C1 descriptor includes restrictions concerning the use of a dictionary and rereading difficult sections, respectively. Attention had to be paid to the uncertainties within the scales as well, especially considering the fact that though some CEFR scales have been empirically validated (see North and Schneider 1998), others have not. Obviously, this does not in any sense undermine the usefulness and value of the CEFR itself, but a future revised version will need to address such issues. Using the Manual at this stage proved to be unproblematic, and the tasks suggested were highly appreciated by the participants.

A brief comment has already been made about the forms in Chapter 4 of the Manual concerning the specification stage. Indeed, while the forms themselves have overall been quite useful in analysing ECL specifications in terms of test content, process of test development, marking process, as well as analysis and post-test reporting, at certain points they seemed to lack consistency, as occasionally overlapping or repetitive entries have been identified (e.g. in reporting). On the whole, however, the specification stage seemed to generate no major problems.

Standardisation seemed to present the first major problem, notably the lack of standardised performance samples in one of the languages involved in the project (Hungarian). This was, indeed, a key issue, as ECL's own performance samples could not be compared to any external point of reference other than the descriptors of the CEFR. The only solution, obviously, was to rely entirely on ECL performance samples. In fact, this proved to be a sound option for two reasons. First, the performance samples provided by the Manual Project in other languages were judged using a very similar procedure, and if judges of the Hungarian samples receive proper training, there is no reason to assume they will be less capable of completing a rating task like this. Second, there was simply no other way to go ahead with standardisation. If standard performances in, for example, oral interaction at level B2 in Hungarian had never been identified before, somebody had to do it the first time. Relying on the CEFR descriptors, this should give the desired results. What is particularly interesting at this point is that two other examination systems in Hungary were also working on linking exams in Hungarian to the CEFR roughly at the same time, but there was no opportunity to accomplish the task as a kind of 'joint venture', even though the quality of the actual linking would probably have been better justified that way.

This issue, however, is relevant in the case of a number of other languages as well. It is likely that no centrally devised project will ever generate and disseminate performance samples in a large number of other European (or non-European) languages, which means that representatives of such languages should be ready to go ahead with producing and – potentially – sharing such performance samples in the future.

Another problem point related to standardisation, however, concerned the performance samples themselves. First, there was very little information on how exactly these samples were chosen and what justified their status. Second, where performances were available in the same language at the same level, they did not always seem to illustrate similar features, which caused a necessity to choose one of them as the 'real one' to rely on. Clearly, future samples would need to go through some generally accepted control stages in order to avoid this problem.

Empirical validation proved to be probably the single most problematic phase of the linking process. Though the Reference Supplement to the Manual (Council of Europe 2004) provided lots of useful information, it could not compensate for some issues that made empirical validation highly problematic in some cases. Mention has already been made of the most important issues, but solutions have not been suggested yet. It seems, once again, that the lack of appropriate reference tasks in less commonly taught languages can only be solved by actually producing such tasks and by supporting their status with appropriate evidence. Of course, this would have to mean a break from test-centred methods, as without a generally accepted set of reference tasks, no other tasks can be empirically validated this way. Candidate-centred methods, on the other hand, are heavily dependent on teacher judgements, whose empirical nature many would question. Yet, there seems to be no other option. Also, it should be remembered that the CEFR itself started out from teacher judgements. Thus, with appropriate familiarisation and careful design, candidate-centred methods could be used quite effectively to solve the problem. The key seems to be familiarity with what the CEFR descriptors truly mean. Hence, increasing teachers' awareness of and knowledge about the CEFR – which appears to be a major task in some European countries – would need to enjoy priority in future projects.

Future directions

In terms of the linking process itself, some points have already been made on what seems to be necessary to do in the future. As to ECL, it should be noted that while this particular project focused on three languages and three levels only, the actual linking has been extended to the other languages and the A2 level as well.

Of course, the difficulties encountered in relation to Hungarian clearly indicate that the most immediate need is to provide better chances for less commonly taught languages. As ECL offers tests in a number of such languages, this seems to be a crucial point. Indeed, since examinations in such languages have a relatively small candidature, it would seem logical for examination providers to co-operate in order to provide a more solid backing to a continuous process of linking. This could happen for instance by setting up mutually beneficial co-operative projects which could involve sharing tasks or candidate responses to be used for empirical validation.

Projects providing support for assessing less commonly taught languages could also fit into a European agenda. Europe, being a multilingual and multicultural entity, seems to be a natural environment for developing and maintaining language tests in less commonly taught languages, and the mandate of the CEFR is also clearly not only related to languages that are taught and learned most frequently.

Another possible future direction is closer co-operation in making a large number of reference tasks available to all involved in linking exams to the CEFR. This would necessitate the development of clear requirements in terms of quality, and some form of quality control. If such circumstances could be guaranteed, empirical validation could be conducted more successfully.

Impact

The impact of the linking project is manifold. First, it contributed to making ECL's tests more easily comparable to the CEFR, which has, by now, become the most widely accepted point of reference in Europe concerning levels of language proficiency. This fact also means that comparisons across various language examinations have become more straightforward.

Also, the project contributed to increasing language testing literacy and, specifically, familiarity with the CEFR. This occurred as a result of involving a number of teachers in the project who had previously not been part of major testing projects but – as a result of the training they received – can now be counted on as raters and judges. Indeed, increased awareness of and familiarity with the CEFR scales is probably one of the most important impacts of the linking project.

It should also be noted that, though ECL's test construction process had included a variety of quality control measures even before the linking project, owing to the extensive use of the Manual and the Reference Supplement, these processes have been further developed, too.

Conclusion

ECL conducted the linking project out of an understanding of the professional necessity of this move as well as because of legal requirements in Hungary. Having completed all major steps of the process at least in part, it is possible to state that all who participated in this effort have learned a great deal from it. One of the most important lessons is that linking itself is never completed; it is only particular tasks that can at certain points be considered linked. This means that ECL, along with all other test providers, will need to continue working on the linking of tasks.

Professionalism comes at a price. But the price paid for appropriate linking is well worth paying for any institution that intends to provide high quality language tests in order to serve the international testing community and, most of all, the candidates. Just like many other testing organisations, this is what ECL is hoping to keep on doing.

References

Council of Europe (2001) *Common European Framework of Reference for languages: learning, teaching, assessment,* Cambridge: Cambridge University Press.

Council of Europe (2003) *Relating language examinations to the Common European Framework of Reference for Languages: learning, teaching, assessment (CEF). Manual: Preliminary Pilot Version, DGIV/EDU/LANG 2003, 5,* Strasbourg: Language Policy Division.

Council of Europe (2004) *Reference supplement to the preliminary version of the manual for relating examinations to the Common European Framework of Reference for Languages: learning, teaching, assessment, DGIV/EDU/LANG 2005, 13,* Strasbourg: Language Policy Division.

North, B and Schneider, G (1998) Scaling descriptors for language proficiency scales, *Language Testing* 15, 217–263.

7 Linking international examinations to the CEFR: the Trinity College London experience

Spiros Papageorgiou
University of Michigan, USA

Abstract

The status of the Common European Framework of Reference for Languages (CEFR) as a common standard among different educational contexts offers international examination providers the opportunity to provide results that are meaningful to test users from different countries. CEFR linkage in such an international context is the focus of this contribution in the volume. The Trinity College London Graded Examinations in Spoken English (GESE) and Integrated Skills in English (ISE) international examinations underwent the procedures for CEFR linkage described in the Manual in order to offer test users in various contexts the opportunity to better interpret results of Trinity qualifications. The methodology and results of the project are described, in particular with regard to the judges' understanding of the CEFR levels during familiarisation activities and the outcome of the Specification and Standardisation stages. Moreover, problems the judges faced and ways to overcome them are discussed and the impact of the linking project on the design of the examinations is considered.

Introduction

Relating international examinations to the CEFR is an essential step in providing test takers with transparent and meaningful results, given the current status of the CEFR as a common standard across different educational systems worldwide. Trinity College London (hereafter 'Trinity'), a UK-based EFL examination provider whose language qualifications are administered in more than 20 countries, embarked on a CEFR linking project in order to offer its test users in various contexts the opportunity to better interpret results of Trinity qualifications. The methodology and results of this project are presented in this paper.

Background, purpose and context of the linking project

Trinity administers two suites of international examinations: the Graded Examinations in Spoken English (GESE) and the Integrated Skills in English (ISE) examinations. As can be seen in Table 1, GESE (Trinity College London 2005a) tests speaking and listening during a one-to-one interaction with an examiner and has 12 levels from Grade 1 to Grade 12. These are grouped into four stages: Initial, Elementary, Intermediate and Advanced.

Table 1: The structure of the GESE suite

Initial Stage Grades 1–3	Elementary Stage Grades 4–6	Intermediate Stage Grades 7–9	Advanced Stage Grades 10–12
1. Conversation	1. Topic discussion	1. Topic presentation and discussion	1. Topic presentation
	2. Conversation	2. Interactive task 3. Conversation	2. Topic discussion 3. Interactive task 4. Listening task 5. Conversation

ISE (Trinity College London 2005b) follows the same structure as GESE for the Interview component as it borrows the content of Grades 4, 6, 8 and 11 for Levels 0, I, II and III respectively. Since the CEFR project, ISE IV, aiming at Level C2, has been added to the suite. In addition, two more components, the Portfolio and the Controlled Written Exam, test writing and reading in an integrated way (see Table 2).

Table 2: The structure of the ISE suite

Levels	Components for all levels
ISE 0 ISE I ISE II ISE III	1. Interview 2. Portfolio 3. Controlled Written Exam

Small-scale internal studies had looked at the content of the Trinity examinations in relation to the CEFR (Davies 2001, Green 2000). However, Trinity decided, following the publication of the Manual, to commission a large-scale external study with the purpose of linking GESE and ISE to the CEFR through the stages described in the Manual. The author was appointed the external co-ordinator of the project in February 2005. The project was completed in June 2006 and the technical report (Papageorgiou 2007) was prepared at Lancaster University and made publicly available.

Design of the linking project and instruments

When the linking project was initially designed, the decision was made to go through all stages described in the Manual. However, it soon became clear that the lack of an external criterion for the External Validation stage at the time the project was conducted would not allow for as much emphasis on this stage as on the other stages.

The design of the project will be described below; however it is worth providing some information about a very important element of the project first: the judges. Bearing in mind that the Manual recommends a minimum of 10 expert judges, the project co-ordinator liaised with the Trinity Chief Examiner to invite 12 participants who would have a variety of responsibilities and posts in Trinity. The judges chosen were involved in examining, marking, monitoring, validation, test design and the administration of Trinity tests. Two were managers in the ESOL department. The panel had some familiarity with the CEFR, as it had already been used in the test syllabuses to describe the level of candidates for both examinations. According to suggestions in the standard-setting literature (Raymond and Reid 2001), this panel appeared suitable, as it had a good knowledge of the exams to be linked to the CEFR and the test-taking population.

Familiarisation stage

This stage was organised as a separate, 2-day meeting in September 2005. It was also repeated as an introductory part to the Specification and Standardisation stages to ensure the judges' good understanding of the CEFR volume overall and its levels in particular throughout the project. Before the meeting the judges were posted a hard copy of the CEFR and were asked to study it carefully. To further help the judges with this potentially challenging reading task, a copy of Norris' (2005) review of the CEFR volume was provided. The judges were also sent an email briefly explaining the stages of the linking process set out in the Manual.

The September meeting started with an introduction by the co-ordinator, where the purpose of the project was explained along with the role of the Language Policy Division of the Council of Europe and documents such as the CEFR. Then, as an initial familiarisation activity, the co-ordinator discussed Section 3.6 of the CEFR volume (Council of Europe 2001:33–36) to introduce the judges to the different levels of performance. The main activities were as follows:

1. **Assigning descriptors to the six main levels:** The original descriptors from Tables 1 and 2 in the CEFR were 'atomised' following the example of a study by Kaftandjieva and Takala (2002), i.e. they were broken down in smaller units and listed in a handout. Without providing any indication about the level, the judges were asked to indicate the level for each descriptor and then, in plenary discussion, explain their decision-making process before the co-ordinator revealed the correct level. All judges' level choices were inserted in an Excel spreadsheet and were shown on a projector. Thirty speaking, 25 writing, 19 listening, 20 reading and 30 global descriptor units were included in the handout. Although the shorter descriptor statements were expected to be more difficult in terms of determining their level, due to the mutilated context, they were nevertheless deemed useful in that they could make the judges focus on the details of the original longer CEFR descriptors.

2. **Filling in table cells:** Table 3 from the CEFR and Table 5.8 from the Manual were given to the judges to further improve their understanding of the speaking and writing levels, due to the emphasis on these skills in the GESE and ISE examinations. The cells were presented without the descriptors, which were given to the judges separately. The judges then had to place the descriptors in the appropriate cells.

The first type of familiarisation activity was repeated on Day 2, as a way to check for descriptors whose level the judges were still not able to properly indicate, and also in order to provide a measure of intra-judge reliability. The latter was examined through Spearman correlations of each judge's ratings on Day 1 and 2. Correlations were high, ranging from .75 to .99, with the vast majority in the area of .85 and above.

Specification stage

This stage took place during a 3-day meeting in November 2005. Forms A1–A8 (general description forms) were prepared before the meeting by staff in the Trinity Head Office, as they contained administrative details that were not always accessible to the judges. Based on the test specifications and judges' recommendations supplied by email prior to the meeting, the following detailed description Forms were chosen:

- For GESE: A8 (Overall Impression), A11 and A13 (Spoken Interaction and Production), A9 (Listening Comprehension) and A19–A21 (Aspects of Competence in Reception, Interaction and Production respectively).

- For ISE: the same forms as for GESE, because of the shared oral and listening components, plus Forms A12 and A14 (Written Interaction and Production), A10 (Reading Comprehension) and A15–A16 (Integrated Skills).

As explained earlier, GESE has 12 levels, called 'grades', which are grouped into four stages. ISE at the time had four levels, from ISE 0 to ISE III. This presented a practical time challenge because the judges would need to fill in the forms for a total of 16 levels. For this reason, the Specification meeting was organised in parallel sessions using three or four teams. This is illustrated in Table 3. Out of the 12 judges of the Trinity project, 10 participated in the Specification stage, as two were unable to attend.

Table 3: Organisation of the parallel sessions for the Specification meeting

Session	Team 1	Team 2	Team 3	Team 4
1. GESE Initial Stage	Grade 3	Grade 1	Grade 2	
2. GESE Elementary Stage	Grade 6	Grade 4	Grade 5	
3. GESE Intermediate Stage	Grade 8	Grade 7	Grade 9	
4. GESE Advanced Stage	Grade 10	Grade 11	Grade 12	
5. Review of GESE Stages	Initial Stage	Elementary Stage	Intermediate Stage	Advanced Stage
6. ISE	ISE I	ISE 0	ISE III	ISE II

Sessions 1−4 were each devoted to one GESE stage. Two teams had three members (Teams 1 and 3) and one team had four members (Team 2). The teams were given a copy of the examination syllabus, the CEFR volume and the relevant Specification Forms mentioned in the bullet points above. At the end of the session the members of each team were asked to explain to the other two teams how they performed the task and what their decision was with regard to the CEFR level. During Session 5 each team was asked to examine the completed forms for the three grades of one stage and point out any inconsistencies or gaps in the way test content was described in relation to the CEFR. Because Team 2 had four members, they worked in pairs. This resulted in the creation of Team 4 for the content description of ISE (Session 6), following a process similar to the description of GESE. The outcome of the Specification stage was the creation of a graphic profile of the content of the two examinations in relation to the CEFR levels, which is further discussed below.

Standardisation stage

This stage took place during a 3-day meeting in February/March 2006. The design was largely based on the procedures described in the Manual:

• Familiarisation activities, which had also been conducted in the previous stages.

- Training with already calibrated samples. Oral, reading and listening samples came from the Council of Europe DVD and CD; however the written samples were taken from Tanko (2004) because the Cambridge ESOL samples contained in the Council of Europe CD were familiar to the judges in terms of the examination suite they were taken from.
- Benchmarking with Trinity samples, where the judges were asked to watch samples of performances by Trinity candidates and rate them using the CEFR scales.
- Standard setting, which was organised despite the fact that the Trinity examinations do not contain any item-based components. However, because it was impossible for the judges to rate a sufficient number of samples due to the large number of Trinity levels (12 for GESE and four for ISE, with three passing scores per level), the judges were asked to answer the following question for every passing score (Pass-C, Merit-B, and Distinction-A) of each Trinity level: At what CEFR level can a candidate obtain each score? The judges made individual judgements about imaginary candidates receiving the passing scores, based on their own expert opinion, rather than rating actual performances, which were done during the benchmarking. A fairly common practice in standard-setting meetings is that more than one round of judgements is required (cf. Hambleton 2001). Between rounds, the panel discusses individual judgements, receives feedback about how test takers performed and repeats the judgements. This was the case with the panel in this study. In the second round of judgements, the judges were asked to focus on the borderline pass candidate, because such a candidate is a holder of the same qualification as a higher ability candidate and therefore elements of the CEFR level aimed at by the examination should be present in a borderline pass performance.

Empirical validation stage

The Empirical Validation stage consisted of:

- Internal validation: An examination of the quality of the ratings given by Trinity examiners, conducted by Alistair Van Moere at Lancaster University. This was also accompanied by observation of rater training and monitoring procedures by the author.
- External validation: The only external criterion that could be used at the time the project was conducted was the intended CEFR level of the examinations in the examination syllabuses that were used when the project was conducted. Though not an empirical study where a common population would take the Trinity examinations and an external one thus allowing for comparisons of performance, the use of the syllabus as

an external criterion offered the opportunity to confirm or reject earlier estimates about the CEFR levels of the Trinity examinations.

Results

Familiarisation stage

Because of the reliance of the linking process on human judgement, the familiarisation activities were analysed statistically to establish the judges' good understanding of the CEFR levels. Due to space limitations it is not possible to present here the full analysis. The interested reader can consult the technical report (Papageorgiou 2007). Table 4 presents partial results from the report. For each set of descriptors in the first type of familiarisation activities, intra-judge reliability was calculated by running Spearman correlations of each judge's level choices in the February/March meeting with their choices in the two rounds of the Familiarisation meeting in September 2005 and the Specification meeting in November 2006. Overall, high levels of intra-rater reliability are observed with only some moderate minimum values for Writing and Listening.

Table 4: Intra-judge reliability (N=12) − summary statistics

Scales	September 1st round			September 2nd round			November		
	Mean*	Min	Max	Mean*	Min	Max	Mean*	Min	Max
Speaking	0.902	0.832	0.958	0.929	0.870	0.972	0.943	0.878	0.980
Writing	0.912	0.760	1	0.898	0.837	0.955	0.917	0.839	0.976
Listening	0.904	0.780	0.947	0.907	0.807	0.960	0.920	0.825	0.960
Reading	0.960	0.916	1	0.962	0.918	1	0.953	0.920	0.970
Global	0.948	0.896	0.979	0.953	0.866	1	0.950	0.909	0.983

*Average using Fisher's Z-transformation

Specification stage

The results of the analysis of the completed Specification forms are presented below. The graphic profiles are an adaptation of Form A23 of the Manual (Council of Europe 2003:63) and show the relationship to the CEFR as recorded by the judges in the Manual Forms. It should be explained here that in Figure 2, Pragmatic and Strategic competences in Reception and Strategic competence in Production could not be described for some GESE Grades because there were no available descriptors for lower levels. The ISE suite is graphically described in Figure 3 for Activities and Figure 4 for Competences.

Figure 1: Graphic Profile of the GESE−CEFR relationship (Overall Impression and Activities)

	Overall Impression	Spoken Interaction	Spoken Production	Listening
C2	Gr12	Gr12	Gr12	
C1	Gr10 Gr11	Gr10 Gr11	Gr10 Gr11	Gr10 Gr11 Gr12
B2.2	Gr9 Gr10	Gr8 Gr9	Gr9	Gr9
B2.1	Gr7 Gr8 Gr9	Gr7 Gr8	Gr7 Gr8	Gr7 Gr8
B1.2	Gr6			
B1.1	Gr5 Gr6	Gr5 Gr6	Gr5 Gr6	Gr5 Gr6
A2.2	Gr4	Gr4	Gr4	Gr4
A2.1	Gr3	Gr2 Gr3	Gr3	Gr2 Gr3
A1	Gr1 Gr2	Gr2	Gr2	Gr2
Below A1		Gr1	Gr1	Gr1

Figure 2: Graphic Profile of the GESE−CEFR relationship (Competences)

	RECEPTION				INTERACTION				PRODUCTION			
	Ling	Sociol	Pragm	Strat	Ling	Sociol	Pragm	Strat	Ling	Sociol	Pragm	Strat
C2	G12	G12	G12		G12	G12	G12		G12	G12	G12	G12
C1	G10 G11	G10 G11	G10 G11	G10 G11 G12	G10 G11	G10 G11	G10 G11 G12	G10 G11	G10 G11	G10 G11	G10 G11	G10 G11
B2.2			G8 G9				G10					
B2.1	G7 G8 G9	G7 G8 G9	G7		G7 G8 G9	G7 G8 G9	G7 G8 G9	G7 G8 G9	G7 G8 G9	G7 G8 G9	G7 G8 G9	G7 G8 G9
B1.2												
B1.1	G4 G5 G6	G4 G5 G6	G4 G5 G6	G4 G5 G6	G4 G5 G6	G4 G5 G6	G5 G6	G4 G5 G6	G4 G5 G6	G5 G6	G4 G5 G6	G5 G6
A2.2	G4		G4	G4	G4		G4	G4	G4	G4	G4	G4
A2.1	G2 G3	G2 G3	G3		G2 G3	G2 G3	G2 G3	G2	G3	G3	G3	
A1	G1 G2	G2			G1 G2	G1 G2	G1 G2	G1 G2 G3	G1 G2	G1 G2	G1 G2	G1 G2 G3
Below A1		G1										

Figure 3: Graphic Profile of the ISE−CEFR relationship (Overall Impression and Activities)

	Overall impression	Spoken interaction	Written interaction	Spoken Production	Written Production	Listening	Reading	Integrated skills
C2								
C1.2								
C1	ISE III	ISE III	ISE III	ISE III	ISE III	ISE III	ISE III	ISE III
B2.2	ISE II	ISE II		ISE II		ISE II		
B2.1	ISE II	ISE II	ISE II	ISE II		ISE II	ISE II	
B1.2			ISE I			ISE I	ISE I	
B1.1	ISE I	ISE I	ISE I	ISE I	ISE I	ISE I	ISE I	ISE I
A2.2	ISE 0	ISE 0	ISE 0	ISE 0	ISE 0	ISE 0	ISE 0	ISE 0
A2.1	ISE 0		ISE 0	ISE 0				
A1								

The creation of these graphic profiles proved a challenging task. Apart from the lack of descriptors for the lower GESE Grades mentioned above, the judges were troubled by a number of descriptors in the CEFR scales which were found irrelevant to test content description. This resulted in the gaps observed in Figure 3 for Written Production and Integrated skills as the judges preferred not to make any claims with regard to levels whose descriptors could not be used adequately. Moreover, the judges noted that there were descriptors from more than one level of a single CEFR scale that were

Figure 4: Graphic Profile of the ISE-CEFR relationship (Competences)

C2												
C1.2												
C1	ISE III	ISE III	ISE III	ISE III	ISE III	ISE III	ISE III	ISE III	ISE III	ISE III	ISE III	ISE III
B2.2												
B2.1	ISE II	ISE II	ISE II	ISE II	ISE II	ISE II	ISE II	ISE II	ISE II	ISE II	ISE II	ISE II
B1.2					ISE I							
B1.1	ISE I	ISE I	ISE I ISE 0	ISE I ISE 0		ISE I	ISE I	ISE II	ISE I	ISE I ISE 0	ISE I	ISE I
A2.2		ISE 0								ISE 0		ISE I ISE 0
A2.1	ISE 0	ISE 0	ISE 0	ISE 0	ISE 0	ISE 0	ISE 0	ISE 0			ISE 0	
A1												
	RECEPTION				INTERACTION				PRODUCTION			
	Ling	Sociol	Prag	Strat	Ling	Sociol	Prag	Strat	Ling	Sociol	Prag	Strat

relevant to some GESE and ISE levels. This was the case for example with ISE 0 for which the judges pointed to descriptors from both A2 and B1. Finally, uneven profiles were observed. For example Grade 12 was most of the time placed at C2, but only at C1 for Listening Comprehension. However, it is not clear whether these uneven profiles were observed due to lower demands by the examinations or higher expectations in some of the CEFR scales.

Standardisation stage

Table 5 summarises the outcome of the Standardisation stage for GESE based on the decisions of the judges, and it shows the expected CEFR level for each GESE Grade for two types of candidates: those who barely pass the examination and those who achieve a comfortable pass. The judges pointed out during the group discussions that this is a more accurate description of their judgements because it reflected the focus on the borderline pass performance during the standard-setting task.

Table 5: CEFR level of borderline and secure pass candidates in the GESE suite

Grades	Level of borderline candidate	Level of secure pass candidate
Grade 12	C1+	C2
Grade 11	C1	C1
Grade 10	B2+	C1
Grade 9	B2+	B2+
Grade 8	B2	B2+
Grade 7	B1+	B2
Grade 6	B1	B1+
Grade 5	B1	B1
Grade 4	A2+	A2+
Grade 3	A2	A2
Grade 2	A1	A1+
Grade 1	Below A1	A1

The minimum expected CEFR level for each ISE level is presented in Table 6. Because the judges were aware of the correspondence between the GESE Grades and ISE levels, this could have affected decision making as can be seen by comparing GESE Grades 4, 6, 8 and 11 with the four ISE levels. This is not unreasonable, since the Interview component in both suites is common. For ISE, unlike GESE, the judges felt that the borderline candidate level represents their decision making sufficiently and that there was no need to indicate levels for higher ability candidates, as they were within the same CEFR band.

Table 6: CEFR level of borderline candidates in the ISE suite

ISE levels	Level of borderline candidate
ISE III	C1
ISE II	B2
ISE I	B1
ISE 0	A2+

Empirical validation

Due to space limitations, the results of this stage will only be summarised here as follows:

- **Internal validation:** Ratings of GESE monitors and examiners for 1,118 candidates in 132 different examination centres during the period May 2004–September 2005 were analysed. On average, examiners and monitors were in exact agreement on the final score to be awarded in over 70% of exams administered, and in 98% of exams they agreed exactly or within one band. This was consistent across all 12 Grades. For ISE Controlled Written Exam, the percentage of exact or within one band agreement for 157 samples (between November 2005 and May 2006) was above 95% for all four levels. However, agreement for 177 Portfolios was lower, ranging from 61% for ISE III to 90% for ISE 0. With regard to examiner training and monitoring, observation of the annual training event for all Trinity examiners was commented positively in the technical report.

- **External validation:** Even though the limitations of using the syllabus as the external criterion are acknowledged in the report, nevertheless results are interesting when comparing the cut score for borderline GESE candidates to what was mentioned about the CEFR level of the GESE Grades in the version of the syllabus used at the time of the project. One third of the GESE Grades was judged to be a band lower when talking about borderline performances, suggesting a lower cut score. Full agreement was observed between judges and the syllabus for the CEFR level of the four ISE levels.

Reflections on the use of the Draft Manual

Problems encountered and solutions found

As with any standard-setting study, the procedures followed were not without problems, even though the judges commented positively on their overall experience. The major issues in the Trinity project had to do with:

- **Fit between test content and the CEFR descriptors.** As clearly explained in the CEFR volume, the scales are not only to be used in a language testing context, but they are primarily intended as learning objectives. Naturally, the judges felt that descriptors and test content would not match exactly in some cases. For example, A1 level in the Global scale states that language learners 'can ask and answer questions about personal details such as where he/she lives, people he/she knows and things he/she has' (Council of Europe 2001:24). Judges noted that GESE Grades 1−3 do not have any questions on behalf of the candidate, but apart from the function of asking questions, A1 descriptors seemed to describe adequately the Trinity context. To address this issue, it was decided that when part of a descriptor does not apply, then it is clearly documented which parts provide an accurate representation of the content of the Trinity examinations, and this was documented in the report.

- **Judging young learners of high proficiency.** The Trinity judges had issues with some of the CEFR descriptors for the higher levels when they are to be applied to younger learners of English. In particular it was difficult to differentiate between the linguistic abilities of highly proficient younger learners and the sociolinguistic and pragmatic abilities which are included in the CEFR descriptors above B2. As with the previous bullet point, the decision made by the panel was to document only the descriptors that accurately describe the Trinity context.

- **Filling in the Specification forms.** Because of the large number of levels (12 GESE Grades and four ISE levels), the judges found the completion of the forms tedious and believed that the finalised version of the forms would be too long, with a lot of information in the forms repeated. The panel decided to refer back to a previous form when a new one would ask the same question. For example Forms A19, A20 and A21 ask more or less the same questions, and after completing A19, judges would just mention 'see Form 19' in A20 and A21. This was very carefully examined by the co-ordinator who collected the completed forms and word-processed them, and also corrected wrong or incomplete reference to the CEFR to ensure that the information was accurate.

Validity, reliability and generalisability of results

In order to secure the validity, reliability and generalisability of results, the following points, described in Hambleton (2001:93) and Kaftandjieva (2004:20), were considered in the project:

- selection of judges who were expected to be able to make accurate decisions about the examinations and the test-taking population
- training of judges to ensure their in-depth understanding of the CEFR and its scales, in order to apply it during the linking project, and statistical analysis of the judges' consistency and agreement
- sequence of activities following the procedures described in the Manual, with the Familiarisation stage repeated as part of Specification and Standardisation
- documentation including not only taking notes and compiling reports, but also recording the sessions in order to clarify points in the sessions that were not clear in the documentation
- feedback given during the Familiarisation session, in order to give judges a picture of their understanding of the CEFR scales
- the judges' high confidence in the results of the project, stated in post-meeting questionnaires.

Limitations and further research

Even though every effort was made to provide valid and reliable results, there are potential limitations that should be considered carefully. The use of internal judges might have affected the results as well as the choice of Trinity performance samples. It will be interesting if a future study is conducted with a different panel of judges and different performance samples. Also, the external validation of the project needs to be conducted in a more detailed manner, with the recruitment of a common test-taking population taking a Trinity examination as well as an external examination aiming at the same CEFR level.

Impact of the linking project

In the light of the project findings, Trinity revised the exam syllabus for administrations from 2007. Revisions included candidates asking questions for Grades 2 and 3 to match the content of A1 descriptors mentioned earlier and the setting of Grade 1 at a pre-A1 level. Adaptations were also made to

Grade 10 requirements to ensure that a borderline candidate would also be a C1 level candidate. The Grade 12 requirements were also revised for similar reasons.

Trinity also included a detailed response to the recommendations made in the technical report. The response listed areas of test development and validation that would be investigated following the publication of the project report.

Conclusion

This contribution presented a linking project for two international examinations. It discussed the design of the project, its results and reflected on the experience of using the Manual, which despite some issues that were raised during the recommended procedures, was overall evaluated as a positive experience by the judges and the examination provider.

References

Council of Europe (2001) *Common European Framework of Reference for Languages: Learning, teaching, assessment,* Cambridge: Cambridge University Press.

Council of Europe (2003) *Manual for relating language examinations to the Common European Framework of Reference for Languages: Learning, teaching, assessment. Preliminary pilot version,* Strasbourg: Council of Europe.

Davies, S (2001) *GESE initial benchmarking against the Common European Framework of Reference for Languages,* unpublished report, London: Trinity College London.

Green, R (2000) *Integrated Skills Exam,* report on mini-pilot, London: Trinity College London.

Hambleton, R K (2001) Setting performance standards on educational assessments and criteria for evaluating the process, in Cizek, G J (Ed.) *Setting performance standards: Concepts, methods, and perspectives,* Mahwah, N J: Lawrence Erlbaum Associates, 89−116.

Kaftandjieva, F (2004) *Standard setting. Section B of the Reference Supplement to the preliminary version of the Manual for relating language examinations to the Common European Framework of Reference for Languages: Learning, teaching, assessment,* Strasbourg: Council of Europe.

Kaftandjieva, F and Takala, S (2002) Council of Europe scales of language proficiency: A validation study, in Alderson J C (Ed.) *Common European Framework of Reference for Languages: Learning, teaching, assessment. Case studies,* Strasbourg: Council of Europe, 106−129.

Norris, J M (2005) Book review of Council of Europe (2001), *Language Testing* 22 (3), 399−405.

Papageorgiou, S (2007) *Relating the Trinity College London GESE and ISE exams to the Common European Framework of Reference: Piloting of the Council of Europe draft Manual,* final project report, London: Trinity College London, retrieved 22 January 2008 from www.trinitycollege.co.uk/resource/?id=2261

Raymond, M R and Reid, J B (2001) Who made thee a judge? Selecting and training participants for standard setting, in Cizek, G J (Ed.) *Setting performance standards: Concepts, methods, and perspectives,* Mahwah, N J: Lawrence Erlbaum Associates, 119−158.

Tanko, G (2004) *Into Europe: The Writing handbook,* Budapest: British Council.

Trinity College London (2005a) *Graded Examinations in Spoken English 2004−2007* (2nd impression), London: Trinity College London.

Trinity College London (2005b) *Integrated Skills in English Examinations 0, I, II, III* (4th ed.), London: Trinity College London.

8 Linking the CILS examinations to the CEFR: the A1 speaking test

Monica Barni, Anna Maria Scaglioso and Sabrina Machetti

CILS Centre, University for Foreigners in Siena, Italy

Abstract

This paper presents the procedures followed by the University for Foreigners in Siena in relating its CILS – Certification of Italian as a Foreign Language – examination to the Common European Framework of Reference for Languages (CEFR). Whilst the link – currently in the Standardisation phase – has been made for all exam levels offered by CILS, this paper will look at that established for level A1 – Adults in Italy module – following the four sets of procedures indicated in the preliminary version of the Council of Europe's Manual (2003), with a particular focus on the speaking test. The paper goes into detail regarding the theoretical, scientific and socio-political motivations leading to the choice of one of the starting competence levels, and emphasises that it required preliminary, radical reflection on the very meaning of assessment and certification. It also highlights the problems faced during this work, some of which were due to basic contradictions found in different parts of the Manual.

Project outline

The project to relate the six CILS examination levels with the CEFR began in 2006. It was co-ordinated by the director of the certification centre, and actively involved a total of 10 experts, including researchers, item writers and raters[1]. These 10 are the only judges attending the seminars organised to work through each of the stages required by the Manual for the linking process. Nonetheless, right from the start, the project was spread and shared through workshops organised and held regularly by the Centre, and attended by students specialising in Language Testing and Assessment – some of them foreigners who have also had first-hand experience of the CILS exam – and exam administrators, working in Italy and abroad[2].

159

The aim of the project is to establish a link between the six CILS examination levels and the CEFR, first and foremost in order to offer a transparent declaration of the content and format of the exam, which can be compared and related to other Italian and European certificates, and to provide the necessary evidence to support this declaration. Alongside this aim, and no less importantly, the linking process seeks to support and contribute to existing research projects on the internal and external validity of the examinations within the certification centre. These projects more generally regard the need for monitoring and constant validation of the certification offered by the CILS centre[3].

Here, we will present and discuss just one part of the project, regarding the link between the CEFR and the level A1 speaking test – Adults in Italy module[4]. The decision to focus on this part was not due simply to the fact that it has already been completed – all the work required by the Manual has actually been finished for levels A1 and A2.

It is a response to two different sets of factors. The first is related to the way in which the A1 speaking test is assessed: the performances are recorded and then assessed centrally by the CILS centre's raters. Establishing a link between the CILS A1 speaking test and the CEFR also implies activities designed to increase the raters' awareness regarding their judgements and to enhance their reliability. This was considered useful precisely for the purposes of an evaluation conducted according to the methods described above, which are relevant to all examination levels offered by CILS.

The second relates to the interest in and the topicality of the basic levels in the context of the certification of Italian as a foreign language. These can be linked to various factors, which we consider to be specific to basic levels and different from the higher levels of communicative autonomy. We will discuss some of these below, because we see this as essential in order to fully understand the extent to which the specific characteristics of the CILS A1 speaking test cannot be excluded from the linking process with the CEFR.

Background and theoretical issues

For CILS and other Italian and European certifications, the explicit description of the starting levels of competence in the CEFR stimulated in-depth reflection. The need for this kind of reflection was felt particularly strongly in Italy, due not least to the varied social conditions found within the country, and in particular, to the presence of immigrants, who currently amount to some three-quarters of a million people (Caritas 2007). Their presence is nothing new, but it is increasingly marked by traits of stability, which changes the condition of the Italian language among foreigners, for a number of reasons. The first of these reasons is that their contact with Italian takes place mainly in Italy. Secondly because contact is largely spontaneous, i.e., it takes place through the very processes of social inter-action between Italians and foreigners. Thirdly, because this spontaneous contact gives rise to a system of formal availability and demand for teaching and learning of Italian, with the consequent need to certify the level of com-petence achieved, whether that competence has been developed naturally and spontaneously or through a formal language course, or a combina-tion of the two, as is most often the case. Finally, there is an increasingly pressing need to expand and develop an *ethical milieu* (Davies 1997) on the issues of assessment and certification of linguistic and communicative com-petence, given the recent legislative proposal that the possession of certified competence in Italian should become the main condition to acquire Italian citizenship.

CILS has taken these needs on board, and ever since the mid-nineties it has been implementing projects to assess the feasibility of an exam designed for immigrants. These projects seek to strike a balance between the recognition of immigrants' specific characteristics and the need to offer them the same certification product offered to any other foreigner coming into contact with Italian, so as to avoid any possible element of segregation or differentiation that might be interpreted as exclusion.

Perhaps the largest and most significant of these projects was launched in 1999, and concluded in 2001 with the construction of basic level CILS exams[5]. Within this project, both the work of theoretical and methodological reflec-tion and the more technical task of constructing the exam progressed along a route that was far from linear. Following and expanding upon the CEFR's stimulation, the project tackled the problem of how to develop an exam that could describe, measure and guarantee, in terms of the social usefulness of the certificates, a competence that cannot be described in terms of commu-nicative autonomy (assuming autonomy to mean the ability of a learner to handle communication between given domains and contexts independently and self-sufficiently). Before defining communicative autonomy, we had to rethink the very concept of linguistic and communicative competence. It is the manifestation of an open system – that of language – which is intrinsically vague and difficult to confine, a system where oscillation of the standard is the rule, not the exception, a system where the dimension of actual use bears considerable weight (De Mauro 1982, Machetti 2006). This makes it impos-sible to refer to the manifestations of this system univocally, with reference to a single standard: particularly in the early stages of competence, there is a range of different linguistic needs that may drive different learners, a range of different domains and contexts generating these needs, and consequently, a range of different kinds of linguistic knowledge and *savoir faire* required to handle them.

From this perspective, communicative autonomy in levels A1 and A2 is not comparable with that of subsequent levels: there is a problem of adequacy and an issue of measurement (Davies 1990). The adequacy problem is due to the fact that in order to respond effectively to certain language needs, the learner requires a variety of knowledge and *savoir faire* that cannot simply be used 'as provided', but need to be adapted each time in order to handle different domains and contexts of communication, as efficiently as the speaker is able. The measurement problem arises because the autonomy seen in the basic levels does not allow us to categorise different learners as one indistinct group, without considering how they have been taught and have learned, the type of contact they have had with the new language, their individual characteristics, etc. It is also due in part to the fact that this autonomy is of a standard below the threshold of both social acceptability (a function of interaction with native speakers, which implies that the foreigner is able to relate to them, presenting him/herself with his/her own identity and ideas) and individual acceptability (felt by the learner him/herself, and a condition for the development of the inner learning process, at least as regards motivation)[6].

As we mentioned, this project concluded with the construction of exams for levels A1 and A2, which, in consideration of issues such as these, is addressed to a differentiated public, with a modular structure to meet the needs of different types of candidates[7].

Project stages: Familiarisation and Specification

At the time of construction of the CILS A1 exam, the test contents had already been amply specified. Its point of reference were the frameworks and conceptual categories used in the CEFR on the one hand, and on the other, language acquisition studies carried out in the context of Italian linguistic scientific research, which show how language learning by foreign adult immigrants is structured in stages that give rise to a systematic set of linguistic varieties[8]. Thus the CEFR linking project offers a chance for analysis and reflection on the procedures used and the product created, and not just a comparison with the operations specified in the Manual. The process also aims to allow the general indications given in the CEFR to be placed in context for the Italian language, detailing and specifying the various descriptors as much as possible, as they tend to be excessively generic, especially for the initial stages of learning.

As mentioned, the model indicated in the Manual was used to organise the process for the CEFR linking project. The first stage (early 2006) was **Familiarisation** using small group activities and plenary discussions, held each time new scale descriptors needed to be dealt with, and for preliminary activities prior to the Specification and Standardisation processes, so that all experts participating in the project could gain shared and in-depth knowledge of the CEFR.

In greater detail, the familiarisation stage required participants to perform the following activities, based on the materials specified below:

- *CEFR, Table 1, Common Reference Levels*: each participant read the table so as to be able to recognise the main characteristics of each level. This was followed by a plenary reflection during which a co-ordinator highlighted the main traits distinguishing each level, also bearing in mind the specifications given in § 3.6 of the CEFR, which was then read and discussed by all participants.

- *CEFR, Table 2, self-assessment grid*: participants reflected on their own level of competence in the foreign languages they spoke, focusing in particular on Spoken Interaction and Spoken Production, and each reported to the other participants on his/her own reflections during a plenary discussion.

- *CEFR, Table 3, qualitative aspects of spoken language use*: participants analysed the table in detail, giving due consideration to the activities previously performed, and with a particular focus on the qualitative aspects of level A1. This activity was further developed by familiarisation with the CEFR scales: *Overall Spoken Interaction (4.4.3.1); Goal-Oriented Co-operation (4.4.3.1); Transactions to Obtain Goods and Services (4.4.3.1); Information Exchange (4.4.3.1); Overall Oral Production (4.4.1.1); Sustained Monologue: Describing Experience (4.4.1.1)*.

The **Specification** stage (mid-2006) aimed to provide both theoretical and empirical evidence of the correspondence between the CILS A1 speaking test and the CEFR. This stage involved three types of activities:

- repetition of Familiarisation activities (*Manual, Chapter 3*: Introductory activities, Qualitative analysis of the CEFR scales)
- completion of control lists specifying the content of the CILS exam, with particular attention to the CILS A1 speaking test
- use of CEFR descriptors;

and was divided into two phases, one of general description and the other of detailed description of the exam.

For the general description of the exam, Form A1 was used (Manual, pages 35–36), whilst Forms A2–A6 (Manual, pages 37–40) were used to provide details on the different aspects of the exam: test development, marking, grading, reporting results and data analysis.

The detailed description phase aimed to provide more information for linking the exam to the CEFR. Having completed the general description of the exam and concurred that their initial impression placed it at level A1 (Form A8), the participants later used Forms A11 (Spoken Interaction), A13 (Spoken Production), A17 (Spoken Mediation), A20 (Aspects of Language

Competence in Interaction), and A22 (Aspects of Language Competence in Mediation) to provide greater detail on the content of the exam and thus to validate the declaration given in Form 8[9].

The results of this work, regarding the spoken interaction, were reported in Form A23, as follows:

Figure 1: Graphic profile of the Spoken Interaction Test CILS A1−CEFR relationship

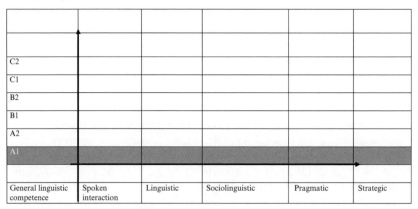

C2					
C1					
B2					
B1					
A2					
A1					
General linguistic competence	Spoken interaction	Linguistic	Sociolinguistic	Pragmatic	Strategic

The graph shows that the variety of tasks and activities, topics of communication and skills proposed by CILS for spoken interaction at level A1 – Adults in Italy module – refers to a basic level of competence strongly rooted in the specific context of language use, and can comfortably be positioned within level A1 of the CEFR. When looking in greater detail at the CEFR's scales and descriptors, the test may in some parts seem to belong to a higher competence level, between A1 and A2. In reality, the test does not exceed the limits of A1, and indeed, this detailed clarification offers us an opportunity to make the CEFR descriptors more specific. Whilst these descriptors must necessarily be generic enough to apply to all languages, there is nonetheless a deeply and broadly felt need for more detailed specifications.

Project stages: Standardisation and Empirical Validation

Standardisation

The **Standardisation** process was performed including each of the three stages: training, benchmarking and standard setting. Training was performed using CILS calibrated examples, which have been used since 2002 by

the certification centre to familiarise its exam administrators with the examination methods. The calibration of these examples is the fruit of discussions held in seminars in 2001 – the first year that the A1 and A2 exams were
offered. It is subject to constant updating, because these materials are used
for the training of future specialists at the teacher-training school for Italian
as a foreign language, for the specialisation course in Language Testing and
Assessment. The format of these examples differs a little from the indications
in the Manual. For example, the test method used was audio, not video and
the examiner was the candidate's interlocutor, rather than another candidate. Again diverging from the indications given in the Manual (2003:70),
participants in the linking project did not feel it would be suitable to use
calibrated examples from other languages – e.g., those available on DVD
for French (North and Lepage 2005). They justified this choice on the basis
of the specific characteristics and features of each individual language, as
process and product cannot easily be described or summarised using standards that are, if not universally, at least transversally valid. Nonetheless,
before starting the seminar, the French calibrated examples were viewed,
and a reading and discussion was held of reports from the 2005 seminar of
the Language Assessment and Certification Centre of the University for
Foreigners in Perugia (Corrigan 2007, Grego Bolli 2006) for the calibration
of their examples.

The Training stage was followed by Benchmarking. This was performed
by submitting a total of 12 local examples of speaking test A1 for assessment by the 10 judges. The selection of clearly different examples meant
each judge was able to view a variety of performances, from those of candidates comfortably within the level to borderline candidates, both those
tending towards A1−, and those closer to A2. The judges were provided
with the CILS scales and some CEFR tables and scales to assist them in the
Benchmarking process[10]. At the end of this phase, having asked the judges to
decide what level each performance belonged to, their opinions were translated into numbers, as shown in the table below and analysed using SPSS (see
the same procedure used by Papageorgiou 2007:41−42).

Table 1: Conversion of CEFR levels into quantitative data

CEFR level	Scale
A1− (below A1)	1
A1	2
A1+	3
A2	4

As we can see from Table 2, the results showed a good level of concordance between the judges.

Table 2: Agreement of judges – CILS A1 speaking test Benchmarking

Stage	Kendall's Coefficient of Concordance			
	Coef	Chi-Sq	DF	P
Benchmarking	0.753516	82.8867	11	0.0000

Participants were directly involved in choosing the method for the standard-setting phase. The advantage of this approach was that the judges immediately became familiar with the standard-setting process as a whole, and at the same time had the opportunity to get to know the different methods first hand, and to understand the pros and cons of each one. This was done following the directions provided by Kaftandjieva (2004:28 ff.), who amongst other things recommends that the method chosen should be appropriate to the situation, realistically usable and implementable, and valid *a priori*. Based on this, the judges opted for the modified Angoff method.

Standard setting was structured into two distinct sessions. In the first session the judges were asked to think of an imaginary candidate – with reference, perhaps, to real candidates they had met in the past whilst administering the A1 speaking test, and to the calibrated examples used in Training. Keeping the CEFR scales used in Benchmarking to hand, they were then asked the question, 'at what CEFR level can a test taker obtain each score?', and were requested to explain the reasons for their choices as clearly as possible[11].

Having done this, the judges discussed and shared the different answers given. An interesting discussion arose from one judge's answer, when he suggested that the scores contained in band (B) correspond to CEFR level A1+, basing this assessment on the breadth of the band. Indeed, whilst all the candidates in question pass the test, the judge pointed out that there is an enormous difference between those who pass with 10/18 and those who pass with 18/18. The second standard-setting session, partly in response to this suggestion, gave rise to some particularly interesting results. The judges were asked to answer the same question again, but this time with particular reference to a single ideal candidate, who gained a borderline score of 10/18, which was still a pass mark. The results were as follows:

Table 3: CEFR level of secure pass and borderline candidates in the CILS A1 speaking test

CILS Level	Level of secure pass candidate	Level of borderline candidate
A1	A1	A1–

The results of the two standard-setting sessions also show a good level of concordance between the judges in establishing a cut-off score for the CILS A1 speaking test in relation to the CEFR, thus confirming the declarations from session 4.

Empirical validation

The link between the CILS exam and the CEFR was completed with the Empirical Validation process. Given the impossibility of providing data on the external validation of our test, since it is still in the planning stage, here we present some of the more prominent aspects regarding its internal validation. For this validation, as we have already mentioned, we were able to draw upon data from research designed to constantly monitor and validate CILS exams and control their quality (Barni and Machetti forthcoming). The statistically processed data from this research was also applied using qualitative analysis procedures: selecting and interviewing a sample of those who had sat a given exam, and asking questions on various aspects of the test, from content to administration methods (Banerjee 2005).

This research brought to light some rather interesting data on the percentage of candidates passing the CILS exams. Here we look at the pass rate in the speaking test; the Manual considers a pass rate that is stable over a certain period of time to be a significant demonstration of a valid link between the exam and the CEFR (Kaftandjieva 2005:26 ff.).

Table 4: CILS A1 speaking test – number and % of pass rate candidates (sessions 2006–2008)

Examination session	Candidates	Pass rate	%
8 June 2006	57	56	98.24%
4 December 2006	40	37	92.50%
7 June 2007	574	557	97.04%
6 December 2007	160	154	96.25%
8 May 2008	88	79	89.77%

The table shows that in the period of time considered – from the June 2006 session to the May 2008 one, for a total of five examination sessions – the pass rate is not only stable, but also very high. Considering the explanation given in section 3 of the predominant weight assigned to this test within the CILS A1 exam for adults in Italy, justified by the kind of contact these candidates have with spoken Italian, the high pass rate is a sign of the good quality of the test, fully reflecting the competence characteristics expected at this level.

These pass rates prove to be even more significant when analysed in detail, looking at the percentage of candidates passing with each possible score.

Table 5: Speaking test CILS A1 – candidates grouped by final score (session 2006–2008)

Examination session		8/6/06		4/12/06		7/6/07		6/12/07		8/5/08
Total candidates		57		40		574		160		88
Score	N°	%	N°	%	N°	%	N°	%	N°	%
Candidates 0			1	2.50%	2	0.35%	4	2.50%		
attaining 5									1	1.14%
each score 6					1	0.17%				
expressed as a 7	1	1.75%			4	0.70%	2	1.25%	4	4.55%
number and as 8			1	2.50%	7	1.22%			2	2.27%
a percentage 9			1	2.50%	3	0.52%			2	2.27%
10	10	17.54%	13	32.50%	40	6.97%	1	0.63%	28	31.82%
11	5	8.77%	6	15.00%	30	5.23%	5	3.13%	12	13.64%
12	9	15.79%	1	2.50%	30	5.23%	2	1.25%	9	10.23%
13	6	10.53%	6	15.00%	54	9.41%	7	4.38%	5	5.68%
14	4	7.02%	3	7.50%	48	8.36%	12	7.50%	4	4.55%
15	4	7.02%	2	5.00%	64	11.15%	28	17.50%	3	3.41%
16	5	8.77%	2	5.00%	86	14.98%	35	21.88%	7	7.95%
17	3	5.26%	2	5.00%	84	14.63%	39	24.38%	1	1.14%
18	10	17.54%	2	5.00%	121	21.08%	25	15.63%	10	11.36%
Pass rate	56	98.24%	37	92.50%	557	97.04%	154	96.25%	79	89.77%

Some reflections on the use of the Manual

The project to link the CILS exams with the CEFR revealed both positive aspects and difficulties. The positive aspects lie in the opportunity offered by the project to reflect once again on the European document, and thus to gain greater awareness both of its strengths and of its weaknesses. In addition to this, the consistency and similarity of opinions of the different experts participating in the project confirm the validity of CILS' decision to assess the tests internally, using these same experts.

The difficulties were essentially of two types. The first had to do with internal limits to the project and the availability of those involved. In our case, the project to link the CILS exams with the CEFR took place in parallel with other projects, and space had to be found for it within the normal, everyday activities of research, planning and examination performed by the centre. This led to a number of organisational problems, often worsened by financial difficulties and by the rather limited number of people who were able to dedicate themselves to the operation full time. Furthermore, it should be emphasised that the culture of assessing linguistic and communicative skills is not yet very highly developed in Italy (Barni and Machetti 2005, Barni forthcoming). Consequently, these reflections are not taken into consideration on an institutional level, and are not adequately supported. The prevalent approach here is a bureaucratic one, oriented towards centralisation and state control, so that the criterion for a good test is not its ethicality, but rather the presence of a ministerial stamp of approval.

The second kind of difficulty had to do with the structure and intentions of the Manual. From 2003 to the present, these difficulties have been met and pointed out by authoritative figures (Alderson 2002, Fulcher 2004a, Fulcher 2004b, Weir 2005), but we feel it would not be superfluous to go over them again in the conclusion of this paper. We present them as questions, because we feel it is useful to view them as issues that are still open, on which there can be new, and we hope fruitful, discussions:

- Is it possible/plausible to establish a perfect link between an exam and the CEFR, comparable with those established for other languages? If so, what happens to the specific characteristics, and above all the strongly social nature of each language?

- What will become of the specific characteristics of non-autonomous competence? Is the core problem of the CEFR to remain that it does not sufficiently perceive the difference between communicative autonomy and non-autonomy, and that it does not relate competence to the different types of users (Hasselgreen 2005)?

- Are the linking procedures proposed by the Manual not perhaps overcomplicated? And could this not lead to both the risk of performing the entire linking process automatically, and that of accepting assessments without further explanation, thus also losing any remaining, positive element of subjectivity?

Notes

1. CILS is an official qualification certifying linguistic and communicative competence in Italian L2. CILS offers six examination levels: CILS A1, CILS A2, CILS Uno-B1, CILS Due-B2, CILS Tre-C1, CILS Quattro-C2. It was established in Italy and around the world following the legal institution of the university (Italian Law n°. 204 dated 17.02.1992), under the general regulations on the Italian university system, and on the basis of a framework-convention stipulated between the Italian Ministry of Foreign Affairs and the university in 1993 and renewed in 2004. Since 2005 the CILS Centre has been an institutional member of EALTA, the European Association for Language Testing and Assessment (www.ealta.eu.org).

2. Thus, in each phase, the project corresponds well both to the requirement of being carried out by experts and to that of involving a range of people who represent as closely as possible those involved in all the different roles within the examination process. With reference to the standard-setting process, Kaftandjieva (2004:28) states that this requirement is a high priority, but difficult to fulfil.

3. CILS is based on sound and systematic scientific research in the sectors

of linguistic theory and its application (standardised for the purposes of assessment), psychometrics, statistics and IT, with a focus on the responsibility inextricably linked to individual and collective assessment operations. The research activities informing the construction of CILS are the following:

– analysis of the position of Italian around the world: analysis of the needs of actual and potential course users; identification of general and local characteristics of available teaching (De Mauro et al 2002, Patat 2004)

– analysis of the possibilities and conditions for usefulness of the certified linguistic and communicative skills in different social contexts: from the world of work to higher education, to specific interests in different local situations (Barni and Villarini 2001, Vedovelli et al, forthcoming)

– analysis of the language's structural characteristics: historic/linguistic conditions, models of use, characteristics of social communication amongst native speakers, general and typological characteristics of texts (Bagna 2003, 2004)

– analysis of linguistic and communicative competence models: definition of development processes and stages of learning (Bagna 2001, Vedovelli 2002, Vedovelli and Villarini 2003)

– analysis of methodological instruments for measuring and assessing competence (Machetti 2007, Vedovelli 2005)

– analysis of the impact and consequences of certification on the education world and on society in general (Barni forthcoming, Barni 2005).

4. The CILS A1 speaking test – Adults in Italy module – involves an individual performance by the candidate, in two separate parts with different types of oral test, one for conversation, the other for solo production. The first test takes the form of a face-to-face conversation: the administrator holds a brief presentation dialogue with the candidate, which is followed by a conversation on a general or personal topic chosen from amongst four proposals. Having chosen the topic, the candidate has 2–3 minutes in which to prepare and organise his/her thoughts. The administrator takes an active part in the conversation (which lasts about 2 minutes), with relevant comments and questions. The second test takes the form of a 1-way speech given face-to-face: the candidate must be able to give an autonomous presentation – without the administrator's intervention – on a topic chosen from amongst four proposals. The candidate has a few minutes to prepare his/her presentation. Altogether, the two tests last for a maximum of 15 minutes. Out of a total of 60 marks for the entire exam, the maximum score a candidate can achieve in this test is 18/18. This is the same score obtainable in the listening comprehension test, whereas for the other two tests in the exam – reading comprehension and written production – the maximum score is 12/12.

5. On this issue, see Vedovelli (1997).

6. For an ample illustration of the different phases and main results of this project, see Barki et al (2003).

7. The modules are designed for immigrant adults in Italy; for the children of immigrants in Italy, aged between 6 and 11 years; for the older children of immigrants in Italy, aged between 12 and 15 years; for foreign youngsters studying Italian abroad, aged between 8 and 15 years; for the children of Italian emigrants (3rd, 4th and 5th generations), aged between 8 and 15 years; for learners with particular difficulties learning Italian, due primarily to the fact that their L1 is from a language typology that is very distant from

Italian (e.g., Asians). The modular structure allows for the expansion of the certificate's functions, which are not limited to describing the structural characteristics of the learner's interlanguage so as to ensure the social value of the certificate, but also extend to diagnosing the potential for development of the language learning process, and to reinforce motivation.

8. For a summary of the results of these studies, see Giacalone Ramat (2003).
9. The results of the description given in Forms 11 and 20 can be found in the Appendix.
10. The CILS A1 scales are those presented in Barki et al (2003:101 ff.); the CEFR tables and scales used are:
    - Manual, Table 4.1 – *CEFR Scales for Communicative Language Activities*
        - scale A11 – Spoken Interaction (CEFR, *Overall Spoken Interaction*)
        - scale A13 – Oral Production (CEFR, *Overall Oral Production*)
    - Manual, Table 4.2 – *CEFR Scales for Aspects of Communicative Language Competence*
        - scale 4.4 – Relevant Qualitative Factors for Spoken Interaction (CEFR, scales for *General Linguistic Range, Vocabulary Range, Grammatical Accuracy, Sociolinguistic Appropriateness, Phonological Control, Cohesion and Coherence, Fluency*)
        - scale 4.5 – Relevant Qualitative Factors for Oral Production (CEFR, scales for *General Linguistic Range, Vocabulary Range, Grammatical Accuracy, Phonological Control, Cohesion and Coherence, Fluency*).
11. For this activity, the different scores assigned to candidates for the CILS A1 speaking test were grouped into two bands: band (A) = from 0 to 9/18; band (B) = from 10 to 18/18.

References

Alderson, J C (2002) Using the Common European Framework in language teaching and assessment, in Alderson, J C (Ed.) *Common European Framework of Reference for Languages: Learning, Teaching, Assessment: Case Studies,* Strasbourg: Council of Europe, 1−8.

Bagna, C (2001) Le varietà di apprendimento dell'italiano L2 e la struttura della CILS, in Barni, M and Villarini, A (Eds) *La questione della lingua per gli immigrati stranieri. Insegnare, valutare e certificare l'italiano L2*, Milano: Franco Angeli, 103−124.

Bagna, C (2003) Il verbo e le sue reggenze: regolarità e anomalie in apprendenti di italiano L2, in Giacomo-Marcellesi, M and Rocchetti, A (Eds) *Il verbo italiano: studi diacronici, sincronici, contrastivi, didattici,* Atti del XXXV Congresso Internazionale di Studi della Società di Linguistica Italiana, Parigi 20−22 settembre 2001, Roma: Bulzoni, 517−534.

Bagna, C (2004) *La competenza quasi-bilingue/quasi-nativa. Le preposizioni in italiano L2,* Milano: Franco Angeli.

Banerjee, J (2005), *Qualitative Analysis Methods. Section D of the Reference Supplement to the Preliminary Version of the Manual for Relating Language Examinations to the Common European Framework of Reference for Languages: learning, teaching and assessment*, Strasbourg: Council of Europe.

Barki, P et al (2003) *Valutare e certificare l'italiano di stranieri. I livelli iniziali*, Perugia: Guerra.

Barni, M (2005) Etica della valutazione, in Vedovelli, M (Ed.) *Manuale della valutazione certificatoria*, Roma: Carocci, 329–341.

Barni, M (forthcoming) *Etica e politica della valutazione*, Atti del XV Convegno GISCEL *Misurazione e valutazione delle competenze linguistiche. Ipotesi ed esperienze*, Milano 6–8 marzo 2008.

Barni, M and Machetti, S (2005) *(The lack of) Professionalism in Language Assessment in Italy*, EALTA Conference, Voss, 2– 5 June 2005, www.ealta. eu.org/conference/2005/programme.htm, accessed 2 July 2008.

Barni, M and Machetti, S (forthcoming) *CILS exams. A validation study (2005–2008)*, Perugia: Guerra.

Barni, M and Villarini, A (Eds) (2001) *La questione della lingua per gli immigrati stranieri. Insegnare, valutare e certificare l'italiano L2*, Milano: Franco Angeli.

Caritas di Roma (2007) *Immigrazione. Dossier statistico 2007. XVII Rapporto*, Roma: Idos.

Corrigan, M (2007) *Seminar to calibrate examples of spoken performance, Università per Stranieri di Perugia, CVCL. Report on the analysis of the rating data*, Perugia, 17–18 December 2005, www.coe.int/T/DG4/Portfolio/ documents/Report_Seminar_Perugia05.pdf, accessed 4 July 2008.

Council of Europe (2001) *Common European Framework of Reference for Languages: learning, teaching, assessment*, Cambridge: Cambridge University Press.

Council of Europe (2003) *Relating Language Examinations to the Common European Framework of Reference for Languages: Learning, Teaching, Assessment (CEFR). Manual. Preliminary pilot version*, Strasbourg: Council of Europe.

Davies, A (1990) *Principles of Language Testing*, Oxford/Cambridge: Basil Blackwell.

Davies, A (1997) Demands of being professional in language testing, *Language Testing* 14 (3), 328–339.

De Mauro, T (1982) *Minisemantica dei linguaggi non verbali e delle lingue*, Roma-Bari: Laterza.

De Mauro, T et al (2002) *Italiano 2000. I pubblici e le motivazioni dell'italiano diffuse fra stranieri*, Roma: Bulzoni Editore.

Fulcher, G (2004a) Deluded by artifices? The Common European Framework and harmonization, *Language Assessment Quarterly* 1 (4), 253–266.

Fulcher, G (2004b) Are Europe's tests being built on an unsafe framework?, *Guardian Weekly TEFL Supplement*, 18 March.

Giacalone Ramat, A (Ed.) (2003) *Verso l'italiano. Percorsi e strategie di acquisizione*, Roma: Carocci.

Grego Bolli, G (2006) *Seminar to calibrate examples of spoken performance in Italian L2 to the scales of the Common European Framework of References for Languages, Università per Stranieri di Perugia, CVCL. Report*, Perugia, 16–17 December 2005, www.coe.int/T/DG4/Portfolio/main_pages/Report%20on%20 Italian%20Benchmarking%20seminar.pdf, accessed 10 July 2008.

Hasselgreen, A (2005) Assessing the language of young learners, *Language Testing* 22 (3), 337–354.

Kaftandjieva, F (2004) *Standard Setting. Section B of the Reference Supplement to the Preliminary Version of the Manual for Relating Language Examinations to the Common European Framework of Reference for Languages: learning, teaching and assessment*, Strasbourg: Council of Europe.

Machetti, S (2006) *Uscire dal vago. Analisi linguistica della vaghezza del linguaggio*, Roma-Bari: Laterza.

Machetti, S (2007) Vaghezza semiotica e linguistica e misurazione della competenza in italiano L2: spunti per una discussione, in Boria, M and Risso, L (Eds) *Laboratorio di nuova ricerca. Investigating Gender, Translation & Culture in Italian Studies,* Atti del II Colloquium in Italian Studies (Cambridge, aprile 2005), Leicester: Troubador, 311−326.

North, B and Lepage, S (2005) *Guide for the organisation of a seminar to calibrate examples of spoken performance in line with the scales of the Common European Framework of Reference for Languages*, Strasbourg: Council of Europe.

Papageorgiou, S (2007) *Relating the Trinity College London GESE and ISE exams to the Common European Framework of Reference: Piloting of the Council of Europe draft Manual*, final project report, February 2007, www.trinitycollege.co.uk/resource/?id=2261, accessed 2 July 2008.

Patat, A (2004) *L'italiano in Argentina*, Perugia: Guerra Edizioni.

Vedovelli, M (1997) La funzione di una certificazione: specificità migratoria vs. generalità della competenza, *Percorsi. Rivista di educazione degli adulti* X, 56−59.

Vedovelli, M (2002) Italiano come L2, in Lavinio, C (Ed.) *La linguistica italiana alle soglie del 2000 (1987−1997 e oltre)*, Roma: Bulzoni Editore, 161−212.

Vedovelli, M (Ed.) (2005) *Manuale della certificazione dell'italiano L2*, Roma: Carocci.

Vedovelli, M and Villarini, A (2003) Dalla linguistica acquisizionale alla didattica acquisizionale: le sequenze sintattiche nei materiali per l'italiano L2 destinato agli immigrati stranieri, in Giacalone Ramat, A (Ed.) *Verso l'italiano. Percorsi e strategie di acquisizione,* Roma: Carocci, 279−303.

Vedovelli, M et al (forthcoming) *Vademecum certificazioni di competenza linguistica in Italiano,* FAPI − Fondo formazione Piccole e Medie Imprese.

Weir, C J (2005) Limitations of the Common European Framework for developing comparable examinations and tests, *Language Testing* 22 (3), 281−300.

Appendix

Table 1: Specification: Spoken Interaction − CILS A1

Categories and References	Short description
Situations, Content categories, Domains (CEFR, 4.1, Table 5)	Home, Education and Work, Travel, Buying in shops, supermarkets and markets, Health, Services
Communication themes (CEFR, 4.2)	Home: lodgings, categories, practical functions and services considered necessary, other; Education: language courses (enrolment, timetables, categories and teaching material); Work: categories and availability; working conditions (working hours, holidays), other; Travel: public transport (timetables, train, plane and bus tickets), street directions, identifying places, other; Shopping in stores, supermarkets, markets: means of transport, books and stationery, food and drink, household cleaning products, clothes, household items, furniture, prices, other; Health: main parts of the body, medicines, illnesses, seeing the doctor, laboratory tests and medical examinations; Services: personal documents, residence permit; domestic utilities, food tastes and preferences, other
Communicative tasks (CEFR, 4.2)	− asking an estate agent for information about renting or buying an apartment − asking a policeman or member of the public for directions to a place − asking for information about a public transport service and buying tickets − asking for information about social services − asking for information about sports activities − asking for information about health services and making appointments with the doctor and for tests − asking for information about sending parcels/paying bills − asking for information about obtaining documents from public offices − asking for information about various types of items on sale and shopping in stores, markets and supermarkets − ordering food and drink in bars and restaurants − buying tickets for the cinema/theatre
Communicative activities a) and interaction strategies b) (CEFR, 4.4.3.1; 4.4.3.5)	a) − casual conversation − informal discussions and meetings − co-operation for a specific aim − transaction to obtain goods and services − exchanging information − interviewing and being interviewed b) − planning (*assessing the situation*) − implementation (*asking for help, turn taking in conversation*)
Text-types (CEFR, 4.6.2)	− dialogues in simple situations − dialogues and interpersonal conversations
Tasks (CEFR, 7.1, 7.2, 7.3)	− tasks were selected with due consideration of the learners' communicative needs outside the classroom, with reference to specific social needs − tasks that enable learners to exhibit communicative functions such as describing, informing, expressing their tastes

**Table 2: Specification: Aspects of Language Competence in Interaction –
CILS A1**

Competence	Description

Linguistic competence: range of lexical and grammatical competence (CEFR, 5.2.1.1, 5.2.1.2)	– Lexical competence: approx. 850 words from the basic vocabulary of Italian, belonging to the following semantic fields: family, home, furniture, clothes, household items, cleaning products and personal toiletries, natural phenomena, shops, public offices, food and drinks, professions, school, body and health, nationalities
	– Grammatical competence:
	– definite and indefinite article
	– gender and number of nouns
	– nouns and descriptive adjectives (for the productive skills noun–adjective agreement is not required)
	– modal verbs
	– active conjugation of auxiliaries *essere* and *avere* and of regular verbs in the following modes and tenses:
	  • present indicative
	  • perfect indicative (subject–past participle agreement is not required)
	  • present infinitive
	  • imperative (active and negative forms in the 2nd person singular and plural)
	– modal verbs: *potere, dovere* and *volere*
	– subject pronouns and recognition of object pronouns
	– possessive, demonstrative and interrogative adjectives and pronouns
	– main adverbs:
	  • of time *(prima, poi, dopo, già, ora/adesso, sempre, mai, oggi, domani, ieri)*
	  • of place *(qui/qua, lì/là, sopra, sotto, giù, dentro, fuori, vicino, lontano, davanti, dietro, a destra, a sinistra)*
	  • other common adverbs *(così, molto, poco, tanto, più, meno, meglio, bene, male)*
	– cardinal numbers (knowledge is required of: numbers 1–20, tens, hundreds, thousands, a million)
	– prepositions, including those combined with the article
	– simple phrases: declaratives, interrogatives introduced by *chi, come, dove, quando, perché, che cosa*, volitives with the imperative
	– complex phrases: co-ordinate clauses introduced by *e* and *ma*
	– subordinate clauses
	  • causal clauses introduced by *perché*
	  • temporal clauses introduced by *quando*
	– final clauses in implicit form, introduced by *per* with the infinitive

Linguistic competence: range of phonological competence (CEFR, 5.2.1.4)	– ability to recognise and use the main intonation patterns (interrogative, declarative and imperative) and distinctive traits needed to handle minimal communication such as the distinction of phonemes (minimal pairs: voiced *vs.* voiceless consonants, long consonants, open *vs.* closed vowels) – ability to express oneself and make oneself understood in Italian, allowing for some uncertainties and pronunciation still rooted in L1

Table 2: (continued)

Competence	Description
Socio-Linguistic Competence (CEFR, 5.2.2)	– ability to interact with one or more interlocutors informally; – ability to apply the simpler rules of courtesy and the conventions governing turn-taking: expressing courtesy in a positive way, showing interest for what the interlocutor is saying, showing admiration, gratitude, the appropriate use of *per favore*, *grazie* etc.
Pragmatic Competence (CEFR, 5.2.3)	– ability to accomplish different communicative functions: ask simple questions, respond and exchange information on familiar topics regarding the family, school or free time, give a simple description of oneself or other people, places, living conditions, etc. and express one's tastes

9 Linking the general English suite of Euro examinations to the CEFR: a case study report

Gergely A Dávid

School of English and American Studies, Eötvös Loránd University, Budapest, Hungary

Abstract

This case study started as a small project focused on the grammar and vocabulary paper, part of the general suite of Euro examinations. In this period all the four phases in *Relating Language Examinations to the Common European Framework of Reference for Languages: Learning, Teaching, Assessment. Manual. Preliminary Pilot Version* (Council of Europe 2003, henceforth, the Manual) were intensively dealt with by a team of Euro item writers. This first stage of the project provided an excellent opportunity to analyse one paper in depth and pilot techniques to be used later. When the project was extended in a second stage, it covered four complete Euro examinations and all the four phases in the Manual were dealt with again. In this stage, the Euro project recreated the measurement scale that the illustrative scales in the Common European Framework of Reference for Languages (CEFR) itself are based on in the sense that CEFR linked thresholds were computed. Using Many-facet Rasch Measurement and a lesser known anchoring technique, the Euro team standardised a range of Euro items and linked them to the CEFR, setting CEFR-related pass marks to their examinations. Reflections on trying out the Manual and on the whole process of linking, which may be useful for others in the field, complement the case study.

The context and the purpose of the Euro linking project

The Euro examinations are proficiency tests of English that comprise reading, listening, writing, grammar and vocabulary, mediation (both ways between English and Hungarian) and speaking papers, each of them at three CEFR levels (B1, B2 and C1). Euro Examinations had had an interest in the *Common European Framework of Reference for Languages* (CEFR, Council of Europe 2001) and the need to strengthen reflective practice among staff led to the case study. Motivation also came from the need to evaluate the appropriacy of the Euro cut-offs because they had never been researched before. In addition, Euro felt they had the experience to build on, having attained accreditation[1] in 2001. Thus in 2005, they decided to undertake a small study in response to the Council of Europe initiative. Initially, the case study focused on the grammar and vocabulary (GV) paper only, which is a test of 40 text-based objective items[2]. I will refer to this initial project as Stage 1. Then in 2007, the Ministry mandated all examinations in Hungary to establish a link to the CEFR, no matter how well the methodology in the Manual had been worked out. The project, therefore, had to be extended, to include four complete Euro examinations (levels B1, B2 and C1 from the general suite and level B2 from their business suite). I will refer to this wider project as Stage 2.

Background in research on language assessment

The Euro projects relied on Messick's principles (1981a, 1981b, 1988, 1995, 1996) about potential sources of invalidity. These were *construct underrepresentation* (when the test measures a lot less than it should, of the ability or particular aspect of language proficiency in focus) and *construct-irrelevant variance* (variation in the scores caused by factors *not* related to what is measured, e.g. test method factors) and the need to *discount rival interpretations* (of test or research results, for example, which go against the interpretation most likely expected and which are often quite simple). One additional principle, by Glaser and Strauss (1967), was that of *data saturation*, i.e. recurrent qualitative evidence which, providing no new insights, may be taken as an indication that the evidence is complete enough for conclusions to be drawn.

Research in language testing also influenced the Euro project in that an examinee-based method was chosen for standard setting, in line with the current trend that Kaftandjieva observed (2004:15). Such methods were attractive to Euro because examiners, all being teachers as well, are more likely to be familiar with a rating situation and the rater's role than with estimating item difficulties in a test-centred exercise. Relevant studies in Cizek (2001) were also consulted.

Like many other institutions, Euro faced the problem of finding enough suitable calibrated or standardised samples (see the introductory chapter in this volume), without which empirical validation can hardly be started. Most reference material (samples) published at the start of the project lacked some of the validity information (procedures, measurements) one would need in order to choose them as reference. Comparability problems were also experienced. Supposing DIALANG reading items were to be used (Council of Europe 2004b), it would turn out that item difficulties and cut-offs are reported (the latter in Table 1), but there is no information about the upper and lower extremes of the DIALANG scale. By contrast, the same information is traceable in North (2000), rendering their scale comparable with other measurements (Table 1). Another case in point may be the *CEFR Performance Samples* video (Migros Club Schools and Eurocentres 2003). The video at first appeared to be the one North (2000) used and which would have been important for the Euro project. A closer inspection, however, revealed that the video includes only four participants from North's well-documented rating conference (p. 329). Thus, it may be stated, North (2000) has the ability calibration data while the video contains a selection of performance samples but the two hardly overlap.

Table 1: The comparison of two probabilistic scales for relevant data (cut-offs and end points)

	The DIALANG reading scale/cut-offs	North and Schneider's scale/ cut-offs
Upper end	no information	4.77
C2	2.01	3.9
C1	1.23	2.8
B2	0.21	0.72
B1	−0.22	−1.23
A2	−0.56	−3.23
A1	−0.94	−4.29
Lower end	no information	−5.68

These problems ultimately make it difficult to make a comprehensive and unified link to the CEFR. The best one could hope for is to use reference items in paper-by-paper comparisons (judgements) with relevant local items and to test these comparisons statistically, to see whether there is a relationship between the reference and local items. With the extension of the project (six papers in four examinations), Euro ought to have found at least 24 well-documented (sets of) reference items and performances.

Problems of incomplete and inadequate reporting led Euro to wonder whether a different approach was possible, through North and Schneider's work (North 2000, Schneider and North 1999). First, it was their work in the 1990s that formed the basis for the illustrative scales in the CEFR (Council of Europe 2001:43–130). Second, the result of their work was a large number of calibrated descriptors, well-documented and comprehensive, covering different skills and papers in one measurement framework. The procedure described below was attractive because it held out the possibility of bringing the three Euro levels together in a single framework, using North and Schneider's calibrations in setting up a CEFR-linked A1–C2 scale of descriptors in Hungary.

MFRM technology was used intensively in the Euro project. The acronym stands for Many-Facet Rasch Measurement (Linacre 2006), an extension of the basic probabilistic Rasch model, itself a branch of the 'IRT family' (Item Response Theory) of measurement models. MFRM is an extension because in addition to the variables of candidate (ability) and items (tasks), it can also be used in 'subjective' rating situations where there are examiners (raters) or other systematic variables of foreign language performance. MFRM can put Messick's ideas about construct-irrelevant variance into practice by removing or neutralising misfitting (inconsistent) elements from datasets in a series of analyses. A misfitting candidate is, for example, someone who keeps guessing, cheats or otherwise scores or loses a point when not expected. Such misfitting elements might be problematic tasks, items and CEFR descriptors, inconsistent respondents such as candidates, examiners, raters and judges. In measurement such elements are seen as 'contaminating' the data and the procedures by which datasets are freed from misfitting elements are called data cleaning procedures[3]. In MFRM analyses four different fit indices help identify the contaminants. MFRM can also put in practice Messick's ideas about construct-irrelevant easiness or difficulty by compensating for rater and task effects (or any additional facets of performance, one of which in our case was the language of CEFR descriptors). Compensation makes measurement more strongly reflect what really needs to be measured, since we are ultimately not interested in the tools of measurement. It is possible to 'construct the construct', as it were, in a series of analyses. Data-cleaning techniques can contribute to the validity of measurement by making it more consistently, or reliably, measure whatever is measured, whereas compensating for performance factors (facets) enhances validity by increasing the dominance of the construct, i.e. construct-relevant variance in determining the outcome of a test, survey, etc.

The design of the linking project

Euro Examinations completed their linking project in two stages. As has been said, in Stage 1 they focused only on one paper (GV), dealing with all the four phases recommended in the Manual. In order to link the complete examinations in Stage 2, they repeated the procedure at a larger scale, modifying some of the techniques as well.

The project members were both full-timers and part-timers, selected on the basis of experience, whether they could be seen as 'holders' of the Euro standard. In Stage 1, the type of test, the fact that the GV paper contained selected-response and short-answer items (marked clerically) demanded that item writers should be the project members, since the standards were to be applied in the test construction stage. In Stage 2, the item writers were joined by some of the designers of the Euro tests and a number of oral examiners.

Given that these roles are often combined in Hungary, for the sake of simplicity, I will refer to them as examiners, even in their judgement roles. I was asked to lead the project as an outside consultant.

The design of Stage 1

In the familiarisation phase, the task was to see whether the item writers were adequately familiar with the CEFR. Taking my cue from the sorting exercise in the Manual (pp. 25−27), I jumbled 133 CEFR descriptors whose level the item writers determined. The descriptors, drawn from 15 relevant scales, including those of linguistic competence and vocabulary scales, were collated as a questionnaire, which was scored on a correct/incorrect basis. The examiners were given feedback and formative discussion followed. If necessary, I was to provide further training for them.

In the specification phase, a content analysis of previous GV papers took place because the specifications did not provide enough information about the construct, i.e. what of linguistic competence needs to be measured and at which level. The project, therefore, fell back on eliciting the information from the item writers because they wrote items on a regular basis. One technique was to *elucidate* from them what made a particular task or paper a good example of the level, in order to see what their *conceptions* of the Euro levels were and whether those were in line with the descriptions in the CEFR. Another substitute for adequate specifications was to have two outside *experts*, of language testing and linguistics, *establish* whether CEFR construct categories (pp. 108−117) were actually represented in the papers. They wanted to know whether papers in different test versions covered the same construct categories and whether Euro levels differed in terms of which construct categories they represented. The experts translated these questions into the key variables of *test administration* (the occasion of test-taking), *type,* or *format of task* (dictation, multiple-choice cloze, modified cloze), the *texts* providing the context for the items, the *authors* of the texts and the *focus* of the item (what construct category the item is targeted at). Since a limited-choice item typically has more than a single focus, the complexity of items could also be analysed. Items with more focuses (in terms of CEFR categories) were considered to be more complex.

In the standardisation phase, the item writers and I further investigated a possible gap between earlier Euro standards and the CEFR, by identifying the differences between their notion of what the minimally acceptable B1, B2 and C1 candidates can do and what the CEFR explicitly specifies as such. I asked them to mark the descriptors (or parts of) they considered 'too demanding'. Next, the item writers held a video rating conference with 11 *CEFR Performance Samples* (Migros Club Schools and Eurocentres 2003) using CEFR criteria (pp. 28−29). The analysis was done in three different ways: comparison of the Euro ratings with North's measures, reliability analysis of the rating conference data and the testing of the agreement between the raters. Finally, Euro attempted to adjust the standards for the GV paper, using candidate performances, which is one of the examinee-centred approaches in Kaftandjieva (2004). The item writers had to convert their conception of the CEFR scales and the oral/aural productions of the video into judgements about a selection of GV papers.

The empirical validation phase started with internal validation. The reliability of the GV tests was established, through the deletion (neutralising) of problematic candidates and items. The stability of the test (across exam dates) was evaluated using MFRM. External validation was also attempted in Stage 1, using item writer judgement data to predict minimum standards (pass marks), but this was inconclusive for two reasons. First, Euro Examinations applied a compensatory pass mark, to which all test papers contributed. Therefore, success could not be predicted from a single test paper. Second, the findings were contradictory in some ways.

The design of Stage 2

In this stage, the phases in the Manual were dealt with again, as recommended, repeating some of the procedures at a larger scale. It is perhaps best if the description begins with the standardisation phase because the requirements of that phase determined what had to be done earlier, in the familiarisation phase. The most central task was to set up a standard via North and Schneider's calibrations and to construct an overall A1−C2 CEFR scale on the basis of the Euro questionnaire data. North and Schneider had had teachers rate students with the descriptors and, using MFRM technology (the same *Facets* software), they calibrated difficulty values for their descriptors, which allowed them to place the descriptors into the A1 to C2 bands. (The right-hand column in Table 1 shows the cut-off points they determined.) It was the calibrations that allowed North and Schneider to decide whether a descriptor was B2, rather than B1 or C1, etc. By administering many of the same descriptors to the Euro examiners, I expected to create a comparable body of response data in Hungary. The Euro experiment, therefore, had to be comprehensive in terms of elements of language proficiency (communicative language activities or skills), scales and languages. Although most of the descriptors had been calibrated in English by North (2000), a comparison with the CEFR (2001) itself would show that some scales, most notably those of reading comprehension, were probably first calibrated in German (Schneider and North 1999). In this way, including German, at least in the standardisation phase of Stage 2, was obviously desirable.

The comprehensive nature of the exercise demanded a long and reliable data collection tool. Two questionnaires, or forms, were taking shape, which included many descriptors from 24 German and 25 English scales. Thirty-seven examiners (including a German team) were selected for Stage 2, taking into account their experience with different levels, papers and tests. While responding, the examiners were to decide the CEFR level of the descriptors, which created a rating situation quite like North and Schneider's in that their teachers also rated descriptors that had no level specification. I made no changes to the wording of the descriptors.

In order to satisfy MFRM technical requirements of connectedness[4], each examiner was to fill in a second questionnaire of descriptors, from 14 scales in Hungarian, which brought the number of responses to about 400 per examiner. This was necessary because if English examiners had responded only to the descriptors in the English questionnaire and the German examiners to the German questionnaire, the two datasets would not have been comparable. The descriptors in Hungarian provided the missing link for the software.

The MFRM analyses based on Hungarian data could not yet be the basis of any claims for a link to the CEFR, of course, since it was a psychometrically unrelated analysis, independent of North and Schneider's measures. Likewise, the difficulty value for each descriptor would necessarily be different from those by North and Schneider because the Hungarian dataset only reflected the judgement of the Euro examiners. Therefore, I selected a batch of descriptors with excellent measurement properties from North (2000) and Schneider and North (1999) to be the link (anchors) between North and Schneider's calibrations and the Euro dataset. In the analysis, I fixed the difficulty values of the anchors at the mean of values taken from North and Schneider's work.

What was done up to this point was mainstream language testing methodology in that test equating is typically based on anchored items. In our case, the batch of North and Schneider's descriptors were the common items. Jones (2002) had also included many of North's fluency descriptors in his own work to anchor the Association of Language Testers in Europe (ALTE) scales. The most important outcome for the Euro project is demonstrated by the MFRM output graph that summarises the difficulties of all 688 descriptors now linked. In Figure 1, ability increases horizontally, from left to right, while probability increases along the vertical axis. The A1 curve, characterising the lowest CEFR level is shown as 0s. It starts high on the left (high probability of low ability), but then falls, plunging towards a point of intersection with the A2 curve, shown as 1s. By contrast, the A2 curve starts low (low probability of somewhat higher ability), rising as ability increases until it reaches its peak, but then falling as the B1 curve is beginning to rise. It was the intersections of the curves and the attached numerical values that were relevant to us. These are called thresholds, above which item (descriptor) difficulties were *more likely to* correspond to A2 rather than A1, or B1 rather than A2, etc. In this sense, out of the many descriptors we have created an overall A1−C2 scale from the Hungarian dataset, which has CEFR-related threshold values (right-hand column, Table 2, further below). Since MFRM technology puts items, raters and candidates on the same logit scale, the threshold values were therefore use in the next phases of linking. These thresholds could first be applied to Euro items and then to carefully selected candidate performances from the spring 2007 examinations, to set CEFR-related standards. MRFM made this possible, via the *step anchoring* approach, which is less well-known than item anchoring. Through *step anchoring* the threshold values (and not difficulty values) from the CEFR-related Euro descriptor calibrations may be fixed in similar MFRM calibrations of examiner judgements of Euro items and also of candidate performances, since the examiners judged both items and candidates according to CEFR levels.

Figure 1: Anchored Euro probability curves

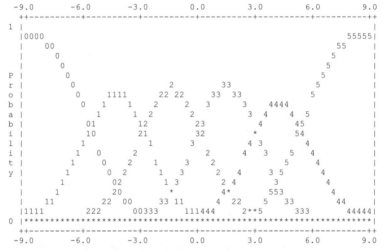

The examiners estimating carefully selected candidates' proficiency was to be the high point of the project because, in my experience, an examination battery can never be perfectly geared in advance to a particular level so that the borderline performances are found exactly at a preconceived passing score. The validation of an examination, i.e. answering the question whether the examination tests the CEFR level that it purports to test must ultimately be the validation of a minimum ability needed for a pass, operationalised as a pass mark. Thus the questions for the external empirical validation phase were whether Euro Examinations passes the candidates that they should in light of the CEFR standards. If not, what passing score (minimum logit ability) allows the same inference to be drawn over time and different administrations?

As I have indicated, the standardisation design principles shaped how familiarisation was to be carried out earlier in Stage 2. The questionnaires were administered to examiners as a summative measure, to test how familiar they were with the CEFR. The complete specifications were also revised in Stage 2, using developments related to the CEFR, such as *The Dutch CEFR Grid (Version 4)* (no date) and the two ALTE CEFR grids for writing and speaking (no date). These were used for most of the papers[5].

Procedures and results

In the reporting below, preference is given to Stage 2 because it covered complete examinations. Stage 1 results are also reported where space allows, as they lend a degree of procedural validity to the whole study.

Familiarisation

At Stage 1, barely 41% of the item writers' answers were correct on average. In response to this poor result, some more analyses were conducted, chiefly of categorical variables, to see how the item writers' awareness of CEFR levels could be characterised. It turned out that, when in doubt, they tended to indicate a level higher than what is in the CEFR. They seemed to be more 'lenient' than the CEFR, as if there was a gap, implying lower Euro standards and likely affecting the level of the tests they wrote. At Stage 2, the mean familiarity reached 50%, only a modest increase over a single year.

Specification

In the elucidation activities, the item writers selected the tasks they thought best represented and supported their choices with explanations, which were recorded. The data was examined for emerging patterns. The original authors of the tasks were also traced, in order to discount the rival hypothesis that the item writers selected their tasks as best representing the level for a different reason, unrelated to the focus of the study, i.e. whether they chose tasks they themselves wrote. If that had been the case, the validity of the insights would be in doubt.

The item writers' conceptions of level B1 matched the CEFR best. By comparison, level B2 was not as sharply conceived, while some CEFR requirements for level C1 were thought to be far-fetched. The responses revealed a gap here, between the item writers' conceptions (expectations) and some C1 descriptors that seemed to specify excessively high requirements. Only three texts (out of the 18) were selected by their original authors, which suggested that item writers' choices of 'best tasks' had probably not been strongly influenced by their own work.

In the expert analyses 265 GV items from six complete, consecutive papers, at three levels, were categorised, according to what each item focused on. Data saturation demanded that, if necessary, more papers be analysed, until no new information was yielded. The analysis was based on the CEFR itself (pp. 108–117) from which the experts made 15 categories with very minor modifications. They trained with a spare B2 GV paper and discussed their findings. Next, they worked individually, now with the papers for the main study, deciding which CEFR category (categories) each item focused on. Then going through all the items together, the experts arrived at agreed (moderated) verdicts.

Statistical analyses of the moderated classifications followed. I analysed item focus for a possible relationship with task type (dictation, MC-cloze, etc.), administration (the test-taking times of December 2003 vs. February 2004), level, text and author. The data being categorical, I chose cross-tabulation (chi-square) to conduct:[6]

1. Overall comparisons, between the six studied tests in the study period.

2. Separate additional comparisons because overall comparisons do not rule out the possibility that relationships might be different, if the two administrations are considered separately or if each level is independently analysed across administrations.

3. An analysis of the stability of the test between two administrations of the same level.

4. Tests of relatedness run in order to find out whether complexity increased with the level.

The experts identified 617 focuses for the 265 items, across which the 15 CEFR focus categories of linguistic competence were fairly well distributed, except those of *Phrasal idioms* and *Fixed frames* (Council of Europe 2001:110–111), which were only represented by a single focus each. There were no observations for *Classes* (p. 113), which may be explained by the characteristics of the English language, where there is very little of verb conjugation and noun declension. On the whole, coverage of the linguistic system appeared to be satisfactory in these tests. The related statistical tests yielded the following results:

1. All analyses of tests across administrations, including the two tests at each level analysed separately, and the tests at three levels together within the same administration indicated that the type of task may have a very powerful effect on what focuses the items were given. Significant relationships were also found with respect to texts and authors. No significant relationships were found to exist between focuses vs. administration and level, which suggested the overall stability of GV.

2. The distribution of focuses across administrations suggested that 'similar ground' is covered any time a test is given. The lack of significant

differences by level suggested that the same 15 CEFR categories were covered at each level, which finding I am inclined to interpret as a reflection of the very general nature of the CEFR categories.

3. The number of focuses increased by level, but the intuitively unwelcome finding was that there was no significant increase in the number of CEFR focus categories represented at the three levels, as if the tests were covering no 'new ground' at the higher levels. This prompted some additional tests, in which item complexity was found to be significantly increasing from one level to the other, according to the Monte Carlo approximation (χ^2 (8) = 15.404, p<0.05).

4. A possible rival interpretation that the increase in the number of focuses was simply a function of the higher number of items at level C1 was checked and rejected.

Overall, the results were reassuring for Euro Examinations. The item writers' conceptions of the levels were mostly in line with the CEFR. In subjective terms, the elucidation tasks rendered better results than the questionnaires in the familiarisation phase, appearing to close much of the gap observed there. The analysis by the experts indicated a good coverage of CEFR categories. The results of the statistical tests were also reassuring to a great extent, especially with respect to stability, but the fact that the focuses varied with the type of task, text and author revealed a method effect, i.e. likely construct-irrelevant variance (Messick 1988, 1995).

Standardisation

Stage 1 showed that there must be some difference between the earlier minimum Euro standards and the projected new CEFR-based standards, although the gap was more convincingly present in some analyses than in others. The account below goes to show that the possibility of a gap between earlier Euro and CEFR standards kept resurfacing with remarkable persistence. A review of many descriptors suggested the gap was not as wide as might have been inferred from a purely numerical stock-take. Quite surprisingly, the item writers selected many descriptors as excessive and far-fetched that North and Schneider had failed to calibrate. In light of the experience, I felt I ought to disregard the uncalibrated descriptors as truly indicative of the CEFR standard, with the result that the gap seemed a lot less formidable.

When the Euro rating conference was analysed, the comparison between the Euro ratings and North's calibrations for the same (few) persons hardly showed any difference, and reliability analyses brought good results too, but for one group of three candidates, the Euro team ratings were conspicuously one level lower. The difference might be explained by the fact that the calibrations did not come from North's rating conference. North (2000) himself placed less trust in calibrations based on teachers rating their own students (pp. 329–333). The agreement of raters bearing the earlier Euro standards in mind brought convincing results (Table 3 in Appendix 1), to be expected after five years of operation. In terms of the newer CEFR standards, however, agreement was not as good (Table 4 in Appendix 1).

Setting up the standard for Stage 2

In Stage 2, the first step was to remove 52 poorly fitting descriptors from the analysis. The left-hand column in Table 2 shows the unanchored thresholds in the Euro data. These values no longer show the effect of the descriptors being in three different languages. Nor do they show the examiners' varying severities, which were bound to come into play when they applied their own personal versions of the CEFR identifying the level of the descriptors.

Table 2: Threshold values in the recreation of North and Schneider's scale

	Unanchored (unanchored)	Anchored (anchored)
C2	3.95	5.36
C1	2.17	3.04
B2	0.1	0.08
B1	−1.93	−2.85
A2	−4.29	−5.62

Data cleaning was followed by the selection of suitable anchors, which were to be the descriptors that showed excellent measurement properties (fit characteristics) both in North and Schneider's original analyses and those obtained in the Euro project. A third requirement was that the difficulty values of the designated anchors were to fall in the same band. In other words, this meant that if an anchor was measured by North and Schneider as B2, its difficulty value also had to be B2 in the still unanchored Euro analysis. Euro examiners were expected to agree with North and Schneider's teachers in their classification of key descriptors. For the comparison, a linear conversion of North's cut-offs was necessary (Appendix 2). As a result, the anchor status of a few descriptors was revoked (marked with an asterisk), bringing the final number to 31 English and German descriptors, to be anchored at mean of their difficulty values from North (2000), and Schneider and North (1999)[7]. In this way, the much needed CEFR-related threshold values were obtained (right-hand column, Table 2). The probability curves betrayed a sound analysis. The appropriately spaced out thresholds indicated roughly equal length middle bands. The curves rose to a comparable height, which suggested that for every band there was a range in the A1–C2 scale where it was the most probable choice, i.e. every band was functional in the anchored Euro standard.

Judgements of Euro items

Workload was balanced and minimised, with each examination separated into three 'packages'. The packages contained all the information the examiners might need such as test papers, sound CDs, marking criteria, etc. The examiners received training. Two packages were assigned to each examiner, in a chain-like judging plan (Appendix 3, ticked cells to indicate papers that judges dealt with), which satisfied the MFRM technical requirement of connectedness. I excluded six English examiners from further work on the basis of their poor familiarisation (questionnaire) results and one more on the basis of poor fit characteristics. In the end, 14 examiners provided 2,797 responses for 76 items, according to the CEFR scale. I processed the responses using MFRM and obtained CEFR-related item judgements.

Standardisation results

The results are shown in Appendix 4, where the top items above the horizontal line may be claimed to be C1, since the line has been inserted where the C1 threshold is. Further below, a second line has been drawn, which indicates peak probability for the category of B2. Above this line, it may be stated that items are less and less likely to be B2 as we move upward, because the shaded zone corresponds to the falling section of the B2 curve in Figure 1, before the intersection is reached. The shaded section, therefore, must indicate the range of B2+. On top of the shaded zone but below the C1 line, an unshaded range indicates the uncertainty due to measurement error: these tasks may or may not be C1. The lower levels can be distinguished in the same way and similar interpretations may be made of them.

Empirical validation

Empirical validation procedures

Stage 2 judgements were based on a sample of complete candidate performances from each of the four examinations, for which complete data sets, analyses and score calculations were available. Candidates were selected if they had good fit indices across all the six Euro papers. Good fit in this case meant candidates whose response patterns could clearly be interpreted as those of a person with high or low ability. Such candidates would answer correctly most of the items they could be expected to answer correctly, as they would get wrong most items they could not be expected to answer correctly. Hard to read scripts that would be difficult for the examiners to judge were not to be included in the sample either. Fifteen to 22 were to be selected at equal intervals over the length of the overall score scale, which is the sum of the scores for the six papers. The interval was determined by the standard measurement error for the examination, computed from values available for each candidate in the MFRM results output. Since this mean error came to about three to four score points out of a maximum of 150 points, the selected candidates were also to be about four points apart, as it was expected that a statistically derived difference might be large (significant) enough to indicate a qualitative difference that examiners would already be able to observe.

Thirteen Euro examiners were given stacks of test papers and scripts, relevant criteria, raw scores, score sheets, keys, sound CDs, etc. and asked to judge the candidates' CEFR level. Care was taken that the test material be as familiar for the examiners as possible. The performances were ordered in stacks from the highest-scoring down to the lowest, in order to make the difficult task of judgement cognitively less demanding and to ensure psychological security so that they could focus all their attention on the task. In order to enhance reliability, there were 3–4 judges working on the same stack. In addition, out of an awareness that candidate strengths and weaknesses result in varied profiles, the examiners were asked to pass judgement paper by paper. MFRM requirements of connectedness were in order, as the judging plan shows in Appendix 5. A total of 1,397 verdicts were analysed with MFRM and the CEFR thresholds were fixed at the same values as before.

Results of empirical validation

From top to bottom in Appendix 6, performances are progressively weaker. The shading, the lines across and the unshaded bands should now be familiar to the reader from the judgements of Euro tasks above. The software-moderated judgements of minimally competent candidates, bolded in Appendix 6, were compared with their official results. For example, at level C1, the result of examinee 778 (coded EA032407BP039987) was reviewed with the expectation that s/he should have passed being a minimally competent pass. Measured at 65%, a Rasch-based percentage result, this person reached the official minimum, 65% at the time. The next 'best' C1-level candidate, 749 (EA032407BP039782), was judged a B2, i.e. a fail. The judges' verdict was again borne out by the official result, which was 61%, clearly below the Euro pass mark. The pass mark for the Pro B2 business examination was found to be similarly appropriate. The conventional pass marks for the B2 and B1 examinations were less appropriate because the minimally competent candidates had obtained higher passing scores previously. The counter-check, however, was successful in the case of all four examinations because all the candidates who were clearly judged to be at a level lower than required, e.g. a candidate taking the B2 examination judged to be a clear B1+, therefore justifiably failed their examination.

Reflections on the use of the draft Manual

On reflection, it transpires that the importance of familiarisation must be emphasised. In the pilot Manual, familiarisation is a formative input technique (p. 27). It prescribes exercises, but then leaves it at the assumption that they have been done and examiners are well-tuned to the CEFR. The Euro experience has taught us that there should be a summative measure as well. Adequate input does not guarantee effectiveness. Euro examiners had not been familiar enough with the CEFR initially and displayed a degree of leniency (lower standards). If familiarity is not tested, examiners may carry their mistaken perceptions with them into subsequent linking phases. This in turn is bound to affect the validity of all later work, including standards, pass marks, etc., since it will not be possible to rule out rival explanations. Familiarisation thus conceived should provide a baseline for linking projects, establishing the credibility of judgements made later. Not surprisingly, Euro has already adopted the Stage 2 questionnaire as a screening test for prospective examiners.

The Euro experience has also taught us about the importance of process. The Manual ought to be reviewed to see whether it adequately stresses the importance of a process of collecting and assessing evidence in one phase and acting on it in the next in a reflective cycle. In the project, further work on familiarisation was done as part of the elucidation activities during the specification phase and then in the standardisation phase, the descriptors were reviewed to explore the gap between the conceptions of Euro examiners and the CEFR.

At a wider level, the experience speaks of the benefits of training in general, and before judgement exercises in particular. The hardest part was to prepare for the judgement of items. An important feature of this was evaluating the quality of the test material *before* moving on to judging its level because I believed that test quality affects the level of challenge. The idea followed Messick's belief (1995) in that construct-irrelevant factors (variance) result in construct-irrelevant difficulty or easiness. If there are imperfections in a item, the challenge for the candidate will either be higher or lower than intended. Another difficult point was preparing for the judgement of polytomous items where the instruction to identify the lowest CEFR level at which the item can be successfully solved, originally meant for dichotomous items, had to be applied at every scale-point of a polytomous item.

The Manual assumes the availability of suitable reference items and samples in adequate numbers. It should be a priority in the CoE project that more adequately reported items and samples are published soon. At the same time, we believe that the solution offered by Euro may be more than a stopgap measure because MFRM methodology offered a comprehensive approach in terms of integrating, i.e. putting four examinations, three levels and two languages on the same scale. Of course, MFRM methodology is no magic wand. There is a lot of truth in North's (2006) comment: 'Logit scales are specific to the analysis that produces them', so putting anchors together from many different sources would definitely have been a mistake. The likely reason for the shorter DIALANG scale, in fact, is the smaller amount of information a computer-mediated test provides. It records only dichotomous responses (only 0 and 1), while responses in North and Schneider's data were on a 5-point scale (0–1–2–3–4). Euro adopted North and Schneider's scale because their data was closer in the number of scale points to the 6-point CEFR scale than the DIALANG scale (and they also used MFRM). Thus, the approach adopted by Euro is more an argument in favour of using a single source of reference, or at least different, comparable sources referenced to each other, much like the ALTE scale has been anchored to North and Schneider's fluency scale (Jones 2002). Last but not least, in a CEFR linking project, the measures that constitute the basis of the CEFR scales must logically be the ultimate point of reference for any other reference items and performances too. In this, the linking of the Euro exams was done as directly as possible.

Reliability and generalisability

Initially, limited financial resources were the reason why Euro opted for GV as the focus of Stage 1, with the rationale that linguistic competences at least underlie all other Euro papers. While it was possible to increase reliability by saturating data and setting the level of analysis 'low', at the level of descriptors and item focuses of which there were many, not much generalisability can be claimed for Stage 1. It is best seen as an intensive probe into the relevant issues, involving key personnel and piloting techniques for Stage 2. Reliability was enhanced by a number of factors in Stage 2, while some of them also contributed towards more generalisable results. The large number of descriptors, involving as many examiners as was possible in the context, the use of data cleaning techniques whereby only appropriately fitting candidates, descriptors and the careful selection and 'deselection' of anchors and examiners were allowed to shape the results. The application of MFRM also allowed Euro to compensate for the leniency of most examiners, as can be seen from the 'pushed up' thresholds in Table 2. These techniques should count towards the validity of the new Euro pass marks and should allow more generalisable conclusions from Stage 2.

Final reflections

As a number of Euro items approached their designated level from below, especially those at C1, the analyst was reminded of some earlier findings about an uncertainty concerning minimum standards for level C1. Thus, only some of the items, bolded in Appendix 4, but not the complete exams may be claimed to be appropriately targeted at the level. It might be advisable for Euro Examinations to use only these as reference tasks in the future. The tasks that were bolded *and* italicised may also be used as reference because they may be claimed to be B1+ or B2+.

The significance of the work done is that CEFR-related thresholds have been identified, which do not need to be recalculated for every examination, but are available for later use. In addition, a range of criterial performances have been identified, pointers to the score that best expresses the minimum at the level. These performances allow thinking about standards in the following way: 'candidate X, judged to be minimally competent, scored m points, while the next one lower down the scale, candidate Y, was judged to be at a level lower than X, so the pass mark, taking the margin of error into account, should fall in between, at the score point of n.' Given a stable and appropriately tuned score conversion and score reporting system, the criterial performances can even be interpolated into tabled examination results in the future, to help identify the most appropriate pass mark. Such stable points of reference are extremely useful because even if an examination is truly referenced to CEFR standards, the raw score equivalents of those standards are bound to fluctuate, due to the action of performance variables in the testing context. Last but not least, there is value in being able to relate different tested levels to each other, i.e. in being able to say how high a score on the B2 examination would translate into a relatively low C1 performance. Such integrated judgements as attempted here might supply that information.

Notes

1. Test producers must go through an administrative and professional audit by the Hungarian Ministry of Education.
2. More information about the examination may be found in English at www. euroexam.org
3. An example of how data cleaning is part of research guidelines is to be found in www.tesol.org/s_tesol/sec_document.asp?CID=476&DID=1032
4. These technical requirements, apart from connectedness, or overlap, in the datasets, include the minimum number of two ratings for the same person (candidate) and by the same person (examiner, judge).
5. For the GV paper, the Dutch Grid was found to be useful in some ways, whereas for Mediation, all the grids were relevant.
6. It should be emphasised that the data were item focuses and not items. If items had been counted the basic assumption that each observation be counted only once would have been violated, since many items had multiple focuses.
7. The anchor status of three poorly fitting descriptors had been revoked (asterisked, **Appendix 2**).

References

ALTE (no date) CEFR Grid for the Analysis of Writing Tasks (input), Version 1.0 [Online] Available: www.coe.int/T/DG4/Portfolio/documents_intro/Manual.html (Date accessed: 27/01/2006).

ALTE (no date) CEFR Grid for the Analysis of Speaking Tasks (input), Version 1.0, prepared by ALTE. [Online] Available: www.coe.int/T/DG4/Portfolio/documents_intro/Manual.html (Date accessed: 27/01/2006).

Cizek, G J (Ed.) (2001) *Setting Performance Standards. Concepts, Methods, and Perspectives*, Mahwah, NJ: Lawrence Erlbaum Associates.

Council of Europe (2001) *Common European Framework of Reference for Languages: Learning, Teaching, Assessment*, Cambridge: Cambridge University Press.

Council of Europe (2003) *Relating Language Examinations to the Common European Framework of Reference for Languages: Learning, Teaching, Assessment. Manual. Preliminary Pilot Version*, Strasbourg: Council of Europe.

Council of Europe (2004a) *Reference Supplement to the Preliminary Pilot Version of the manual for Relating Language Examinations to the Common European Framework of Reference for Languages: Learning, Teaching, Assessment. Manual*, Strasbourg: Language Policy Division.

Council of Europe (2004b) *Relating Language Examinations to the CEFR. Reference reading items and writing tasks. Preliminary pilot version of the Manual and related documents* [CD- ROM].

Council of Europe (2005) Final Report of the Dutch CEFR Construct Project, in Council of Europe (2005) *Relating Language Examinations to the Common European Framework of Reference for Languages: Learning, Teaching Assessment. Reading and Listening Items and Tasks: Pilot Samples Illustrating the Common Reference levels in English, French, German, Italian and Spanish*, [CD-ROM].

Alderson, J C, Figueras, N, Kuijper, H, Nold, G, Takala, S, Tardieu, C (no date) The Dutch CEFR Grid (Version 4) [Online]. Available: www.lancs.ac.uk/fss/projects/grid

Glaser, B and Strauss, A (1967) *The Discovery of Grounded Theory*, New York: Aldine.

Jones, N (2002) Relating the ALTE Framework to the Common European Framework of Reference, in Alderson, J C (Ed.) *Common European Framework of Reference for Languages: Learning, Teaching, Assessment. Case studies*, Strasbourg: Council of Europe Publishing, 167–183.

Kaftandjieva, F (2004) Standard Setting, in Council of Europe (2004a) *Reference Supplement to the Preliminary Pilot Version of the manual for Relating Language Examinations to the Common European Framework of Reference for Languages: Learning, Teaching, Assessment. Manual*, Strasbourg: Language Policy Division, 1–43.

Linacre, J M (2006) Facets: Rasch Measurement Computer Program, Version 3.59 [Computer software], Chicago: Mesa Press.

Messick, S (1981a) Constructs and their vicissitudes in educational measurement. *Psychological Bulletin* 89, 575–588.

Messick, S (1981b) *Evidence and Ethics in the Evaluation of Tests*, research report, Princeton, N J: Educational Testing Service.

Messick, S (1988) Validity, in Linn, R L (Ed.) *Educational Measurement*, New York: American Council on Education/Macmillan.

Messick, S (1995) Validity of psychological assessment, *American Psychologist* 50 (9), 741–749.

Messick, S (1996) Validity and washback in language testing, *Language Testing* 13 (3), 241–256.

Migros Club Schools and Eurocentres (2003) *CEFR Performance Samples. English*, [Video] Strasbourg: Language Policy Division of the Council of Europe.

North, B (2000) The Development of a Common Framework Scale of Language Proficiency, in Belasco, S (General Editor) *Theoretical Studies in Second Language Acquisition* 8, New York: Peter Lang Publishing.

North, B (2006) Personal communication.

Schneider, G and North, B (1999) *Die Entwicklung von Skalen zur Beschreibung, Beurteilung und Selbsteinschätzung der fremdsprachlichen Kommunikationsfähigkeit. Nationales Forschungsprogram NFP33: Wirksamkeit unserer Bildungssysteme*, project report, Berne, Swiss National Science Research Council, August 1999.

TESOL (2003) TESOL Quantitative research guidelines, www.tesol.org/s_tesol/ sec_document.asp?CID=476&DID=1032 (Date accessed: 30/09/2003).

Appendices

Appendix 1: Rater agreement on test 2003

Table 3: Agreement of raters on classification if the conventional Euro standards are applied (2003)

			B1	B2	C1
N			4	4	4
Kendall's Coefficient of Concordance (W)			.802	.928	.924
Chi-Square			54.566	81.654	70.190
df			17	22	19
Asymp. Sig.			.000	.000	.000
Monte Sig.			.000(a)	.000(a)	.000(a)
Carlo Sig.					
	99% Confidence Interval	Lower Bound	.000	.000	.000
		Upper Bound	.000	.000	.000

a Based on 10,000 sampled tables with starting seed 2,000,000.

Table 4: Agreement of raters on classification if the CEFR standards are applied

			B1	B2	C1
N			4	4	4
Kendall's Coefficient of Concordance (W)			.755	.781	.791
Chi-Square			51.357	68.708	60.116
df			17	22	19
Asymp. Sig.			.000	.000	.000
Monte Sig.			.000(a)	.000(a)	.000(a)
Carlo Sig.					
	99% Confidence Interval	.000	.000	.000	.000
		.000	.000	.000	.000

a Based on 10,000 sampled tables with starting seed 2,000,000.

Appendix 2: Designated anchors from North and Schneider's work

Serial	Name	North and Schneider's measures and cut-offs	Unanchored local analysis	Expected values
	highest	4.77		8.36
	C2	3.9		6.17
246	264	3.61	4.37	5.71
224	39	3.38	5.96	5.35
*245	262	3.18	4.28	5.03
	C1	2.8		4.43
193	145	2.07	4.21	3.28
239	211	2.04	2.91	3.23
183	89	1.78	3.76	2.82
	B2+	1.74		2.75
170	33	1.57	2.03	2.48
169	19	1.5	1.77	2.37
591	647	1.47	2.22	2.33
	B2	0.72		1.14
146	171	0.64	0.58	1.01
596	671	0.51	0.97	0.81
581	864	0.34	1.13	0.54
134	131	0.14	0.88	0.22
537	670	0.07	0.31	0.11
152	189	−0.07	−0.01	−0.11
136	134	−0.18	0.25	−0.28
	B1+	−0.26		−0.41
167	273	−0.31	−0.78	−0.49
139	137	−0.39	−0.49	−0.62
108	13	−0.45	−0.97	−0.71
130	110	−0.86	−1.03	−1.36
546	710	−0.86	−1.38	−1.36
*144	155	−1.23	−1.46	−1.95
	B1	−1.23		−1.95
74	162	−1.34	−3.49	−2.12
538	672	−1.36	−2.47	−2.15
60	114	−1.61	−2.93	−2.55
65	125	−1.61	−2.2	−2.55
88	215	−1.90	−2.93	−3.01
92	224	−1.91	−2.64	−3.02
	A2+	−2.21		−3.50
91	221	−2.37	−3.66	−3.75
76	164	−2.67	−3.87	−4.22
*78	*166*	*−2.8*	−4.25	−4.43
	A2	−3.23		−5.11
10	101	−3.5	−5.54	−5.54
12	*108*	*−3.86*	−5.33	−6.11
8	86	−4.01	−5.75	−6.35
	A1	−4.29		−6.79
	Lowest	−5.68		−8.18
	Min	−5.68		−8.18
	Max	4.77		8.36
	Range	10.45		16.54

Appendix 3: Plan for the collection of judgements on Euro items

Judges	B2 06 2007			ProB2 06 2007			B1 03 2007			C1 03 2007		
	Speaking Lis Read	GV Med	Writing	Speaking Lis Read	GV Med	Writing	Speaking Lis Read	GV Med	Writing	Speaking GV	Reading Writing	Lis Med.
Futár Ernőné	✔	✔										
Tornóczi Ági		✔	✔									
Vácziné Arnold Éva			✔	✔								
Gorondy Judit				✔	✔							
Östör Zsuzsa					✔	✔						
Lukácsi Zoltán						✔	✔					
Nádasdy Vilma							✔	✔				
Török István								✔	✔			
Ács Nagy Mari									✔	✔		
Ziegler Szilvia										✔	✔	
Újszászy Anna	✔											✔
Berkovics Ildikó	✔	✔										
Budainé Farkas Éva		✔	✔									
Rezes Molnár Hilda			✔	✔								
Barthalos Judit				✔	✔							
Csekéné Véber Gabriella					✔	✔						
Kéry Dóra						✔	✔					
Góra Ágnes							✔	✔				
Sályi Katalin								✔	✔			
Udvardiné Somkuti Zsuzsa										✔	✔	
Köves Nikoletta											✔	✔
Tóthné Dr. Udvardi Katalin	✔											✔

Appendix 4: Linked Euro tasks

Analysis of tasks, based on eudesc7j.sd 07-03-2007 18:49:39
Table 7.4.1.1 Tasks Measurement Report (arranged by mN).

Num Tasks	Obsvd Score	Obsvd Count	Obsvd Average	Fair-M Avrage	Model Measure	S.E.	Infit MnSq	ZStd	Outfit MnSq	ZStd	
213 C10307 Listening 3	82	20	4.1	3.88	3.88	.36	0.7	0	0.7	0	
232 C10307 Reading 2	70	18	3.9	3.72	3.48	.37	0.9	0	0.9	0	
202 C10307 GramVoc 2	172	45	3.8	3.68	3.40	.24	0.6	-2	0.6	-2	
203 C10307 GramVoc 3	170	45	3.8	3.64	3.29	.24	0.9	0	0.9	0	C1
231 C10307 Reading 1	68	18	3.8	3.61	3.21	.37	1.0	0	1.0	0	
201 C10307 GramVoc 1	162	45	3.6	3.47	2.84	.24	0.6	-2	0.6	-2	
222 C10307 Mediation 2	66	18	3.7	3.45	2.79	.37	0.6	-1	0.6	-1	
241 C10307 Long text writing	64	18	3.6	3.39	2.65	.38	2.9	4	2.9	4	
245 C10307 Writing2 Option C	305	87	3.5	3.35	2.52	.17	2.4	7	2.4	7	
242 C10307 Writing1 Compulsory	303	87	3.5	3.32	2.46	.17	2.8	8	2.8	8	
91 Pro B20607 Reading 1	47	15	3.1	3.29	2.35	.44	1.0	0	1.0	0	
31 B20607 Reading 1	34	10	3.4	3.26	2.28	.52	1.2	0	1.2	0	
102 Pro B20607 GramVoc 2	58	20	2.9	3.23	2.21	.38	0.6	-1	0.6	-1	
112 Pro B20607 Mediation 2	29	10	2.9	3.23	2.21	.54	0.9	0	0.9	0	
221 C10307 Mediation 1	96	28	3.4	3.22	2.18	.31	0.7	-1	0.7	-1	
83 Pro B20607 Listening 3	92	30	3.1	3.22	2.16	.31	1.2	0	1.2	0	
211 C10307 Listening 1	82	24	3.4	3.21	2.15	.33	0.7	-1	0.7	-1	
224 C10307 Mediation 4	82	24	3.4	3.21	2.15	.33	0.7	-1	0.7	-1	
191 C10307 Speaking	297	90	3.3	3.18	2.05	.18	2.0	5	2.0	5	
111 Pro B20607 Mediation 1	91	32	2.8	3.18	2.04	.30	1.0	0	1.0	0	
23 B20607 Listening 3	66	20	3.3	3.16	2.01	.37	1.4	1	1.4	1	
212 C10307 Listening 2	60	18	3.3	3.14	1.92	.39	0.6	-1	0.6	-1	
244 C10307 Writing2 Option B	285	87	3.3	3.13	1.90	.18	2.9	8	2.9	8	
243 C10307 Writing2 Option A	282	87	3.2	3.09	1.80	.18	2.7	7	2.7	7	
113 Pro B20607 Mediation 3	77	28	2.8	3.08	1.77	.32	0.7	-1	0.7	-1	
82 Pro B20607 Listening 2	78	27	2.9	3.04	1.63	.33	1.2	0	1.2	0	
103 Pro B20607 GramVoc 3	54	20	2.7	3.03	1.62	.38	0.9	0	1.0	0	
52 B20607 Mediation 2	46	15	3.1	3.03	1.61	.44	0.6	-1	0.6	-1	
94 Pro B20607 Reading 4	60	21	2.9	3.01	1.54	.38	0.6	-1	0.6	-1	B2+
53 B20607 Mediation 3	127	42	3.0	2.99	1.49	.27	0.7	-1	0.7	-1	
233 C10307 Reading 3	75	24	3.1	2.98	1.47	.35	2.4	3	2.4	3	
101 Pro B20607 GramVoc 1	105	40	2.6	2.96	1.41	.27	1.0	0	1.0	0	
42 B20607 GramVoc 2	89	30	3.0	2.93	1.32	.32	0.7	-1	0.7	-1	
92 Pro B20607 Reading 2	49	18	2.7	2.87	1.14	.40	1.0	0	1.0	0	
32 B20607 Reading 2	36	12	3.0	2.87	1.13	.50	1.0	0	1.0	0	
43 B20607 GramVoc 3	87	30	2.9	2.87	1.12	.32	1.0	0	1.0	0	
93 Pro B20607 Reading 3	57	21	2.9	2.87	1.12	.37	1.5	1	1.4	1	
223 C10307 Mediation 3	36	12	3.0	2.81	.96	.50	5.0	4	5.0	4	
225 C10307 Mediation 5	36	12	3.0	2.81	.96	.50	5.0	4	5.0	4	
33 B20607 Reading 3	41	14	2.9	2.80	.92	.46	1.1	0	1.1	0	
34 B20607 Reading 4	41	14	2.9	2.80	.92	.46	1.5	1	1.5	1	
51 B20607 Mediation 1	129	46	2.8	2.77	.83	.25	1.0	0	1.0	0	
54 B20607 Mediation 4	38	14	2.7	2.72	.68	.46	1.9	1	1.8	1	
21 B20607 Listening 1	34	12	2.8	2.70	.63	.50	1.4	0	1.4	0	
114 Pro B20607 Mediation 4	28	12	2.3	2.67	.56	.49	2.7	2	2.7	2	
41 B20607 GramVoc 1	162	60	2.7	2.66	.53	.22	0.9	0	0.9	0	
124 Pro B20607 Writing Option 3	143	58	2.5	2.61	.36	.23	4.7	9	4.7	9	B2
81 Pro B20607 Listening 1	43	18	2.4	2.54	.18	.40	0.7	-1	0.7	-1	
64 B20607 Writing Option 3	274	112	2.4	2.54	.17	.16	2.8	9	2.8	9	
172 B10307 Mediation 2	33	15	2.2	2.40	-.23	.44	1.3	0	1.3	0	
63 B20607 Writing Option 2	257	112	2.3	2.39	-.27	.16	2.8	9	2.9	9	
122 Pro B20607 Writing Option 1	126	57	2.2	2.34	-.41	.23	3.0	7	3.0	7	
22 B20607 Listening 2	44	18	2.4	2.31	-.49	.40	1.0	0	1.0	0	
123 Pro B20607 Writing Option 2	126	58	2.2	2.31	-.50	.22	3.0	7	3.1	7	
62 B20607 Writing Option 1	245	112	2.2	2.28	-.58	.16	2.4	7	2.4	7	
121 Pro B20607 Writing Compulsory	123	58	2.1	2.25	-.65	.22	3.0	7	3.0	7	
11 B20607 Speaking	142	60	2.4	2.23	-.71	.22	3.3	8	3.3	8	
143 B10307 Listening 3	48	20	2.4	2.22	-.76	.38	0.8	0	0.8	0	
61 B20607 Writing Compulsory	237	112	2.1	2.21	-.79	.16	2.2	6	2.2	6	
154 B10307 Reading 4	32	14	2.3	2.10	-1.09	.46	0.6	-1	0.6	-1	
71 Pro B20607 Speaking	141	73	1.9	2.10	-1.11	.20	3.5	8	3.5	8	

Num Tasks		Obsvd Score	Obsvd Count	Obsvd Average	Fair-M Avrage	Measure	Model S.E.	Infit MnSq ZStd	Outfit MnSq ZStd	
171 B10307 Mediation 1		86	48	1.8	2.00	-1.42	.25	1.3 1	1.4 1	B1+
162 B10307 GramVoc 2		49	30	1.6	1.84	-1.88	.31	1.4 1	1.4 1	
152 B10307 Reading 2		24	12	2.0	1.82	-1.93	.50	0.0 -4	0.0 -4	
153 B10307 Reading 3		28	14	2.0	1.82	-1.93	.46	0.0 -5	0.0 -5	
161 B10307 GramVoc 1		95	60	1.6	1.79	-2.02	.22	1.8 3	1.8 3	
142 B10307 Listening 2		35	18	1.9	1.76	-2.10	.41	0.2 -3	0.2 -3	
163 B10307 GramVoc 3		44	30	1.5	1.67	-2.36	.31	1.5 1	1.5 1	
173 B10307 Mediation 3		61	42	1.5	1.66	-2.40	.26	1.2 0	1.2 0	
141 B10307 Listening 1		21	12	1.8	1.56	-2.67	.49	1.9 1	1.9 1	B1
181 B10307 Writing Compulsory		44	34	1.3	1.50	-2.84	.29	1.5 1	1.5 1	
183 B10307 Writing Option B		59	46	1.3	1.49	-2.87	.25	1.8 3	1.8 3	
174 B10307 Mediation 4		23	18	1.3	1.48	-2.90	.40	1.7 1	1.7 1	
151 B10307 Reading 1		16	10	1.6	1.41	-3.10	.53	1.0 0	1.0 0	
182 B10307 Writing Option A		53	46	1.2	1.36	-3.25	.25	1.5 2	1.5 2	
131 B10307 Speaking		91	60	1.5	1.33	-3.33	.22	0.9 0	0.9 0	A2+
Mean (Count: 76)		95.9	36.8	2.7	2.67	.54	.33	1.5 1.7	1.5 1.7	
S.D.		76.5	27.7	0.7	0.65	1.88	.11	1.1 3.5	1.1 3.5	

RMSE (Model)   .35 Adj S.D. 1.85 Separation 5.27 Reliability .97
Fixed (all same) chi-square: 3335.4 d.f.: 75 significance: .00
Random (normal) chi-square: 75.1 d.f.: 74 significance: .44

Appendix 5: The plan to judge local Euro performances

Judges	Euro	EuroPro	B2 0607 Speaking Lis Read	B2 0607 GV Med	B2 0607 Writing	PROB2 0607 Speaking Lis Read	PROB2 0607 GV Med	PROB2 0607 Writing	B1 0307 Speaking Lis Read	B1 0307 GV Med	B1 0307 Writing	C1 0307 Speaking GV	C1 0307 Reading Writing	C1 0307 Lis Med.
Tornóczi Ági	X		▨	▨	▨									
V. Arnold Éva		X				▨	▨	▨						
Östör Zsuzsa		X							▨	▨	▨			
Lukácsi Zoltán	X								▨	▨	▨			
Berkovics Ildikó	X		▨	▨	▨									
Barthalos Judit		X							▨	▨	▨			
Köves Nikoletta												▨	▨	▨
Simanovszky K.	X		▨	▨	▨									
Gorondy Judit		X				▨	▨	▨						
Nádasdy Vilma	X								▨	▨	▨			
Török István	X											▨	▨	▨
Reszler Zita	X											▨	▨	▨
Borsos Viola	X		▨	▨	▨									

Appendix 6: CEFR-linked local Euro candidate performances

Analysis of examinees, based on locitc.sd
Table 7.1.1 Candidates Measurement Report (arranged by mN).

Num	Candidates	Obsvd Score	Obsvd Count	Obsvd Average	Fair-M Avrage	Measure	Model S.E.	Infit MnSq	ZStd	Outfit MnSq	ZStd	PtBis	
777	EA032407BP039964	76	18	4.2	3.88	3.90	.38	0.4	-2	0.4	-2	.19	
972	EA032407PE039901	76	18	4.2	3.88	3.90	.38	0.5	-2	0.5	-2	.07	
759	EA032407BP039839	73	18	4.1	3.71	3.46	.38	0.6	-1	0.6	-1	.39	
937	EA032407MF039971	73	18	4.1	3.71	3.46	.38	0.2	-4	0.2	-4	.03	
778	EA032407BP039987	71	18	3.9	3.60	3.18	.37	0.4	-2	0.4	-2	.35	C1
4920	EI060207SF042585	74	21	3.5	3.49	2.90	.35	0.5	-2	0.5	-2	.60	
4883	EI060207SF041394	72	21	3.4	3.39	2.65	.36	0.9	0	0.9	0	.14	
4214	EI060207BS042118	71	21	3.4	3.35	2.52	.36	0.8	0	0.8	0	.31	
749	EA032407BP039782	66	18	3.7	3.33	2.48	.37	0.6	-1	0.6	-1	-.05	
917	EA032407EG001144	65	18	3.6	3.28	2.34	.38	0.6	-1	0.6	-1	.10	
3997	EI060207BD039385	69	21	3.3	3.25	2.26	.36	0.6	-1	0.6	-1	.12	
4943	EI060207VE041781	69	21	3.3	3.25	2.26	.36	0.8	0	0.8	0	.24	
868	EA032407BS03B634	64	18	3.6	3.23	2.20	.38	0.6	-1	0.6	-1	.35	
542	PI060207BI041943	54	17	3.2	3.19	2.07	.41	0.4	-1	0.4	-1	-.23	
658	EA032407BP038196	63	18	3.5	3.18	2.06	.38	1.0	0	1.0	0	-.20	
680	EA032407BP039482	63	18	3.5	3.18	2.06	.38	0.6	-1	0.7	-1	.05	
936	EA032407MF039970	62	18	3.4	3.13	1.91	.38	1.0	0	1.0	0	-.08	
4991	EI060207ZE042362	66	21	3.1	3.11	1.85	.37	0.9	0	0.9	0	.02	
4511	EI060207GC041425	65	21	3.1	3.06	1.71	.37	1.6	1	1.6	1	.18	
484	PI060207BP041329	51	17	3.0	3.01	1.55	.42	0.4	-2	0.4	-2	-.19	
560	PI060207BO041627	51	17	3.0	3.01	1.55	.42	0.4	-2	0.4	-2	-.19	
574	PI060207MF041861	50	17	2.9	2.95	1.37	.42	0.2	-3	0.2	-3	.07	
881	EA032407BS039775	58	18	3.2	2.93	1.30	.40	1.1	0	1.1	0	.20	
916	EA032407EG001118	58	18	3.2	2.93	1.30	.40	0.4	-2	0.4	-2	.44	
4910	EI060207SF041725	62	21	3.0	2.92	1.29	.38	1.0	0	1.0	0	-.08	
531	PI060207BI041594	49	17	2.9	2.89	1.19	.42	0.7	0	0.7	0	-.53	
3754	EI060207BP041511	61	21	2.9	2.88	1.15	.38	0.2	-3	0.2	-3	.23	
554	PI060207BN041994	48	17	2.8	2.83	1.02	.42	0.4	-2	0.4	-2	-.20	
3748	EI060207BP041505	60	21	2.9	2.83	1.00	.38	0.7	0	0.7	0	-.18	
930	EA032407MF000429	56	18	3.1	2.82	.98	.40	0.3	-2	0.3	-2	.20	
4694	EI060207NY041459	59	21	2.8	2.78	.86	.38	1.6	1	1.6	1	.05	
474	PI060207MF039791	47	17	2.8	2.77	.84	.42	0.5	-1	0.5	-1	-.14	
334	EE032407BP039870	42	18	2.3	2.67	.54	.40	1.0	0	1.0	0	.45	
355	EE032407BS039726	42	18	2.3	2.67	.54	.40	0.4	-2	0.4	-2	.56	
405	EE032407SF039942	42	18	2.3	2.67	.54	.40	1.0	0	1.0	0	.52	
4387	EI060207DE041095	56	21	2.7	2.64	.45	.37	0.9	0	0.9	0	.09	B2
520	PI060207BI029919	44	17	2.6	2.60	.33	.41	0.7	-1	0.7	-1	-.16	
589	PI060207SF041400	44	17	2.6	2.60	.33	.41	0.7	-1	0.7	-1	-.39	
583	EA032407BP000213	51	18	2.8	2.54	.16	.41	0.4	-2	0.4	-2	.33	
549	PI060207BN040999	42	17	2.5	2.48	.00	.41	0.7	-1	0.7	-1	-.22	
875	EA032407BS039722	50	18	2.8	2.48	-.01	.40	0.5	-1	0.5	-1	.26	
3999	EI060207BD042403	52	21	2.5	2.45	-.10	.37	1.5	1	1.5	1	.04	
4217	EI060207BS042124	52	21	2.5	2.45	-.10	.37	1.2	0	1.2	0	.23	
958	EA032407MK039881	49	18	2.7	2.42	-.17	.40	0.5	-1	0.5	-1	.40	
388	EE032407MK039900	35	18	1.9	2.27	-.59	.40	0.7	-1	0.7	-1	.38	
409	EE032407VE039957	35	18	1.9	2.27	-.59	.40	0.2	-3	0.2	-3	.32	
3995	EI060207BD039228	48	21	2.3	2.25	-.65	.37	1.7	1	1.7	1	.01	
364	EE032407BT040066	34	18	1.9	2.22	-.75	.40	0.2	-3	0.2	-3	.46	
527	PI060207BI041569	37	17	2.2	2.19	-.85	.42	0.8	0	0.8	0	-.09	
348	EE032407BA039781	33	18	1.8	2.16	-.92	.40	0.7	0	0.7	0	.16	
472	PI060207BP039737	36	17	2.1	2.13	-1.02	.42	0.3	-2	0.3	-2	-.44	
323	EE032407BP039583	32	18	1.8	2.11	-1.08	.40	1.0	0	1.0	0	.31	
335	EE032407BP039892	32	18	1.8	2.11	-1.08	.40	0.5	-1	0.5	-1	.16	
358	EE032407BS039734	32	18	1.8	2.11	-1.08	.40	0.6	-1	0.6	-1	-.05	
4337	EI060207BV040643	43	21	2.0	2.02	-1.35	.38	1.5	1	1.5	1	.24	
4528	EI060207GJ041816	43	21	2.0	2.02	-1.35	.38	0.6	-1	0.6	-1	.26	
546	PI060207BN038384	34	17	2.0	2.01	-1.37	.42	1.1	0	1.1	0	-.35	
3853	EI060207BP041687	42	21	2.0	1.97	-1.49	.38	0.9	0	0.9	0	-.04	
349	EE032407BA039912	29	18	1.6	1.95	-1.56	.40	1.0	0	1.0	0	.18	
392	EE032407MK039907	29	18	1.6	1.95	-1.56	.40	0.6	-1	0.6	-1	.41	
360	EE032407BS039780	27	18	1.5	1.84	-1.87	.40	0.5	-1	0.5	-1	.52	
389	EE032407MK039902	27	18	1.5	1.84	-1.87	.40	0.7	-1	0.7	-1	.25	

Num	Candidates	Obsvd Score	Obsvd Count	Obsvd Average	Fair-M Avrage	Measure	Model S.E.	Infit MnSq	Infit ZStd	Outfit MnSq	Outfit ZStd	PtBis	
4396	EI060207DE041887	39	21	1.9	1.83	-1.91	.37	1.4	1	1.4	1	.10	
528	PI060207BI041583	28	16	1.8	1.76	-2.12	.42	1.6	1	1.6	1	-.08	
4501	EI060207ER190267	35	21	1.7	1.64	-2.46	.37	0.8	0	0.8	0	.39	**B1**
385	EE032407MK039894	23	18	1.3	1.62	-2.50	.40	0.6	-1	0.6	-1	.25	
387	EE032407MK039898	23	18	1.3	1.62	-2.50	.40	1.0	0	1.0	0	.44	
533	PI060207BI041889	27	17	1.6	1.60	-2.57	.41	1.0	0	1.0	0	-.26	
316	EE032407BP039494	22	18	1.2	1.57	-2.66	.40	0.4	-2	0.4	-2	.34	
4768	EI060207PI042198	33	21	1.6	1.54	-2.73	.37	1.7	1	1.7	1	.23	
313	EE032407BP039437	20	18	1.1	1.45	-2.98	.40	0.5	-2	0.5	-2	.44	
366	EE032407BT040075	18	18	1.0	1.34	-3.30	.40	1.0	0	1.0	0	.52	
384	EE032407MK039891	15	18	0.8	1.16	-3.80	.41	0.6	-1	0.6	-1	.52	
327	EE032407BP039625	13	18	0.7	1.04	-4.14	.42	0.8	0	0.8	0	.49	
312	EE032407BP038305	10	18	0.6	0.86	-4.68	.43	0.9	0	0.9	0	.61	
Mean (Count: 75)		46.7	18.6	2.5	2.52	.10	.39	0.7	-1.1	0.7	-1.1	.15	
S.D.		17.0	1.5	0.9	0.70	2.01	.02	0.4	1.4	0.4	1.4	.27	

RMSE (Model)   .39 Adj S.D. 1.97 Separation 5.02 Reliability .96
Fixed (all same) chi-square: 1990.6 d.f.: 74 significance: .00
Random (normal) chi-square: 74.0 d.f.: 73 significance: .45

10 Relating the GEPT reading comprehension tests to the CEFR

Jessica R W Wu and Rachel Y F Wu

The Language Training and Testing Center, Taiwan

Abstract

English learning and assessment in Taiwan has been undergoing a critical change, particularly in relation to the establishment of a common standard of English proficiency through the adoption of the Common European Framework of Reference for Languages (CEFR) by the Ministry of Education, starting in 2005. This article describes a project initiated by the Language Training and Testing Center (LTTC[1]) to relate the General English Proficiency Test (GEPT) reading comprehension tests in Taiwan to the CEFR. Firstly, this paper introduces the background, purpose and context of the linking project. Secondly, the article reports on the process and product of the project which was conducted by following the procedures and methods in both the preliminary draft of a Manual for *Relating language examinations to the CEFR* (Council of Europe 2003) and the Dutch CEFR Construct Grid (Alderson et al 2006). In addition, as the CEFR framework is a rather new input to the Taiwanese English as a Foreign Language (EFL) context, the impact of using the CEFR as a common framework of reference on language teaching and testing in Taiwan is discussed. Drawing from previous experience with the linking project from a local exam board's perspective, the article offers reflections on the process and contributes to the ongoing and increasingly important discussion of the CEFR.

The Taiwanese context

The use of English language tests

With the development of Taiwan's economy and the shift in Taiwan to a more international outlook, there has been a strong identification in recent years of the need for residents to acquire competency in English. This interest has been supported by government policies concerning the use of English language assessment.

In 2005, the Ministry of Education (MoE) adopted the CEFR, *Common European Framework of Reference for Languages: learning, teaching, assessment* (Council of Europe 2001), as its source for the establishment of target levels of English ability for EFL learners in Taiwan. Following that move, the government recommended that certain English proficiency tests available in Taiwan be mapped against the CEFR levels to assist score users in choosing tests that they considered appropriate for their needs. Among the recommended tests were general English proficiency tests, e.g. Cambridge Main Suite and GEPT; tests for academic purposes, e.g. International English Language Testing System (IELTS) and Test of English as a Foreign Language (TOEFL); and tests for workplace English, e.g. Business Language Testing Service (BULATS) and Test of English for International Communication (TOEIC).

Currently in Taiwan, a score on an external English test is influential in enabling individuals to graduate from educational institutions or obtain job promotions. The following are some concrete examples.

- **English ability of college and university students**

The MoE has encouraged universities and colleges to establish a regulation requiring that all students attending these institutions achieve a pass in a test of English prior to graduation. The number of students who achieve a passing level in a test will be taken into account in evaluating the quality of a college or university. According to the MoE, university graduates must achieve scores equivalent to the CEFR B1 level (Threshold) or above in an English language test; and for technological and vocational colleges, they should demonstrate a minimum proficiency in English at the CEFR A2 level (Waystage).

- **English ability of teachers**

Like students, teachers at all levels of the educational system are urged to take an English test. Teachers in elementary and secondary schools are expected to achieve a score on a test of English equivalent to the CEFR B1 level, and teachers of English in elementary and secondary schools are expected to achieve a score equivalent to the CEFR B2 level (Vantage).

- **English ability of government employees**

Government employees are also required to demonstrate a minimum proficiency in English at the CEFR A2 level. Those with better command of English enjoy enhanced prospects for promotion.

Governmental support and developing social trends have resulted in an enormous increase in the population of English language test takers in Taiwan. In 2006, the number of test takers sitting for the four most popular

English tests, GEPT, IELTS, TOEFL, and TOEIC, reached a record high of 600,000. Among them, the GEPT was the most widely used, accounting for over 80% of the total number of test takers (approximately 500,000).

The General English Proficiency Test (GEPT)

The GEPT is a 5-level criterion-referenced EFL testing system implemented in Taiwan to assess the general English proficiency of EFL learners. In 1999, the MoE lent its support to the LTTC in its development of the GEPT. The aim of the GEPT is to promote the concept of life-long learning and to encourage the use of the communicative approach in English teaching and learning. The test was created in response to comments from educators and employers about the general lack of ability to communicate in English among Taiwanese English learners, partly due to the previous 'old-fashioned' approach to English teaching, which over-emphasised the importance of grammatical accuracy.

Each level of the GEPT consists of four components of assessment: listening, reading, writing, and speaking. The GEPT is being used by various government institutions and schools for entry, classroom achievement, and graduation requirements. So far, about 2.7 million EFL learners in Taiwan have taken the GEPT since its first administration in 2000.

A number of studies related to the GEPT have been conducted by the LTTC on: parallel-form reliability (Weir and Wu 2002); the concurrent validity of the GEPT Intermediate and High-Intermediate tests (LTTC 2003); mapping the GEPT to the Common English Yardstick for English Education in Taiwan (LTTC 2005); the written language of test takers (Kuo 2005); test impact (Wu and Chin 2006, Wu 2007), and test form and individual task comparability (Weir and Wu 2006).

The use of the CEFR in Taiwan

As noted earlier, the MoE adopted the CEFR with the aim of using it as a yardstick to inform assessment of learners' proficiency in English. This move has indeed created a new context for English language learning and assessment in Taiwan.

As background to the idea of locating different tests in relation to the CEFR framework, Taiwan is a very competitive free-market society and people expect to be offered choices. In addition, the government, for various reasons, does not feel it is appropriate for them to choose one test or one kind of test over another. Under such circumstances, a positive result is that Taiwanese EFL learners and/or score users are free, to some degree, to make their own choices as to which test to take; however, as a natural consequence, this leads to a pressing need for score equivalence, i.e., knowledge of how scores from two different tests relate to one another and to what extent they can be considered equivalent. Therefore, the MoE determined that the CEFR could function as a common basis on which comparisons between different tests of English could be made, and thus meeting the demand for score comparability. Also, adopting the CEFR, the MoE intended to enable test developers to relate their examinations to a single scheme so that more interpretable and meaningful score results could be offered.

Despite the good intentions, the reaction to the introduction of the CEFR by the MoE has been mixed due to problems that have arisen, primarily in the area of test comparability. In addition, the extent to which the introduction of the CEFR may stimulate positive developments in EFL education in Taiwan is definitely one of the questions facing the LTTC and other local professionals in language testing and teaching.

- **Test comparability**

A number of language testers have addressed concerns about the issue of test comparability. For example, Bachman (1995) remarks that any comparability study needs to take account of more than just score equivalences; other aspects such as test content and performance must also be investigated. In line with this, Davies, Brown, Elder, Hill, Lumley and McNamara (1999) and Taylor (2004) also suggest that the concept of test comparison is problematic, because each test is designed for a different purpose and a different population.

Acknowledging the concerns noted above, at the time when the MoE was creating the 'table of approximate score comparability' for the purpose of comparing English language tests commonly used in Taiwan, including those provided by international test developers (i.e., BULATS, Cambridge Main Suite, IELTS, TOEFL, TOEIC) and those provided by local test developers (i.e., CSEPT, GEPT, FLPT), the LTTC alerted the Ministry to the potential misuses of the 'table'. One of the misuses we think most likely to occur is that test users may focus on the notion of 'score equivalence' only, rather than on variations in the features and constructs between different tests. When the test construct is ignored, test users may choose to use a less difficult test (e.g., one with no speaking or writing component, or one that uses only multiple-choice items) to achieve a 'passing' score more easily. Our warnings were accepted by the MoE and later were included in the 'table'. However, since the launch of the 'table', the warning messages have been disregarded by test users, and problems associated with misuses of the 'table' have arisen as predicted. Sadly, we have to note that the concept of a 'CEFR-aligned' test has not been correctly realised in our country.

Having noted these problems, however, we believe that the CEFR can play a useful role in Taiwan. We believe adoption of the CEFR has potential for improving language teaching and testing in Taiwan, but that misuse, such as using the Framework as a medium to compare different tests must be avoided. Therefore, as a local exam board that develops and administers high-stakes language tests, the LTTC recognises its obligation to interact with our stakeholders concerning the correct meaning of the term 'CEFR-aligned' tests. For this purpose, in July 2005, the LTTC decided to launch a research project: Mapping the GEPT onto the CEFR. Furthermore, in order to carry out the mapping project appropriately, the LTTC officially registered with the Council of Europe (CoE) to participate in the project for piloting the Manual for *Relating language examinations to the CEFR*.

- **New challenges and responsibilities**

As the full title of the CEFR shows, it is a framework not only for assessment but also for learning and teaching. Although for the present, the government in Taiwan seems to have adopted the CEFR only as a new standard for assessment, its potential for affecting how learning and teaching are viewed and implemented in Taiwan should not be ignored. As in many other Asian countries, there is a very exam-oriented culture in Taiwan, and exams, particularly high-stakes ones, such as the GEPT, can have a significant impact on teaching and learning (Wu and Chin 2006). Therefore, by relating the GEPT to the CEFR, which may make GEPT scores more interpretable and transparent, we may be able to increase teachers' and learners' understanding of what 'communicative language ability' really means. In other words, provided that teachers can understand what a GEPT test taker with a particular score is able to do in terms of the criteria specified in the CEFR framework, they will gradually consolidate the theoretical criteria with their teaching and assessment practices employed in the classroom.

The article will next describe in detail the GEPT–CEFR mapping project undertaken by the LTTC.

Mapping the GEPT onto the CEFR

This project for relating the GEPT to the CEFR followed the 'internal validation' procedure, including Familiarisation, Specification and Standardisation (Judgment session only), proposed by the draft Manual for *Relating language examinations to the CEFR* (CoE 2003), with the intention of re-examining the GEPT to ensure that its test development and administrative procedures conform to the internationally accepted code of practice, and also to present various features of the GEPT to its stakeholders in a more comprehensive way.

It was found that the Specification provides a well-covered outline, which includes the major features of language examinations, and that the forms which the Manual provides not only are useful tools for re-examination of language tests but also facilitate detailed reports on the quality of tests.

Familiarisation

To familiarise those who would be involved in the Specification and Standardisation procedures with the CEFR, the Familiarisation was conducted in January 2007. A total of 20 people who are experienced professionals in English teaching or testing participated in the Familiarisation session. The scheme followed the procedures provided in Chapter 3 of the Manual. CEFR Chapters 1, 2 and 3 were distributed to the participants for self-study before they attended the 2-stage Familiarisation session.

The first-stage Familiarisation session began with a 30-minute introduction to the background, including aims and overview of the CEFR, followed by small group discussions focusing on the questions presented at the end of the subsections in the CEFR: 'How to use scales of descriptors of language proficiency' (p. 40); 'Conditions and constraints' (p. 50); 'Communication themes/communicative tasks and purposes' (pp. 53 and 54); 'Productive activities' (pp. 61 and 63); and 'Receptive activities' (pp. 68 and 71). After the discussions, the participants tried to relate the GEPT to the CEFR using Table 1, the global descriptors of the CEFR. Then, the participants self-assessed their English proficiency level using Table 2 (Self-assessment grid) in the CEFR as a wrap-up activity.

In the second-stage Familiarisation session, the participants sorted slips of individual proficiency statements from lower level to higher level and then compared their results with the CEFR level descriptors. Various scales of reading comprehension descriptors in the CEFR, DIALANG self-assessment statements, and self-assessment statements in CEFR Table 2 were reconstructed in the activities.

During the familiarisation process, Table 2.1: the Common Reference Levels (CoE 2003:18−19) was found to be especially useful. The descriptions under Salient Characteristics illustrate and exemplify the corresponding descriptors in a clear and straightforward manner. Some participants found that the descriptor scale reconstruction activities were sometimes confusing to them since the original descriptors were broken down into constituent sentences, and that it was difficult to guess the level of independent sentences because some descriptors were phrased in very similar ways. However, the discussion results based on the participants' estimation showed that there was global agreement on the rationale for relating the four levels of the GEPT to the CEFR levels.

Specification

The CEFR is potentially a useful reference document for reviewing test specifications at different levels of proficiency, and the Manual facilitates detailed reporting on the quality of tests. However, based on our experience gained from the CoE's Project of Piloting the Manual, the qualitative analysis procedures provided in the Manual's specification forms seem to include only administrative procedures, Forms A1 to A7, and text-level specifications, Forms A10 and A19; specifications of item-level comprehension operations, which should be equally important when test constructs are examined and compared, are overlooked (Alderson et al 2004:44). Therefore, we applied the Dutch CEFR Construct Grid to analyse different levels of the GEPT reading comprehension tests, in the hope of differentiating the difficulty levels of the GEPT reading comprehension tests in terms of the CEFR levels.

Method

The first four levels of the 2006 GEPT reading comprehension tests (excepting the Superior level, since the Superior level GEPT was not administered in 2006) were analysed mainly with the help of the Dutch CEFR Construct Grid. Although the content analyses only covered the most recent year of the test forms and, therefore, may not present a complete picture of the GEPT reading comprehension tests, we believe the results should be able to exemplify the test constructs of the different levels of the GEPT reading comprehension tests. An overview of the GEPT reading comprehension tests is provided in the appendix.

A total of nine judges participated in the Specification session. All judges attended the Familiarisation session and felt confident to proceed to the Specification session. For each level of the GEPT reading comprehension tests, the analysis was carried out by a different pair of judges, grouped based on their familiarity with that particular GEPT level. The ninth judge double-checked the results of the analyses of all four levels.

Table 1: Number of texts and items analysed per GEPT level[2]

GEPT	No. of Tasks	No. of Items
Elementary level	12	40
Intermediate level	14	50
High-Intermediate level	16	70
Advanced level	7	40

Text dimensions

In the Dutch CEFR Construct Grid, text dimensions fall into four categories: text sources, text types, communication themes and domains. The present study adopted these categories to analyse the texts used in the GEPT reading papers.

• Text sources

Figure 1 shows text sources of the GEPT reading comprehension tests. Through all levels, most texts were based on information from newspapers and magazines. It is important to note that in order to compose texts of suitable difficulty level for the target examinees, all texts in the Elementary, Intermediate, and High-Intermediate levels of the GEPT reading comprehension tests are developed and written by the GEPT item writers, and authentic passages only appear in the Advanced level.

Figure 1: Text sources of the texts in the GEPT reading comprehension tests (%)

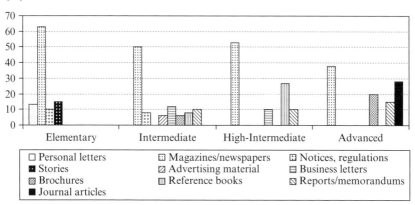

• **Text types**

There are five text types in the Dutch CEFR Construct Grid: descriptive, narrative, expository, argumentative, and instructive. Figure 2 shows the results of classifying the GEPT reading text types; from the Elementary level to the Advanced level, the distribution of text types shifts from a greater number of descriptive and narrative text types to a greater number of expository and argumentative text types, which corresponds to the rationale of the CEFR.

Figure 2: Text types in different levels of the GEPT reading comprehension tests (%)

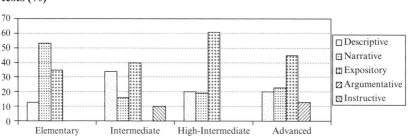

- **Domains**

Figure 3 shows the results of classifying the GEPT reading text domains. It appears that for all levels of the GEPT, most reading texts are within the public and educational domains, and that the percentage of the texts in the personal domain decreases as the GEPT level advances.

Figure 3: Text domains in the GEPT reading comprehension tests (%)

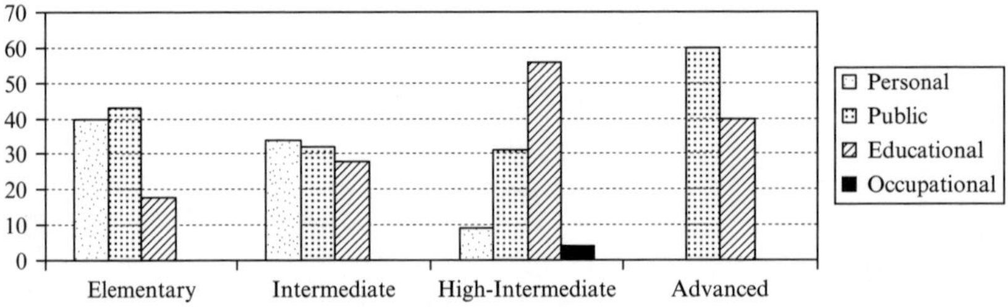

- **Communication topics**

Table 2 shows the range of communication topics which the GEPT reading comprehension tests cover. The CEFR list of communication topics includes only relatively concrete subjects, e.g. daily life, education and weather. Therefore, topics related to more conceptual matters, such as culture/customs, science, history, literature, and fine arts, which typically appear in the High-Intermediate and Advanced levels of the GEPT

Table 2: Communication topics in the GEPT reading comprehension tests (%)

	Elementary	Intermediate	High-Intermediate	Advanced
Health and body care	√	√	---	√
House, home environment	√	√	---	---
Daily life	√	---	√	---
Relations with other people	√	√	---	---
Services	√	√	√	---
Culture/Customs	√	---	√	---
Free time, entertainment	---	√	---	√
Travel/Transportation	---	√	√	√
Education and training	---	√	---	√
Places	---	√	√	√
Food and drink	---	---	√	---
Science	---	---	√	---
History	---	---	√	---
Literature/Fine Arts	---	---	√	√
Other	---	---	√	---

reading comprehension tests, were added to the categories. The results show that there is a wide variety of communication topics in the GEPT reading comprehension tests.

The linguistic and cognitive complexity of texts

In the Dutch CEFR Construct Grid, linguistic and cognitive complexity is characterised in terms of the degree of abstraction, grammar and vocabulary range. To display, in terms of degree of abstractness, the tendency of the difficulty level to increase in the GEPT reading comprehension tests, an abstraction score for each level was computed using the Dutch approach; values for the degree of abstraction were assigned to each text: 1 for 'only concrete', 2 for 'mostly concrete', 3 for 'fairly extensive abstract' and 4 for 'mainly abstract'. The result suggests the GEPT reading comprehension tests reflect the tendency described in the CEFR: as the GEPT level advances, more abstract texts are included. Similarly, a grammar score for each level is computed; values for the range of grammar used are assigned to each text: 1 for 'only simple structures', 2 for 'mainly simple structures', 3 for 'limited range of complex structures' and 4 for 'wide range of complex structures'. The result suggests that the GEPT reflects the expected tendency described in the CEFR; the Elementary Level texts contain only simple grammatical structures, while the Intermediate, High-Intermediate and Advanced Level reading texts tend to contain a greater number of more complex grammatical structures. In addition, the result of vocabulary range analysis suggests that as the level of GEPT advances, the range of vocabulary expands.

The three dimensions are potentially good indicators for displaying the tendency described in the CEFR levels. However, during the Specification the judges noted that the categories lacked clear definition and precision. They found it difficult to make reliable judgments and could only justify their decisions through an intuitive understanding of the classifications, for example, of the four distinct levels of abstractness as described above and of the degree of grammatical complexity.

As an alternative measurement of structural complexity, the average number of words in a sentence of each GEPT level was calculated by WordSmith (version 4.0; a lexical analysis software published by Oxford University Press). Figure 4 shows the average sentence length for different levels of the GEPT reading comprehension tests; as the GEPT level advances, longer sentences are used.

To provide estimates of the difficulty and complexity of texts used in the GEPT reading comprehension tests, readability formulas were also employed. Figure 5 shows two sets of readability scores produced by the Dale-Chall (Chall and Dale 1995) and Fry (1968) formulas, indicating that as the level of GEPT advances, the range of vocabulary expands and text difficulty increases.

Figure 4: Average sentence lengths in the GEPT reading comprehension tests (number of words)

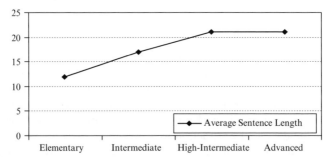

Figure 5: Summary of readability analysis

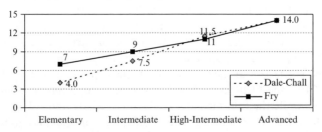

Dimensions of question types

In consideration of the large volume of candidates who participate in each test administration, the Elementary, Intermediate and High-Intermediate levels of the GEPT adopt multiple-choice questions only. The Advanced level, with a relatively small number of candidates, can accommodate a wider variety of question types, i.e. multiple-choice questions, matching, short-answer questions and summary completion.

Operations

• Task dimension

In terms of the task-level operations of the GEPT reading comprehension tests, the GEPT Elementary to High-Intermediate levels assess careful reading only, while the Advanced level tests both careful reading, in Part 1, and expeditious reading, in Part 2, and the two parts are timed separately. Weir (2005:9–10) proposes that the expected reading speed, which does not appear in the CEFR, be considered as an independent variable when operations of the reading process are analysed, since it may affect individuals' choices of reading strategies and the difficulty level of the reading tasks. Figure 6 shows the expected speed of reading in the GEPT reading

Figure 6: Reading speed of the GEPT reading comprehension tests (words per min.)

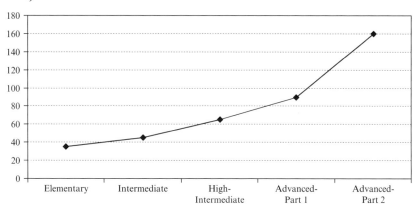

comprehension tests. The data indicates that as the GEPT level advances, the expected reading speed increases.

- **Content dimension**

Figure 7 shows the content of the operations in the reading items for different levels of the GEPT. As the GEPT level advances, the items become more cognitively challenging, but there is a drop in the Advanced level. The construct of the GEPT Advanced level reading comprehension test is different from those of the other levels of the GEPT reading comprehension tests in that it consists of both careful reading and expeditious reading. The operations

Figure 7: Content of the operations in the GEPT reading items (%)

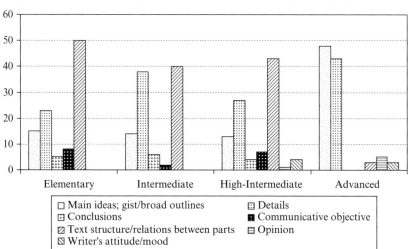

in the expeditious reading items include search reading to understand the main points of the texts and scanning to locate specific details. Therefore, the percentages of main idea and detail questions in the Advanced level GEPT appear to be significantly higher than in the other levels.

The judgment process

To consolidate the claim that the GEPT is related to the CEFR, after the Specification was completed, the Standardisation of judgment process was carried out in April 2007. The process followed the training and standard-setting procedures that the Manual proposed. A total of 15 judges, who are experienced professionals in English teaching or testing, participated in the 1-day session. All participants attended the Familiarisation session prior to the Judgment session. The Judgment session included a half-day training session in the morning and a half-day standard-setting session in the after-noon. During the morning session, the participants were trained to relate their interpretations of the CEFR levels to calibrated sample items. The exemplars employed in the session included a total of 13 calibrated samples of reading texts, along with the corresponding items, provided by the CoE[3], and 12 relevant scales in the CEFR (Table 1: Common Reference Levels: global scale; five tables in Section 4.4.2.2, including Overall reading compre-hension, Reading for correspondence, Reading for orientation, Reading for information and argument and Reading instructions; Identifying cues and inferring table in Section 4.4.2.4; General linguistic range table in Section 5.2.1; Vocabulary range and Vocabulary control tables in Section 5.2.1.1; Grammatical accuracy table in Section 5.2.1.2; and Sociolinguistic appropri-ateness table in Section 5.2.2).

During Phase I Illustration and Phase II Controlled Practice in the morning session, the participants were trained to assimilate the rationale behind the CEFR levels using nine calibrated sample tasks and the CEFR scales through consultancy with other participants and the co-ordinators. In the following phase, Individual Assessment, the participants then rated the CEFR levels of four calibrated tasks individually, and the co-ordinators checked whether they reached a general consensus. During the training session, the descriptors in Reading for information and argument (CoE 2001:70) were the most frequently consulted scale.

After the participants reached consensus on the CEFR levels of 13 cali-brated samples in the morning session, the Standard-setting session in the afternoon adopted the method applied by the DIALANG project to deter-mine 'the minimum CEFR level needed by a candidate to successfully perform' on a given level of the GEPT. The participants used an Item Rating Form, adapted from Form B5 provided in the Manual, to estimate the dif-ficulty of the GEPT reading tasks and items in terms of the CEFR levels. The tasks and items from different levels of the GEPT reading comprehension tests were sampled according to the following criteria: text types, communication topics, operations and content questions. The GEPT items were then arranged in random order for the participants, who judged the difficulty of the items in terms of the CEFR levels.

The overall rater agreement for the GEPT items was 0.91 (Spearman-Brown), suggesting that the participants reached a generally satisfactory degree of consensus on the minimum CEFR level required for the GEPT sample items. The judges considered that in order to perform satisfactorily on the GEPT Elementary level questions, candidates need a minimum level of CEFR A2 or A2+; on the Intermediate level questions, a minimum level of B1 or B1+; on the High-Intermediate level questions, a minimum level of B1+ or B2; and on the Advanced level questions, a minimum level of B2+, C1 or C1+. The spread of estimates is wider at the Advanced Level due to the fact that, based on the different demands of cognitive processes, the linguistic complexity of the texts in the expeditious reading section is set to be lower than that of the texts in the careful reading section. Overall, the mean required minimum CEFR level increases as the GEPT level advances. The results were summarised in Table 3. Figure 8 shows a graphic profile of the relationship between the GEPT to CEFR levels.

Table 3: Minimum required CEFR level for each GEPT level

GEPT level	No. of Items	A2	A2+	B1	B1+	B2	B2+	C1	C1+	Mean CEFR level	
		2	2.5	3	3.5	4	4.5	5	5.5		
Elementary	20	5	15	0	0	0	0	0	0	2.40	A2+
Intermediate	11	0	1	6	4	0	0	0	0	3.14	B1
High-Intermediate	22	0	0	2	7	13	0	0	0	3.75	B2−
Advanced	17	0	0	0	0	0	7	2	8	5.01	C1

Some reflections

Drawing from previous experience with the linking project, in the next section we will offer some reflections on the process, including comments on use of the draft Manual and the impact of using the CEFR on teaching professionals. We hope that our experience and the reflections from the local exam board's perspective can contribute to the ongoing and increasingly important discussion of the CEFR.

Figure 8: Graphic profile of the relationship between the GEPT to CEFR levels

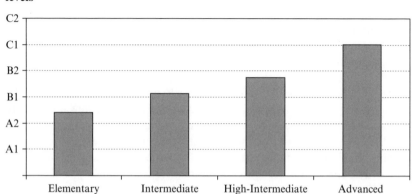

Comments on the use of the draft Manual

The findings of this GEPT–CEFR mapping project reveal that based on the results of content analysis, the four levels of the GEPT reading comprehension tests correspond generally to the CEFR A2 to C1 levels. The content analyses guided by the framework of the Dutch CEFR Construct Grid and supplemented by statistical data regarding sentence lengths and readability scores indicate that the GEPT reading texts become more complex as the GEPT level ascends. Similarly, the analysis of the items shows an increase in the diversity of the operations involved, from the Elementary level to the Advanced level, which corresponds to the CEFR rationale.

As an exam board, we encountered some difficulties when applying the Draft Manual to relate our test to the CEFR. The major obstacle we found when applying the CEFR 'Can Do' statements was that while the quality of a learner's performance is a major indicator of his or her proficiency level, few descriptions of how well he or she is expected to perform at a particular CEFR level are included (Fulcher 2004:256, Weir 2005:8). Furthermore, as Weir (2005) notes, some test conditions that obviously affect task difficulty, e.g., expected reading speed, response format, text length and cognitive demands of task/item, are left out of the CEFR, thus hindering the validity of the linkage between the GEPT and the CEFR levels. Also, the scales of Vocabulary range and Grammatical accuracy in the CEFR vaguely classify lexical and grammatical complexity into six levels. Thus, we agree with Fulcher's comment (2004) that although the Specification provided in the Manual facilitates detailed reports on the quality of the tests, its lack of precision and clear guidelines make comparison of constructs and difficulty level between different testing systems difficult. To remedy this problem, we have used instruments, such as readability formulas and WordSmith, to provide more concrete information about the linguistic complexity of the GEPT reading comprehension test.

For non-professionals in the language testing field, i.e. examinees, teachers and other stakeholders involved in the assessment process, the content and format of the Specification forms are not readily comprehensible. The general public is more familiar with subtest-oriented categories, e.g., the four skills of listening, reading, writing and speaking, while the Specification presents various communicative language activities in separate forms; for example, speaking-relevant activities include Form A11 Spoken Interaction, Form A13 Spoken Production and Form A17 Spoken Mediation. It would be helpful to provide users with guidance on how the relevant forms can be applied so that they can better meet the needs of the stakeholders.

Impact observed

For the sake of transparency, a talk introducing the GEPT–CEFR linking project was given in July 2007 in Taipei to a group of English teachers, which also served to investigate the impact of the recognition of the CEFR. A questionnaire survey of the audience was conducted immediately after the speech. We collected 46 valid questionnaires, and most of the respondents were English teachers in colleges. The survey results are summarised in the following:

- 60% of the audience had heard of the CEFR before the talk. Only 17% of the audience knew what the CEFR meant, and 24% of them responded that the CEFR was unfamiliar to them.
- More than 80% of the audience thought that the talk helped them understand the CEFR.
- 80% of the audience responded that the talk helped them understand the purpose of and procedure for calibrating language tests against the CEFR, and 76% of them thought that the GEPT–CEFR linking project helped them understand the GEPT as well.
- 50% of the audience thought that information about the relationship between the CEFR and an English test is useful for them to choose a test or judge the quality of a test.
- 98% of the audience showed interest in understanding the CEFR further.
- 41% of the audience was in favour of the MoE's policy of adopting the CEFR as a means to encourage English learning and to support language testing and assessment in Taiwan. The respondents gave a variety of reasons, including:

- The CEFR can serve as an internationalised, authoritative standard, and can also help language tests in Taiwan achieve international standards.
- A common, internationalised, and credible criterion like the CEFR can facilitate correspondence and comparison between different tests.
- The CEFR is a practical and feasible tool, as long as it is employed in compliance with valid calibration procedures.
- The GEPT−CEFR linking project helps them consider the complementary relationship between language teaching and language testing.

- However, 22% of the audience was against the policy for various reasons, including:
  - It is inappropriate to use the CEFR as a model to assess English language education in Taiwan because it is more commonly used in Europe, where the context, including the needs for learning and testing, and learners' cultural background, is rather different from that in Taiwan.
  - The CEFR is not yet widely known by people in Taiwan. The MoE should be more active in helping teachers to become familiar with the CEFR.
  - The MoE is too domineering in enforcing its policy, although the existing English curriculum in colleges does indeed need improvement.

To sum up, though the survey was small, it revealed some impact of the use of the CEFR in Taiwan. The impact is largely positive in the sense that the CEFR itself has been viewed as a common standard for English learning, teaching and testing. Moreover, the GEPT−CEFR linking project has aided in increasing teachers' knowledge of the CEFR and the GEPT, and the relationship between these two. More importantly, it has encouraged teachers to rethink their teaching and assessment practices in their classrooms. However, some concerns about adopting the CEFR as part of a country's educational policy were raised. In particular, it was anticipated that more work needs to be done to deal with the cultural differences and to increase teachers' familiarity with the CEFR.

Notes

1. The LTTC, founded in 1951, is a non-profit cultural and educational foundation, dedicated to meeting Taiwan's social and economic development needs through research, development, and administration in the language teaching and testing fields.

2. The Elementary, Intermediate, and High-Intermediate levels are administered twice a year, and the Advanced level once a year. All reading tasks administered in 2006 are included in the analyses, except Part I (sentence completion) of the Elementary, Intermediate, and High-Intermediate levels, since the present approach does not seem to provide an adequate means for analysing of the sentential level item type.
3. Reading and Listening Items and Tasks: Pilot Samples illustrating the common reference levels in English, French, German, Italian and Spanish (CoE 2005).

References

Alderson J C et al (2004) *Specification for item development and classification within the CEFR: the Dutch CEFR construct project*, paper presented at workshop on research into and with the CEFR, University of Amsterdam.

Alderson, J C et al (2006) Analysing tests of reading and listening in relation to the Common European Framework of Reference: The experience of the Dutch CEFR Construct Project, *Language Assessment Quarterly* 3 (1), 3–30.

Bachman, L F (1995) *An Investigation into the Comparability of Two Tests of English as a Foreign Language*, Cambridge: UCLES/Cambridge University Press.

Chall, J S and Dale, E (1995) *Readability revisited: the new Dale-Chall readability formula*, Brookline, MA: Bookline Books.

Council of Europe (2001) *Common European Framework of Reference for Languages: learning, teaching, assessment*, Cambridge: Cambridge University Press.

Council of Europe (2003) *Relating language examinations to the common European framework of reference for languages: Learning, teaching, assessment. Manual. Preliminary pilot version*, Strasbourg, France.

Council of Europe (2005) *Relating language examinations to the Common European Framework of Reference for Language: Learning, teaching, assessment (CEFR) – Reading and Listening Items and Tasks: Pilot Samples illustrating the common reference levels in English, French, German, Italian and Spanish*.

Davies, A, Brown, A, Elder, C, Hill, K, Lumley, T and McNamara, T (1999) *Dictionary of Language Testing*, Cambridge: UCLES/Cambridge University Press.

Fry, E (1968) A readability formula that saves time, *Journal of Reading* 11 (7), 265–71.

Fulcher, G (2004) Deluded by artifices: The Common European Framework and Harmonization, *Language Assessment Quarterly* 1 (4), 253–266.

LTTC (2003) Concurrent Validity Studies of the GEPT Intermediate Level, GEPT High-Intermediate Level, CBT TOEFL, CET-6, and the English Test of the R O C College Entrance Examination, *LTTC Research Report*, Taipei: Language Training and Testing Center.

LTTC (2005) Mapping the GEPT to the Common English Yardstick for English Education in Taiwan (CEY), *LTTC Research Report*, Taipei: Language Training and Testing Center.

Noijons, J and Kuijper, H (2006) *Mapping the Dutch Foreign Language State Examinations onto the Common European Framework of Reference*, Arnhem, the Netherlands: National Institute of Educational Measurement.

Taylor, L (2004) Issues of test comparability, *Research Notes* 15, 2–5, available at www.CambridgeESOL.org/rs_notes/rs_nts15.pdf (accessed July 2005).

Weir, C J (2005) Limitations of the Common European Framework for developing comparable examinations and tests, *Language Testing* 22 (3), 1–20.

Weir, C J and Wu, J (2002) Parallel-Form Reliability – A Case Study of the GEPT Spoken Performance Test, *Proceedings of the Fifth International Conference on English Language Testing in Asia*, Tokyo.

Weir, C J and Wu, J (2006) Establishing test form and individual task comparability: a case study of a semi-direct speaking test, *Language Testing* 23 (2), 167–197.

Wu, J (2007) English language assessment in Taiwan: Where do we go from here?, *The Proceedings of 2007 International Conference and Workshop on TEFL & Applied Linguistics*, 574–586, Taipei: Crane Publishing Co Ltd.

Wu, R Y and Chin, J S (2006) *An Impact Study of the Intermediate Level GEPT*, paper presented at the 9th International Conference on English Testing in Asia, Taipei, November.

Appendix: Overview of the GEPT reading comprehension tests

GEPT level	Part	Item Type	No. of Tasks	No. of Items	Time (mins.)	Task Focus	Overall Descriptor
Elementary	1	Vocabulary & Structure	15	15	35	Completing a sentence by recognising correct syntax and lexis	An examinee who passes this level can understand simple written English related to daily life. He/she can read street signs, traffic signs, shop signs, simple menus, schedules, and greeting cards.
	2	Cloze	2	10		Processing a text to understand relationships between sentences	
	3	Reading Comprehension	4	10		Processing a text thoroughly to comprehend main ideas, supporting details and implied meanings	
Intermediate	1	Vocabulary & Structure	15	15	40	Completing a sentence by recognising correct syntax and lexis	An examinee who passes this level can read short essays, short stories, personal letters, advertisements, leaflets, brochures, and instruction manuals. At work, he/she can read job-related information, company notices and operation manuals, as well as routine documents, faxes, telegrams and email messages.
	2	Cloze	2	10		Processing a text to understand relationships between sentences, and between parts of the text	
	3	Reading Comprehension	5	15		Processing a text thoroughly to comprehend main ideas, supporting details and implied meanings	

High-Intermediate	1	Vocabulary & Structure	15	15	50	50	Completing a longer sentence by recognising correct syntax and lexis	An examinee who passes this level can read written messages, instruction manuals, newspapers, and magazines. At work, he/she can read general documents, abstracts, meeting minutes, and reports.
	2	Cloze	2	15	50		Processing a text to understand relationships between sentences, and between parts of the text	
	3	Reading Comprehension	6	20			Processing a longer text thoroughly to comprehend main ideas, supporting details and implied meanings	
Advanced	1	Careful Reading	4	20	40	50	Processing a long and complex text thoroughly to comprehend main ideas, supporting details and implied meanings	An examinee who passes this level can understand all sorts of written English from a wide variety of sources, including magazine and newspaper articles, literature, professional periodicals, and academic publications.
	2	Skimming & Scanning	3	20	20		• Processing a text quickly and selectively to get the gist of the text • Processing a text quickly and selectively to locate specific information	

Section Three
Large-scale multilingual assessment frameworks at national level

11 Asset Languages: a case study of piloting the CEFR Manual

Neil Jones, Karen Ashton and Tamsin Walker

University of Cambridge ESOL Examinations, UK

Abstract

Asset Languages (AL) emerged from the UK's National Languages Strategy, launched in 2002 to address serious problems in language education. The strategy included the Languages Ladder, a new voluntary recognition system. AL, the assessment system developed to deliver it, is a framework for lifelong learning encompassing six levels and 25 languages. AL took the Common European Framework of Reference for Languages (CEFR) as an important point of reference, and has relevance as a case study, both for what we did and did not use of the pilot Manual. Our approach was determined above all by the need to impose consistency across languages in the way scales were constructed and levels determined. We describe our approaches to objectively and subjectively assessed skills, explaining where we followed the pilot Manual and other procedures we used. We argue that the Manual should encourage methodological innovation, and also that CEFR linking procedures should be seen as integral to test construction and administration, rather than a one-off exercise.

Asset Languages

Asset Languages (AL) qualifications, accredited by the UK's Qualifications and Curriculum Authority (QCA), are being developed at six stages in 25 languages and across three contexts (primary, secondary and post-16 education). For each language, the skills of reading, writing, speaking and listening are assessed separately.

Asset Languages (AL) emerged as part of the UK's National Languages Strategy launched in 2002 to address serious underperformance in languages (DfES 2002). The strategy included the Languages Ladder, a new voluntary recognition system intended to complement existing national qualifications frameworks. The remit of the Languages Ladder, and of AL, as the assessment system developed to deliver it, is to provide a framework for lifelong learning: i.e. a learning ladder of accessible targets, related to meaningful proficiency levels. By conceiving comparability between languages in terms of functional proficiency the system differs fundamentally from most other UK schools qualifications, which view comparability in terms of equivalence of learning effort or general academic ability.

The Languages Ladder itself is a document produced and owned by the Department for Children, Schools and Families (the UK Ministry of Education[1]), describing proficiency via 'Can Do' descriptions of six stages subdivided into three grades per stage (DfES 2003). The AL development team has treated the Languages Ladder as broadly equivalent to the CEFR, and has made close reference to the CEFR in the course of its development. The Languages Ladder is articulated in terms of learning stages, rather than levels achieved, which means that it is only the top grade within each LL stage which can be seen as achieving the corresponding CEFR level (Figure 1).

Figure 1: CEFR levels and Languages Ladder stages

	Languages Ladder: Learning stages	CEFR: Proficiency levels
	Intermediate 9	B1 Threshold
Working at *Intermediate*	Intermediate 8	*Working towards B1*
	Intermediate 7	
	Prelim 6	A2 Waystage
Working at *Prelim*	Prelim 5	*Working towards A2*
	Prelim 4	
	Breakthrough 3	A1 Breakthrough
Working at *Breakthrough*	Breakthrough 2	*Working towards A1*
	Breakthrough 1	

Context of study

Our purpose in undertaking the work reported in this case study was to develop effective practical procedures for the construction and operation of a complex multilingual assessment framework, and to contribute more generally to the development of a practically and theoretically sound framework for the validation of Cambridge ESOL language assessments.

As part of this work we have made reference to the pilot version of the Manual for *Relating language examinations to the CEFR* (Council of Europe 2003), the Dutch construct grid (Alderson, Figueras, Kuijper, Nold, Takala and Tardieu 2004), as well as extensive reference to the Common European Framework of Reference (CEFR) itself (Council of Europe 2001). However, our use of the Manual has been critical, selective and pragmatic, rather than systematic. The Languages Ladder's relation to the CEFR remains to some extent implicit: the DCSF provides 'approximate' equivalences between LL and CEFR levels, and places little emphasis on the latter (something which reflects the general lack of awareness of the CEFR in British education). For this reason we have no requirement, and no intention, to make a public case for the alignment of AL to the CEFR.

We offer the experience of developing AL as a case study for the pilot Manual because we believe it can usefully complement the procedures described there. Many of the procedures we used are not treated in the draft version of the Manual, at least not quite as we used them. We must stress that this does not of itself imply a criticism of the pilot Manual, but rather reflects the specific challenges which AL presented us. Developing a framework of 25 different languages and seeking to achieve comparability between them in functional terms requires an explicit cross-language focus.

The pilot Manual does not explicitly treat cross-language comparability. The case described there, and the case to which it appears to have been largely applied, is that of the single language and even the single language exam at a single level. The comparisons involved are between the exam and the CEFR reference levels, as described by the scales. Comparison with another language is thus indirect, mediated by the text of the CEFR. The Manual's procedures rely heavily on the mobilisation of human judgments, and evidently, judgment must play a major role. However, within a multilingual, multilevel framework, judgment regarding individual languages and levels should be severely constrained. This consideration was the major determinant of our approach to constructing the AL framework.

We also stress that the methods described here have not all been thoroughly validated or proven to guarantee success. Such large developments take place within severe constraints of time, resource and availability of data. We have recognised the iterative nature of framework construction, and the need to adopt practical solutions when faced with differing degrees of uncertainty. However, we believe that the general principles we have used in shaping our approach are appropriate to the goal of constructing a multilingual assessment framework.

Validity within the test construction process

In this section we would like to make some general comments about test validity in relation to the pilot Manual. The Manual stresses that it is not a guide to how to construct valid tests, but this cannot be wholly true. The central concern of the Manual is how to make criterion-referenced interpretations of test performance (where the criterion is the CEFR) – and this is the central problem of test validity, at least in the current orthodox view of what validity is. Thus if the claim of alignment to the CEFR is an important one for a given exam, it must be seen as integrated into every stage of the design and administration cycle that impacts on validity. It cannot be a one-off exercise, although the current organisation of the Manual seems to suggest that it might be treated as such.

This raises the question of who the Manual's users might be, and how the Manual might best help them improve the quality and validity of their tests. In language assessment there are more small, modestly resourced operations than there are large, well-resourced ones. It would be good if the Manual's educative potential for quality assurance were made as clear as possible. This is envisaged on page 125 where it is stated that composing the internal report 'could contribute to the ongoing process of continuously improving the quality of the examination involved, e.g. construction of the test, test development, feedback for item writers and raters, etc.'.

This purpose would be served if the organisation of the Manual related more explicitly to the scheme of such a testing cycle, where the relevant aspects of validity are clearly located. Users who have existing tests may find that they are able to relate their own reality to such a scheme, and find a place for CEFR-focused validation activities within it. In this case they may be able to address different aspects simultaneously at different points in the cycle. Those developing a new test may be able to follow a more sequential set of steps – although even in this case, the reality of test development is that various things must happen simultaneously or in a tight iterative cycle: developing a test to a targeted standard is a process of progressive approximation.

Figure 2 illustrates a model for test validation as a 5-step process from test construction through to 'real world' interpretation. The steps make up the chain of inference through which interpretations are supported: each step asks a question and indicates the kind of evidence needed to answer it (Kane, Crooks and Cohen 1999, Mislevy, Steinberg and Almond 2002, Weir 2005a).

Relating this to the purposes of the Manual one can readily identify points where CEFR-related validation fits in. It strikes us, for example, that many activities in the Manual relate usefully to *training*. This in turn can be related to stages in the validity argument: training item writers at the test construction phase, training raters to support evaluation, generalisation and extrapolation at steps 2, 3 and 4, and so on. Figure 3 sketches this out.

Figure 2: Steps in a validity argument: from test design to framework alignment

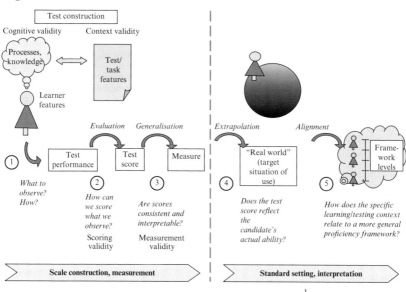

Figure 3: Pilot Manual sections in a test construction cycle

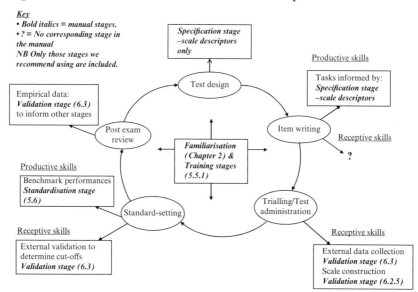

Sections in the Manual (shown in *italics* in the boxes) are linked to relevant stages of the test design cycle. Thus for an existing test the Validation stage (using the Manual's terminology) could be done first, so that standardisation and specification are informed by empirical data. Familiarisation with the CEFR is seen as of central importance at all stages.

Another reason for locating CEFR linking within the broader context of test validity and the overall testing cycle is to make clearer, especially for smaller and perhaps less sophisticated testing organisations, that there are two distinct aspects to the problem: *scale construction* and *standard setting*. As the pilot version of the Manual itself makes clear, having a valid and reliable approach to test construction is a pre-requisite for addressing standards, because without it the standard may simply fluctuate from session to session. Thus effort put into developing an item-banking, IRT-based approach to test construction may pay more dividends than the same amount of effort devoted to repeated standard setting. Ideally, standards are set once and then maintained over time by effective scaling procedures. This is something which the Manual could emphasise more strongly.

Developing the Asset Languages Framework

This section is organised around the process of developing the AL framework, making reference to stages where the CEFR and the Manual were made use of, as well as to the other procedures and sources of evidence which were utilised. The objectively marked tests are treated separately from the performance tests.

Objectively marked tests (Reading and Listening)

General approach to design, specification, item writing

CEFR and Languages Ladder scales were useful as indicative of general linguistic/functional level and appropriate tasks. Waystage and Threshold learning objectives were also referred to (Van Ek and Trim 1990a, 1990b).

For general guidance as to level, Cambridge ESOL test papers also provided an initial useful model. The Main Suite exams (Key English Test (KET), Preliminary English Test (PET) and First Certificate in English (FCE)), associated with A2 to B2, were particularly relevant. Why do such exemplars seem so useful? As noted below, simply describing the content of test tasks in terms of the CEFR's taxonomies of *conditions, constraints, texts, themes, domains* and *tasks* does not help much in identifying their level. This is because in classroom-based learning these contextual variables are carefully selected and manipulated to provide a supportive context for learning, the major determinant of progression being, naturally, linguistic. It is the configuration of these variables, particularly the linguistic challenge, which accounts for difficulty. Testing reflects this. Just as learning tasks are structured to enable learning, testing tasks are structured to enable learners to display their competence. This is why exemplars, illustrating quite widely shared, conventional understanding of what is appropriate at a level, are useful. The CEFtrain project (www.ceftrain.net) which sets out to introduce the CEFR and train in using the CEFR scales for assessment, very sensibly takes exemplification, rather than content description, as its starting point.

Reference to the pilot Manual

Manual Chapter 4 (Specification) was not referred to in the process of test design, but a *post-hoc* study in applying the descriptive categories to AL was undertaken for this case study.

We concluded that many of the categories of context variables do not relate to level of proficiency (in line with the findings of Alderson et al 2004). Thus they do not serve the purpose of justifying a link to a CEFR level, even if for other test design purposes they might be relevant. They also foster the feeling that what is expected is a needs analysis of a quite specific, adult group of learners, which for most general language tests is not useful. This is particularly the case with forms A8 to A18 dealing primarily with CEFR Chapter 4 on language in use. In attempting to complete these one feels that the final step of identifying the CEFR level from a table is not well informed by the task of description that leads up to it. It would almost make more sense to start with the CEFR scale and work backwards in the other direction.

Forms A19 onwards deal with CEFR Chapter 5 (Language competence) and are much easier to work with.

Our feeling about these forms, relating to Chapters 4 and 5 of the CEFR respectively, relates to the criticism which has been made of the CEFR that it has more to say about the social dimension of language in use than it does about the cognitive dimension of language competence. This perception is doubtless fuelled by the exaggerated attention given by most readers to the illustrative scales in Chapter 4. Assessment requires the cognitive dimension to be more fully articulated (Weir 2005a, 2005b, Shaw and Weir 2007).

A suggestion is that the order of presenting these two sets of forms should be reversed.

Other related areas of work

The following pieces of work all relate to the construct validity of the objective papers, by investigating sources of task difficulty. The central theme is that what tasks actually test, and thus their effective level of difficulty, may be due to a range of factors not captured in the categories of description proposed by the Manual. In practice it is very important for test developers to be sensitive to these issues. A mismatch between the apparent level of a task, in terms e.g. of textual features, and its actual difficulty may indicate a construct validity problem.

What is tested – Breakthrough

This study involved qualitative analysis of early versions of AL Breakthrough French, German, Italian and Spanish tests in Reading, Listening, Writing and Speaking (Walker 2005). For Reading and Listening quantitative analysis of response data was also available, identifying tasks which were unexpectedly easy or difficult. For these objective tests it was striking how many items depended on a single word, irrespective of whether the intended focus was on word, sentence or text level. Cognates also seriously affected difficulty. Dependence on specific vocabulary was recognised as an issue for this early learning stage. Item writing practices identified as effective in ensuring phrase/sentence level understanding were identified, such as simple use of distractors, so that for example a negative sentence has to be distinguished from a positive.

Reading – Study on comparability of German, Japanese and Urdu

This project, undertaken as part of a PhD study by a member of the development team (Ashton 2009) used a learner-centred mixed-methods approach focusing on beginner to intermediate (A1–B1 in CEFR terms) secondary school readers of German, Japanese or Urdu in England. For the majority of these learners, English is their first or strongest language. Self-assessment 'Can Do' surveys and think-aloud protocols were used in the study. The self-assessment survey was used to compare the ability of approximately 150 learners across each language and to compare their perception of the construct of reading at each level. 'Can Do' statements were taken from a number of sources including the Bergen 'Can Do' study (Hasselgreen 2003), CEFR statements, CEFR portfolio statements (Lenz and Schneider 2004), National Curriculum for Modern Foreign Languages statements (in use in England[2]) and Languages Ladder statements. Data analysis included Rasch, factor analysis and multiple regression analysis.

The think-aloud protocols were used to explore and compare the strategies and reading processes that learners of these languages use. Findings from these two data sources were analysed separately before triangulating across both sources. The research demonstrates that the construct of reading in the National Curriculum for Modern Foreign Languages in England is not endorsed by any of the learner groups. For all language groups and levels, the CEFR portfolio statements provided the best representation of the students' perception of the construct. At A1 for all language groups, the level is predominantly defined by what learners cannot do rather than by what they can do. In other words, it is the fact that learners cannot perform these functions that is salient. At A2, the factor scores were positive meaning that the level is defined by what learners can do.

In terms of the use of a common proficiency framework across learners of different languages, findings show that the same three factors best represent learners' understanding of reading proficiency across all three languages. However, there are also strong differences. For example, the difficulty of script acquisition in Japanese impacts on learners' understanding of the construct, while learners of both Japanese and Urdu were unable to scan texts in the way learners of German were able to. Urdu learners under-rated their ability, not taking into account the wide range of natural contexts in which they use Urdu outside the classroom. The data also illustrates how Urdu learners use their spoken knowledge of Urdu as a resource when reading.

Reading Grid study

This concerns an unpublished comparative study of GCSE (General Certificate of Secondary Education) and AL French Reading tasks. The purpose was to develop using the subjective judgment of experts a grid of task features describing the nature of what is tested, and relate these both to difficulty and to construct validity. The grid was then used to review further tasks. Available item calibrations could be used to verify the predictive power of the grid. The intention was to use the grid to aid item writers in test construction and as a tool to enable comparisons to be made across different assessments, e.g. different languages and versions as well as assessments with different testing purposes. At task level, it takes into account features included in the Dutch construct grid (Alderson et al 2004), such as text length, topic, text source, discourse type, domain, intended operations and linguistic features. As assessment tasks of reading typically elicit some testing or task focused strategies that may not be present in reading outside an assessment context, it was felt that such strategies needed to be included in the grid. Cognitive operations that candidates use, particularly focusing on what they have to do and understand in order to answer each item, were looked at in detail. Aspects such as how easy it is for candidates to find the relevant section of text, the quantity and difficulty of the language needed to respond to each item, the similarity of this language to English and whether there was alternative or more than one piece of information that leads to the answer are included in the grid. Other features include the extent to which the task is scaffolded (e.g. for Asset Languages the questions are in English which provides extra support in understanding the text), the extent to which existing knowledge and task familiarity impact on answering each item and particular strategies that the task elicits. The final item on the grid asks whether it is possible to assign a CEFR level 'in terms of what the learner is likely to be able to do if they are successful at the task'. Current literature and consultation guided the development of the grid which was then trialled in a day-long workshop with three experts. The grid has since been used in a training day with subject officers across the full range of languages assessed by Asset Languages and work is in progress to have the grid incorporated into editing meetings with language specialists and item writers.

Experts were commissioned to use the grid on a number of Asset Languages and GCSE French reading assessments covering levels A1, A2, B1 and B2. This data was looked at together with item level data. Findings are summarised below.

Assessments at and working towards A1

The analysis suggests that despite a text length of 50–60 words, only one or two words are needed in the target language in order to respond to each item. Item level statistics showed that where the vocabulary was particularly easy, contained cognates, or where there was alternative information, items were relatively easy. More difficult items contained difficult vocabulary, no cognates and no alternative information.

Experts found it difficult to give a CEFR level and tended to do this at text level (e.g. '*I can understand a short, simple letter*') rather than on the basis of the cognitive operations that the candidate actually performs. It was found that the CEFR level of the texts is different to the level of the cognitive operations. For example, even though the text is a short, simple letter (A2), it is mainly at high frequency word or very short phrase level that candidates need to engage (A1). Information in texts is easy to locate and data from other research such as verbal protocols suggests that candidates work through in this way working between the text and questions rather than reading the text as a whole.

While the text is in the target language, Asset Languages has the questions and multiple-choice answers in English, which is typically the candidate's first language. This scaffolds students' understanding of the text and is likely to also impact on task difficulty. This use of English may also promote the strategy of keyword translation, which is a common strategy at this level.

Assessments at and working towards A2

The results here were very similar to those at A1 where the easiest items required reading less text containing less complex language, sometimes with cognates. Where there was more alternative information this also impacted on item difficulty.

Candidates generally needed to read and understand phrases and sentences although there was the occasional poorly constructed item where candidates may have been successful by understanding one or two single words.

The most difficult task at Preliminary requires the entire text to be read and understood and ordered correctly. This task is probably operating above the level due to the level of knowledge of textual cohesion that is required.

Again, it was found that the experts found it difficult to assign a CEFR level for the cognitive operations that the candidate uses. Again, they tended to use a CEFR descriptor that matched the text rather than the necessary cognitive operations.

Assessments at and working towards B1

The results here were different to those found at the lower levels. More text (sentences to whole text) of more difficult language had to be understood in order to answer the questions. As the focus is not on word or short phrase level, cognates or words close to English only rarely impacted on item difficulty.

At this level, it is more difficult to isolate the factors which impact on item difficulty. It was apparent that scaffolding in the form of English summaries, information in English in the rubrics etc. helped to make tasks easier.

As at A1 and A2, there was some mismatch between the level of the assigned CEFR descriptor and the necessary cognitive operations, although much less of a mismatch than at earlier levels. The CEFR descriptors better match what candidates are doing at this level.

As found at A2, the most difficult task requires the entire text to be read and understood and ordered correctly. The language for this task is clearly more sophisticated than that in the A2 task. Again this task is probably operating above the level due to the level of knowledge of textual cohesion that is required.

The text of the Reading Grid itself is provided in the Appendix.

The study thus provided some useful insights into the causes of task difficulty. It is worth noting that the factors identified here are of great importance for item writing, as they impact on the validity of tests. These factors are not well treated in the pilot Manual.

Comparative reading reviews

These addressed concerns that tasks for particular AL languages were diverging from the intended level. Development staff and language experts reviewed sample tasks and identified issues to be addressed. Interestingly, not knowing the language(s) in question was not a bar to useful participation, at least at the lowest levels. Given at least one expert in the language a number of issues could quickly be identified: text length, the amount of distraction or irrelevant text, the spacing of elements within the text referenced by particular items, and so on. A general issue concerns languages using non-Latin scripts, where simply decoding text presents a far greater cognitive load at lower proficiency levels. This suggests that reading texts in such languages need to be shorter. Specific character lists were specified from the outset for initial levels of Chinese and Japanese.

Scale construction and standard setting

These two stages in constructing an assessment framework for objective items are logically ordered: first construct a scale and then set cut-offs on it.

In practice the two stages have had to proceed side-by-side in the AL development, and indeed, the process is still unfinished as the higher levels are developed and added. For many less widely spoken languages there is as yet insufficient response data and collateral information to consider the process complete.

Scale construction is based on an IRT (Rasch) model and an item-banking approach. Data for linking the levels vertically has come from pretesting, where it has been possible to include items linking two levels; and also from common-person linking in both live and non-live situations, where learners have taken tests at two levels.

The scaling and standard-setting approach is based on the notion of a template scale which by default applies to all languages. The shape of this scale, i.e. the proportional intervals between levels, is based on the model of the Cambridge ESOL Common Scale, which is the measurement scale underpinning the Cambridge ESOL main exam suite, covering levels A2 to C2 of the CEFR. The underlying idea is that the measurable distance between two levels on a proficiency scale reflects the empirically observable difference between the levels, which is equivalent to a certain learning gain. The relation between learning and observable gains is well known: at low levels a little learning makes a big observable difference; at higher levels it may take years of learning to move up a level, as is shown in Figure 4.

Figure 4: Relationship of effort and observable difference

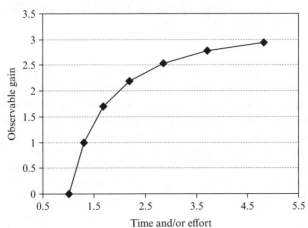

Time and/or effort

Also there is some logic in the progression which we observe in the Cambridge ESOL Common Scale. At low levels learners develop rapidly, so several target levels are needed perhaps quite closely spaced in time. These targets also serve an important motivational function, as at this early stage many learners may not be studying intensively, or be at all keen on language study. Learners at high levels are likely to be more committed students, so it is acceptable that levels should demand much more time and effort to achieve; at the same time the next level must remain accessible, even if that means settling for smaller observable gains. The scale makes sense as a framework for learning.

This rationale explains quite well the shape of the Cambridge ESOL Common Scale, even though its empirical construction was a *post-hoc* exploration of a system which had developed piecemeal over the best part of a century. Pending any better evidence it is reasonable for us to work on the basis that the proportional intervals on a scale for objectively measured skills should be the same across languages, as they define levels as a particular function of effort and observable learning gains. Jones (2005) has more detail.

This approach allows us to impose the necessary coherence on the AL framework: the requirement to align a large number of elements (six levels, many languages) is met by working from a model of the framework as a whole downwards to the elements within it, rather than working upwards from individual standard-setting decisions. The approach is also potentially amenable to validation, and facilitates gradual and progressive amendment, as evidence accumulates.

The template scale is thus a central idea in the AL approach to scaling, although for many languages difficulty in achieving a reliable vertical link in response data has meant that standard setting has had to proceed on a by-level basis. In practice this has given even greater importance to the use of teacher ratings, collected as collateral data about candidates, during pre-testing and live test administration. To date these have played a major role in both standard setting and, effectively, scale construction. Teacher ratings were initially elicited by reference to National Curriculum levels, which are broadly in line with Languages Ladder stages, at least for the most popular modern foreign languages like French. It was believed that these were the most familiar proficiency levels for primary and secondary school teachers to use. Subsequently ratings have been elicited by reference to the Languages Ladder/CEFR, using an instrument that draws on both scales.

Teacher ratings are used as follows. At pretesting teachers are asked to give a single rating of level for each of the candidates. The level rating corresponds to an ability on the template scale, so that the IRT analysis of pretest data can be anchored to the scale via the estimated ability of candidates. When live tests are constructed, the item difficulties anchored in this way can be used to estimate the ability corresponding to different scores in the test, and hence the score corresponding to each grade threshold on the scale.

Reference to Manual

Thus the approach to standard setting falls under the procedures discussed in Chapter 6 of the pilot Manual under 'external validation'. No operational use has been made of task-centred standard setting as described in Chapter 5.

Other related areas of work

Experimental approaches to standard setting and cross-language comparability include the use of 'Can Do' statements, and task-centred alignment of reading.

Plurilingual 'Can Do' study

'Can Do' questionnaire instruments have been developed for self-assessment or teacher rating for the four AL skills. Trial questionnaires have been assembled using 'Can Dos' from a range of sources: National Curriculum, Languages Ladder, CEFR including ELP, the Bergen study, the Association of Language Testers in Europe (ALTE) etc., and response data collected to identify a coherent subset (some of these sources work better than others). A limited amount of data has so far been collected where learners taking AL tests in two different languages provide self-ratings for each language. The purpose of the study, which replicates a design adopted for the Business Language Testing Service (BULATS), another Cambridge ESOL multilingual test, is to evaluate the potential of this approach as a way of verifying cross-language alignments of objective tests. This is an attractive idea to the extent that self-ratings by plurilingual informants should reflect reasonably well their *relative* competence in the two languages. The tendency of individuals' self-ratings to vary widely in terms of judgments of *absolute* level should thus not be a problem.

Task-centred alignment of reading using rankings

This was a small-scale study based on data collected at a workshop during the Vilnius ALTE conference (October 2007). The purpose is to evaluate whether rankings of tasks, based on raters' judgements of difficulty, could be used for cross-language alignment, and whether the quality of such an alignment might be estimated on the basis of comparison with known empirical difficulties available for each language separately. This area of study is being taken forward in the context of the development of the European Survey on Language Competence (ESLC) by the *SurveyLang* consortium, in which Cambridge ESOL is a partner[3]. A ranking approach to cross-language comparison of speaking is reported in North and Jones (2009:17).

Subjectively marked tests (Writing and Speaking)

Design, specification, item writing

The same approach was taken with the performance skills as with the objective tests described above. Comparability across languages was sought through the use of English exemplars, as further described below.

Standard setting, rater training and standardisation

The challenge of developing a common understanding of levels given the wide range of languages in the AL framework and the different contexts in which they are learned and taught (community languages and modern foreign languages) was addressed through the use of exemplars in English. Even though English is not a language in the AL framework, this was seen as the most direct way of setting an initial target. Video exemplars of AL speaking tests were filmed in EFL (language school) and ESL (primary school) contexts. Writing samples were collected in the same way.

It was important that the exemplars represented the standardised AL test format. Using available English exemplars from other Cambridge ESOL exams would have introduced extraneous difficulties. Using the AL format focused attention on specific issues of how the same construct and the same notion of level could be implemented in perhaps very different languages. The exemplars also demonstrated the central importance of task to perceptions of level of performance, as they included examples of the same learner taking the test at two levels – typically appearing more fluent and confident at the lower level, but struggling at the higher one.

In addition to the English exemplars, exemplars were also to be produced for each language, although these were only available initially for the most common languages (French, German, Spanish, Italian). These were used for standardising raters for each language, and also in cross-language comparisons of standard.

Reference to Manual

The use of standardised English exemplars, in the absence of such exemplars for a given language, is envisaged in the Manual. The benchmarking of these English exemplars was done by AL staff already familiar with the CEFR, making reference to available CEFR exemplars in English, French and German, as well as to the text of the CEFR. We found some problems of interpretation using the available exemplars due to the differences compared to AL in test format (paired vs. single), task (open-ended discussion vs. more guided tasks) and context (adult vs. secondary or primary; community-based learners vs. MFL learners).

A problem to be engaged with was assigning the lower AL grades, because (as shown in Figure 1 above) these correspond to less-than-complete achievement of the target level, i.e. to the CEFR level below.

Benchmarking of language-specific exemplars where these were available was done by teams of language experts guided by AL CEFR-expert staff. These sessions incorporated familiarisation with the CEFR as described in the Manual, and reference to the English exemplars where these were available. There were construct issues to address as well as issues of level, as many language experts came with previous experience of other UK language qualifications (Entry level, GCSE, A-Level). Reference to the CEFR was also very useful in understanding what determined the level (range, task), as well as what expectations of performance should be, in terms e.g. of accuracy, fluency or communication.

Initial standardisation of language experts for the wider range of AL languages was based on the English exemplars. Procedures as suggested in the pilot Manual were followed. Even in a large conference involving many different languages this approach was very effective in arriving quickly at an understanding of levels. This in itself, of course, does not necessarily mean that examiners were able successfully to transfer this common understanding to their own languages.

Other related areas of work

In an approach to ongoing verification of standards, cross-language comparisons have been undertaken for the more commonly spoken languages in AL, based on the AL exemplar materials for those languages, or on speaking and writing samples from live exams (the speaking being recorded). Such sessions have depended on the plurilingual competence of the respective language experts, but have proved fruitful (things might be different when the higher levels are compared).

Specific queries regarding standards may also arise in the operational conduct of exams. In one case a multilingual expert was asked to adjudicate on the standard applied across languages (French, German) in a particular session. Such issues are understandable when teams of markers and moderators are still relatively inexperienced.

Conclusions

The Asset Languages project is challenging in a number of ways. Comparability between such diverse languages and learning contexts is a difficult notion to concretise. The context of learning and language use of community language learners differs from that of the modern foreign language learner, whose exposure to the language may be largely or exclusively in a formal setting. The place of literacy in learning differs where the script itself presents a long-term learning challenge. Adult learners and primary school children differ in their purposes for learning and in the cognitive maturity they bring to it. Relating these different contexts to a single frame of reference requires specific arguments and justification, and must in the end be tempered by realism: we are after usefulness rather than some absolute truth.

These are important issues for AL, and they also remind us that the CEFR itself in its current form has certain limits. It deals well with that range and kind of ability achievable within a normal foreign language learning career: that is, based on formal study possibly supplemented by informal learning experiences. Being focused on Europe, moreover, it does not strongly distinguish the development of oracy and literacy. Whether the CEFR could usefully be extended, or related to some larger meta-framework, to encompass, for example, the languages of education depends in the first instance on finding compelling reasons for wishing to do so. Fleming (2008) reports on the Council of Europe Language Policy Division's work in the area of Languages of Education, where the need for a different kind of framework to the CEFR is debated.

Asset Languages in common with all assessment projects has been developed within practical constraints, and fully implementing all the stages of the test design, construction and administration cycle will require an iterative approach. Finally the degree of perfection achieved will vary by language depending on its popularity and the consequent availability of data. These factors weigh on the construction of any claim to alignment to the CEFR. The Asset Languages project continues to seek methods which serve the purpose.

We would like the Manual, in terms of its style, organisation, and above all in the significance it attaches to particular procedures, to encourage rather than discourage this search for approaches which work for particular purposes. The current guidelines for reporting envisage users applying the Manual rationally, selectively, 'contributing to a body of knowledge and experience' and 'adding to the compendium of suggested techniques'. We very much endorse this approach to using and perhaps further developing the Manual.

Notes

1. The Department for Children, Schools and Families (DCSF) was formerly known as the Department for Education and Skills (DfES).
2. A number of documents are available from the CILT (National Centre for Languages) website: www.cilt.org.uk/faqs/nat_cur.htm
3. The SurveyLang website is: www.surveylang.org

References

Alderson, J C, Figueras, N, Kuijper, H, Nold, G, Takala, S, Tardieu, C (2004) *The Development of Specifications for Item Development and Classification within the Common European Framework of Reference for Languages: Learning, Teaching, Assessment. Reading and Listening. The Final Report of the Dutch CEFR Construct Project*, project report, Lancaster University, Lancaster, UK, retrieved from: www.eprints.lancs.ac.uk/44/

Ashton, K (2009) *Comparing proficiency levels in an assessment context: the construct of reading for secondary school learners of German, Japanese and Urdu*, PhD study, University of Cambridge.

Council of Europe (2001) *Common European Framework of Reference for Languages*, Cambridge: Cambridge University Press.

Council of Europe (2003) *Relating language examinations to the CEFR. Manual; Preliminary Pilot Version*, retrieved from: www.coe.int/T/E/Cultural Co-operation/education/Languages/Language Policy/Manual/default.asp

DfES (2002) *Languages for all: languages for life*, Department for Education and Skills, retrieved from: http://publications.teachernet.gov.uk/eOrderingDownload/DfESLanguagesStrategy.pdf

DfES (2003) *The Languages Ladder*, Department for Education and Skills, retrieved from: www.teachernet.gov.uk/languagesladder/

Fleming, M (2008) *Languages of schooling within a European framework for languages of education: learning, teaching, assessment*, conference report, Strasbourg, France: Council of Europe, retrieved from: www.coe.int/t/dg4/linguistic/Source/Prague2007_ConferReport_EN.doc

Hasselgreen, A (2003) *Bergen 'Can Do' project*, Strasbourg: Council of Europe.

Jones, N (2005) Raising the Languages Ladder: constructing a new framework for accrediting foreign language skills, *Research Notes* 19, Cambridge ESOL, retrieved from: www.CambridgeESOL.org/rs_notes/rs_nts19.pdf

Kane, M, Crooks, T and Cohen, A (1999) Validating measures of performance, *Educational Measurement: Issues and Practice* 18 (2), 5–17.

Lenz, P and Schneider, G (2004) *A bank of descriptors for self-assessment in European Language Portfolios*, Strasbourg: Council of Europe, retrieved from: www.coe.int/T/DG4/Portfolio/documents/descripteurs.doc

Mislevy, R J, Steinberg, L S and Almond R G (2002) Design and analysis in task-based language assessment, *Language Testing* 19 (4) 477–496.

North, B and Jones, N (2009) *Further Material on Maintaining Standards across Languages, Contexts and Administrations by exploiting Teacher Judgment and IRT Scaling*. Council of Europe: Strasbourg, retrieved from: www.coe.int/t/dg4/linguistic/manuel1_EN.asp

Shaw, S D and Weir, C (2007) *Examining Writing: Research and practice in assessing second language writing*, Studies in Language Testing Volume 26, Cambridge: Cambridge University Press.

Van Ek, J A and Trim J L M (1990a) *Threshold 1990*, Cambridge: Cambridge University Press.

Van Ek, J A and Trim J L M (1990b) *Waystage 1990*, Cambridge: Cambridge University Press.

Walker, T (2005) *What is tested – Breakthrough*, Cambridge ESOL internal report AVR006.

Weir C (2005a) *Language Testing and Validation*, Basingstoke: Palgrave Macmillan Ltd.

Weir C (2005b) Limitations of the Common European Framework for developing comparable examinations and tests, *Language Testing* 22 (3), 281–300.

Appendix

Reading Grid study

This study is described in the paper above. The bare text of the Reading Grid document is given below, without layout, or the grid boxes in which users recorded their analysis of a reading task. The Dutch grid handout refers to the project reported in Alderson et al (2004).

Test level and test part

Text features

- Length
- Domain *(e.g. personal, public, occupational, educational etc.)*
- Language of the rubric
- Topic
- Source *(see Dutch grid handout)*
- Intended operations *(see Dutch grid handout, e.g. gist, detail, opinion)*
- Discourse type *(see Dutch grid handout, e.g. expository, narrative)*
- Linguistic features *(e.g. linguistic, syntactic, functional, high/low frequency language)*

Task features

'Know where to look'

How easy is it for students to determine where in the text the answer is? (e.g. six sentences, six questions, words relating the question to the text)

'How much?'

How much text do students need to understand in order to answer the question?, e.g. word, phrase, sentence or whole text level?

'What?'

What language do students need to understand in order to answer the question?

'Frequency of language'

Is the language that students need to understand in order to answer the question high frequency, low frequency etc.?

'Relationship to English'

Is the language that students need to understand in order to answer the question close to English, are cognates used? etc.

'Alternative information'

Is there alternative information/extra support that helps students to answer the question?

'Scaffolding'

Is there extra support, e.g. do the questions scaffold understanding of the text for students?

'Schema'

To what extent does the task genre awaken existing schemata for the student?

'Existing knowledge'

Can students predict the answer, using existing knowledge? Is this helpful/not helpful in answering the question?

'Task familiarity'

To what extent does task familiarity/unfamiliarity impact on answering the question?

'Particular strategies'

Are there particular strategies that the task elicits?, e.g. matching tasks may elicit process of elimination strategy.

'Other features'

Are there other features that may impact on difficulty?, e.g. the layout, 'doesn't say'.

'CEFR level'

In terms of what the learner is likely to be able to do if they are successful at the task. Is it possible to assign a CEFR level or CEFR 'Can Do' statement to what they can do?

12 Mapping the Dutch foreign language state examinations onto the CEFR

[Summarised report of a Cito research project commissioned by the Dutch Ministry of Education, Culture and Science]
José Noijons and Henk Kuijper
Cito, Institute for Educational Measurement, the Netherlands

Abstract

In this report an account is given of the content specification and the stand-ardisation of the state examinations of reading comprehension in the foreign languages French, German and English as carried out by Cito. For this the procedures as described in the draft Manual published by the Council of Europe have been followed (Council of Europe 2003). To arrive at valid speci-fication and standardisation, project members first had to get familiar with the Common European Framework of Reference for Languages (CEFR) in the familiarisation phase. And later, when external judges were asked to determine the minimum CEFR level of the items that occur in the reading comprehension examinations, these judges also had to get familiar with the CEFR.

Project members performed a content analysis of the examinations of reading comprehension during the specification process. The issue has been to find out to what extent examinations of reading comprehension at all sec-ondary school levels did indeed contain texts and items that show an increase in CEFR level. To be able to answer this question a CEFR-related descriptive model was used with which the texts and items have been described.

It proved possible to indicate for each of the examinations of reading comprehension for the various school types what the mean minimum reading comprehension level of a candidate should be in terms of the CEFR in order to be able to answer the questions in an examination correctly. In addition to this we have been able to indicate for nearly all the examinations used, what the minimum scores should be to reach the relevant CEFR levels. We have compared these minimum scores per examination with the State Examination Committee's cut-off scores.

Introduction

In 2003 the Dutch Ministry of Education, Culture and Science commissioned SLO, the Dutch Institute for Curriculum Development, and Cito, Institute for Educational Measurement, to carry out a linking project which had the following objectives:

A. To establish links between the existing examinations in French, German and English and the Common European Framework of Reference, CEFR (Council of Europe 2001), following the steps as outlined in the (preliminary pilot version of the) Manual published by the Council of Europe.
B. To study the possibilities of developing more comprehensive CEFR-related examinations in the foreign languages.

The project defined a number of goals, resulting in the production of the following:

1. A qualitative analysis of the examination syllabuses and examinations (2003 and 2004) for lower secondary pre-vocational level and for higher secondary/pre-university level French, German and English.
2. A new set of specifications for the examination syllabuses 2007 at the higher levels based on the CEFR for the skills of reading, listening, writing, spoken production and spoken interaction.
3. A classification of the items in the examinations for French, German and English at five levels within the terms of the CEFR by judges and stakeholders, with a computation of cut-off scores at relevant CEFR levels.
4. A psychometric validation of the above-mentioned examinations.
5. A set of sample items illustrating those 'Can Do' statements at each CEFR level that are not tested in the present examinations.
6. Prototypes of CEFR-based examinations of reading in French, German and English at relevant levels.
7. Inclusion of research data in the syllabuses for the state examinations in the foreign languages that will be produced within the framework of the revision of the examination syllabuses for higher secondary and pre-university level.
8. Publication of a final report.

Linking procedures

The aim of the Manual published by the Council of Europe has been to propose possible procedures for finding evidence to relate examinations to the CEFR. In the Manual three methods of linking are identified:

1. Specification of the content of the examinations.
2. Standardisation of judgements.
3. Empirical validation by means of data analysis of test results.

With the first method the claim of links to the CEFR is made on the basis of specification only. This method (with variations) has been followed by a number of institutes in Europe and outside. The second method may lead to a stronger claim of links, because it is based on specification AND standardisation. The third method may result in claims that are confirmed by empirical verification. Methods 1 and 2 have now been carried out by Cito and are described in this report. Cito has been carrying out activities relating to method 3 since.

Within the various methods the following phases have been identified:

- *Familiarisation:* making sure that those persons involved in the linking procedure are thoroughly acquainted with the goal, the set-up and the levels of the CEFR (Introduction phase).
- *Specification:* mapping out the extent to which the coverage of the examination syllabuses and the state examinations of reading comprehension can be related to descriptors of the CEFR.
- *Standardisation:* asking judges (language teachers, representatives from politics and industry) through a procedure as described in the Manual to classify a selection of the examination questions that were used in the research project, in terms of CEFR (that is, linking them with CEFR levels). On that basis it can be determined what score a candidate should get in a particular examination in order to be able to say that he/she masters a level that is relevant to CEFR for that particular examination.
- *Empirical validation:* psychometric validation of the results collected in the standardisation procedure.

In this report the activities that relate to all four phases are described. Some aspects of empirical validation (validation through comparison with other CEFR-related examinations) are not reported upon here.

Familiarisation

The first phase in the linking process described in the Manual is that of familiarisation. The Manual points out that it is important for all those involved in the linking process to familiarise themselves with the CEFR. The familiarisation process in this project has involved five steps:

1. Familiarisation with the global and specific aims, objectives and functions of the CEFR.
2. Discussions with reference to the questions that are put at the end of each chapter in the CEFR about the relevance of the chapter in question for the work situation of the user of the CEFR.
3. Discussion about the global descriptors of the CEFR and the levels that go with them. Project members (content specialists) made a first, preliminary link of the Dutch education levels to the CEFR.
4. Self-assessment of one's own proficiency level for project members in two foreign languages with the help of the self assessment grid (Table 2 in the CEFR).
5. Sorting specific CEFR descriptors. The descriptors all pertained to reading, the skill that is tested in the state examinations.

The discussions among project members showed that there was global agreement on the CEFR levels attained in Dutch foreign language education. It must be emphasised here that these estimates were not based on any empirical evidence. All project members estimated their own CEFR levels. Most of them had university degrees (BA or MA) in one or more foreign languages.

Content specification

The second phase in the linking process as outlined in the Manual and carried out in the Dutch linking research is called the *specification* phase. The Manual describes what specification in the linking process involves: describing the extent to which an examination covers the categories and levels of the CEFR. The Manual identifies two separate forms of description:

1. A description of the examination in its own right.
2. A content analysis of the examination (in terms of the CEFR).

In this section the results are reported of the content analysis of the state examinations of reading comprehension in terms of the CEFR. This content analysis of the examinations consists of a description of the examinations through the scales of communicative activities and the scales of communicative competence in the CEFR.

Content specification in relation to the scales for communicative activities

Within the context of linking the state examinations of reading comprehension in French, German and English to the CEFR, the examinations of the year 2004, for all regular school types have been analysed with the help of the four global descriptors and the accompanying detailed descriptors of *Taalprofielen* [Language Profiles] (Liemberg and Meijer 2004). These global descriptors correspond to the scales of communicative activities for reading in the CEFR.

Taalprofielen identifies the following global descriptors:

- Reading correspondence
- Reading for orientation
- Reading for information and argument
- Reading instructions.

These global descriptors in turn are subdivided into detailed descriptors ('Can Do' statements).

In the standard-setting phase (see below) a minimum CEFR level has been estimated that would be required to successfully respond to items from each examination for each school type. Based on the estimation of the minimum CEFR level for an individual item a mean minimum CEFR level could be computed for each examination. On the basis of the above estimations, the examinations have been analysed with the descriptors for the level or the levels to which the required minimum level corresponded.

For reasons of efficiency judges were instructed to assign only one global descriptor to each item. The descriptor that was selected had to be the most appropriate. The next step was to determine to which detailed descriptor each reading item mainly referred to. The assigning of descriptors to the items was carried out by two judges in close consultation.

The project has found the following:

- The distribution of the items in the examinations across the four global descriptors is not balanced. The items that focus on reading for information appear most often. This has partly to do with regulations in the examination models which prioritise this type of reading.
- The current examination syllabus and the examination model that is derived from it, are in fact very global as far as the texts and tasks are concerned. The diversity of the source material mentioned in the descriptors in *Taalprofielen* corresponds with the great variety of text materials that can be used for the state examinations. This variety has been confirmed by the fact that the examination texts represent a great variety of what is described in the CEFR for text type, text source and communication topics.
- It is exactly this very wide variety that makes an extensive revision of the current examination syllabuses less opportune. It is for this reason that constructing new examination prototypes has not been deemed advisable.
- Although not all four global descriptors are equally represented in the examinations, it appears that the skills that are described in the detailed

descriptors are all represented in the examinations. Reading skills which are described under the global descriptors show a great deal of overlap. When one concludes for instance that *reading correspondence* does not occur very often, this does not mean that the skills as described in the detailed descriptors under reading correspondence are not represented in the examinations. For both *reading correspondence* and *reading for information*, candidates have to be able to understand the main ideas and detailed information in texts. It is likely that when a candidate is able to demonstrate this skill when reading an article from a magazine – as is mentioned with *reading for information* – he or she can also show this skill when reading correspondence. The difference then is not in the reading comprehension, but in the type of text.

• When revising the examination models one could nonetheless consider the necessity of having the missing detailed descriptors appear more explicitly in the examinations. One can think of work-related correspondence, *reading for orientation* and *reading instructions* for instance for the lower-level examinations. The global descriptor *reading for information* appears most frequently in the examinations. The detailed descriptor *reading of texts for pleasure* that goes with this particular global descriptor does not appear in the state examinations at all.

• Redistribution of the present attainment targets may be considered so that there is more correspondence with the relative importance that is given to each of the descriptors within the CEFR at the various levels. In other words: the present distribution of attainment targets does not reflect the CEFR sufficiently.

Content specification in relation to the scales for communicative competence

The levels in the CEFR represent an increasing degree of language ability. Language learners can deal with increasingly more text types in many more domains and situations, as their proficiency level increases. Their ability to handle linguistically and cognitively more complex texts with an increasing accuracy also increases. This aspect of the language ability is described specifically in the scales for communicative competence and within those even more specifically in the scales for communicative linguistic competences.

In the following paragraphs additional information is given about the texts and items in the state examinations of reading comprehension in German and English in relation to the CEFR. For the examinations in French not enough data was available to carry out such an analysis. However, it can be assumed that the results presented here for German and English in relation to the CEFR will also apply to the state examinations of reading comprehension in French. After all, the examinations in German, English and

French are developed following the same examination syllabus and the same examination model.

In the CEFR content aspects and levels of language tasks have been described. The language development from a lower to a higher level can be described as the increase in the ability to perform more and more language tasks with text types of an increasing difficulty level. The question is to what extent the state examinations of reading comprehension contain texts and items that show an increase in difficulty level from the lowest streams to the highest streams as is to be expected from the standard-setting process (see below). To be able to answer this question a descriptive, CEFR related model is needed to describe texts and items.

A research project into such dimensions in the CEFR has been carried out in the *Dutch Grid project* (Alderson, Figueras, Kuijper, Nold, Takala and Tardieu 2006). In this European project the CEFR has been analysed for the extent to which it contains clear instructions and guidelines for the description and development of test tasks at various CEFR levels. It is concluded that the CEFR is a useful instrument, but that clear guidelines for test development and test description at the various levels cannot be found in the CEFR. The following problems for test construction on the basis of the CEFR have been identified:

1. Terminology: are some technical terms synonyms or not?
2. Omissions, when a concept or characteristic needed for test specification simply is not present.
3. Inconsistencies, when a characteristic is mentioned at one level and not at another level, where the same characteristic occurs at two different levels, or when at the same level a characteristic is described differently in different scales.
4. The absence of definitions, when terms are presented, but not defined.

The problem is not so much in the descriptive criteria in the CEFR being absent, but rather in the fact that there is a lack of explicitness, structure, consistency and precision, aspects which are of vital importance for test construction.

On the basis of a thorough analysis of the CEFR, the Dutch Grid project has developed a new descriptive model, related to the CEFR, for reading and listening items and texts. The model attempts at describing the relevant dimensions of the CEFR in a more systematic way. This descriptive model is available on the web at www.ling.lancs.ac.uk/CEFRgrid. The Dutch Grid contains descriptive dimensions for texts and items in reading and listening. The text dimensions can be subdivided into a content category and a category referring to cognitive and linguistic complexity. Table 1 gives a survey of these dimensions. For each dimension it is shown if the descriptive structure is derived directly from the CEFR, or is an adaptation of the CEFR, or is derived from a different taxonomy.

Table 1: Descriptive dimensions of the Dutch Grid for reading

Text dimensions	
Content	Source
Text source	Directly from CEFR
Text type	DIALANG
Domain	Directly from CEFR
Topic	Directly from CEFR
Cognitive and linguistic complexity	
Abstraction level	Adapted on the basis of CEFR
Vocabulary	Adapted on the basis of CEFR
Grammatical complexity	Adapted on the basis of CEFR
Text length	Adapted on the basis of CEFR
CEFR-level estimate	Directly from CEFR
Reading item dimensions	
Question type	Adapted on the basis of CEFR
Operations	Adapted on the basis of CEFR
CEFR-level estimate	Directly from CEFR

In the linking study the Dutch Grid has been used to provide a first description of the items of the examinations of reading comprehension. This description has also been used for the selection of the examination items for the standardisation phase.

The analyses are based on the state examinations of reading comprehension in German and English in the years 2003 and 2004. For each of the two languages the analyses have been carried out by two persons. In the manual of the Dutch Grid it is recommended to have each text and item analysed by more than one person and to discuss the findings. Considering the great number of texts and items included in this project this plan could not be carried out for financial and organisational constraints. Nonetheless we consider the results to be sufficiently valid to report them here. These results can be considered as indicative. Clear trends can be recognised and the information is useful for further construction of the examinations.

For content specification in relation to the scales for communicative competence the project has found the following. The CEFR presupposes that higher levels will show an increase of the linguistic and cognitive complexity of reading texts which language learners should be able to understand. This presupposition also goes for the reading tasks which they have to be able to perform. This development is described specifically in the scales for communicative competences. The content description carried out for the examinations of reading comprehension in German and English shows that this increase of linguistic and cognitive complexity in the examinations is specifically found at text level. The texts become more complex grammatically; the abstractness of the texts increases and the vocabulary becomes increasingly more extensive and more varied. The descriptions of the items indicate that as the level of the examinations is higher, examinees should be able to perform a wider variety of operations.

Standardisation

The Manual distinguishes two main phases in this process:

- the judgement process
- data analysis for validation of the standards.

Judgement process

An overview of the various steps that were made in this process is given below.

- *Definition of goals for the decision procedure*

The aim of the judgement process is that judges determine the minimum CEFR level needed by a candidate to successfully perform on a given language test. In other words, to determine cut-off scores for each examination at which a candidate can be said to have acquired a CEFR level that is relevant to the aim of the specific examination. The standard-setting algorithm that was used is described here briefly. The data is collected by the so-called basket procedure. A judge is asked to put each item into a labelled basket corresponding to the minimum CEFR level that is needed to carry out the task in the item. There are five baskets, called A1, A2, B1, B2 and C1+, corresponding to the levels that the examination syllabuses aim at (and beyond). C1+ refers to the levels C1 and C2. If an item is placed in basket B1, this means that according to the judge, a person at level B1 should be able to carry out the task correctly and by implication mastery is assumed at all higher levels (persons at levels B2 and higher). It cannot be expected, however, that a person at level A2 (or lower) will be able to carry out the task correctly. This method of standard-setting has been developed for the project DIALANG (DIALANG 2002). The method was used because it has been shown to be manageable and to yield reliable and useful results. Moreover, several members of the linking project were familiar with this method.

- *Selection of reading items*

Ideally all the items in the state examinations of reading comprehension in French, German and English under review should be judged during the standard-setting. However, this would have meant that for each language judges would have had to rate a total of circa 250 reading items (to go with over 50 texts). It is clear that this would have been too strenuous a task to perform during one session. It was therefore decided to create representative samples from the five examinations per language.

- *Selection of judges*

In order to raise the validity of the standard setting judges were recruited from the teaching profession at secondary schools (at which the students are trained to take the foreign language examinations) and at institutes for higher and university education where such teachers are trained. These lecturers from higher education also train teachers for primary schools, which is relevant in the case of English, because in primary schools English will be taught at the lowest level (A1). Other judges were recruited from the business world and from private language institutes. A last group of judges included a politician and members of the State Examination Committees (CEVO). There were a number of reasons why project members have been excluded from the standard setting. Some project members had been responsible for constructing the items to be judged. Although it would have been useful to know how they would relate items to CEFR levels, their familiarity with the items might yield biased results.

- *Training of judges*

Judges were trained in much the same way as in the Familiarisation phase of the project, to get familiar with CEFR categories and levels. This training was given by the same person who had trained project members. A lively discussion on the relevance of the CEFR for various purposes developed. The judges were then given a number of texts with items to judge following the basket procedure described above. For each item in the training session the following question was put to the judges:

> *Please indicate for each item which level (A1, A2, B1, B2 or C1+) is minimally required to carry out the task correctly. (Circle for each item the number in the column with the answer of your choice.)*

Text	Tasks	Level				
		A1	A2	B1	B2	C1+
1	1	1	2	3	4	5

The training of the judges at this stage took place in three separate language groups (French, German and English) each consisting of 15–20 judges. The training was led by project members. During the discussions in the language groups the judges reached agreement on the required minimum level for each of the four items selected for training. These items were not included in the actual standard setting.

- *The judgement sessions*

After the training the judges were given sets of texts and items in the randomised order described above. Judges took between two and three hours to rate all the items using a rating form as described above. There have been no complaints of this task having been too strenuous. As a matter of fact, many of the judges expressed their willingness to take part in future standard-setting sessions for listening, speaking and writing tasks.

- *Data collection procedures*

The rating forms have been collected and the data has been transferred to optical reading forms. Data collected included: rater ID, language and ratings (1 to 5, corresponding to A1 to C1+) per item.

Data analysis for validation of the standards

The next phase in the standard-setting procedure has been the data analysis to validate the accuracy of the standards. The data analysis comprises two operations:

1. Determining rater agreement and rater reliability.
2. Determining minimum scores for relevant CEFR levels on each examination.

Rater agreement and rater reliability of French reading items:
reliability (α):   0.9395
agreement (Rho2):   0.9279
Rater agreement and rater reliability of German reading items:
reliability (α):   0.9567
agreement (Rho2):   0.9432
Rater agreement and rater reliability of English reading items:
reliability (α):   0.9755
agreement (Rho2):   0.9728

The project has found the following relating to rater agreement:

- Rater agreement for all the items presented to judges was over .90 for all three languages. This would indicate that judges agree sufficiently on the minimum CEFR level required for each item to be mastered.
- Judges have placed the items taken from the lowest level examination at the lower end of the CEFR scales and they have placed items taken from the higher level examinations at the higher end of the CEFR scale. This difference in level corresponds with the range in the Dutch examination levels.
- External judges seem to agree with the item writers on the level of difficulty of sets of items.
- Data analysis shows that for French and English, judges are of the opinion that a higher CEFR level is needed to be able to successfully answer the questions if moving up through the examinations from low level to high level.

- For German, judgements suggest that CEFR levels required for mastery of the items at a higher level are in a less consistent order of increasing difficulty.

Determining minimum scores for relevant CEFR levels in each examination

The next step in the data analysis phase has been the determining of minimum scores on a state examination needed by a student to be able to claim that he or she is at a relevant CEFR level. Also, we would like to know what the actual cut-off score as determined by the State Examination Committee (CEVO) would mean in terms of mastery of CEFR levels. For this purpose we have extrapolated the data found in the 'basket' procedure to the actual examinations taken by students in 2004. The method that has been followed to link the above-mentioned scores and cut-off scores to CEFR levels is being illustrated below for English. After that the most important conclusions for French and German will follow.

Results standard setting for the English examinations

Below an overview of the findings with the state examinations of reading in English will follow: the scores that go with the cut-off scores sufficient/insufficient as set by CEVO and the scores that go with the relevant cut-off scores with CEFR levels. We will indicate how the judgements of CEVO of what is a sufficient performance match with the judgements of relevant CEFR levels.

In Table 2 an overview is given of the number of examinees whose responses have been analysed as part of quality control procedures for the examinations and to determine cut-off scores and reliability estimates (Cronbach's alpha) with unweighted and weighted scores. Weights are used in Item Response Theory (IRT) analyses that are at the basis of standard-setting procedures.

Table 2: Examinations in English: number of respondents, reliability estimates with unweighted (unw.) and weighted (w.) scores

Level	N	A (unw.)	α (w.)
Vwo (pre-university)	1858	0.823	0.838
Havo (higher secondary)	2036	0.782	0.807
gl/tl (lower secondary)	2683	0.744	0.783
Kb (lower secondary – short)	2131	0.834	0.849
Bb (lower secondary – basic)	2250	0.841	0.855

The basic counting in the standard-setting procedures has been the average (across judges) cumulative number of reading items that has been put in each basket, starting with the lowest basket A1. A fictitious example is given in Table 3. From the table, we know that on average 3.2 items were put in basket B1 and 1.9 items (on average) were put in a lower-level basket. So (on average) 5.1 items should be mastered at level B1. In the standard setting this number is interpreted as a *minimum requirement for B1*. And therefore the cut-off score A2/B1 is positioned at 5/6.

Table 3: An example of the outcomes of the standard-setting procedure

Level	Frequency	Cumulative frequency
A1	0.8	0.8
A2	1.1	1.9
B1	3.2	5.1
B2	8.0	13.1
C1	1.9	15

When items are calibrated using Item Response Theory (IRT), different items may be given different weights. When these weights are taken into account one might replace the column frequency in Table 3 by a column with the average weight of the items put into each basket and then cumulate these weights across levels. These cumulative weights can then be interpreted as the minimum weighted score on a test consisting of all the items used in the standard setting. If the calibration is reliable, these cumulative weighted scores can be converted into a measure on the latent trait. An example is given in Table 4.

Table 4: Results for the highest school level examination in English (pre-university)

Level	Theta	Unweighted score	Weighted score
A1	−0.980	0.00	0.00
A2	−0.939	0.07	0.20
B1	−0.478	1.60	5.73
B2	−0.182	9.07	32.20
C1	1.277	15.00	54.00

A sample of 15 items taken from the vwo examination was rated by 15 judges. The maximum unweighted score therefore is 15 and the maximum weighted score (based on an analysis of the whole examination vwo) for these 15 items is 54. When we consider level B2, the cut-off score for unweighted scores at B1/B2 is 9/10; for weighted scores it is 32/33 and on the theta scale the cut-off is −0.182. For the A2/B1 cut-off point, the theta value is −0.478. This operation can be used to apply the standard setting to larger tests than the sample of items that has been presented to the judges.

We may consider applying two methods here:

1. In the calibration, weighted scores can be transformed into theta estimates. For the pre-university examination in English we then find the following results (see Table 5). They suggest that the cut-off score for B1/B2 is 126/127. For A2/B1 we could choose either 28/29 or 29/30 (since we have results with three decimals). The disadvantage of this procedure is that it requires the use of weighted scores, which may be impractical in real applications: test scores of pupils are in fact reported in unweighted *total* scores.

Table 5: Correspondence weighted score – theta in the highest school level examination in English (pre-university)

Weighted score	Theta estimate
28	−0.490
29	−0.478
30	−0.468
. . .	. . .
126	0.181
127	0.189

2. We can, however, also estimate theta on the basis of unweighted scores. The results of applying this method are given in Table 6. For B1/B2 the cut-off score is at 33/34, whereas for A2/B1 the cut-off score is at 8/9.

Table 6: Correspondence unweighted score – theta in the highest school level examination in English (pre-university)

Unweighted score	Theta estimate
8	−0.490
9	−0.478
10	−0.468
. . .	. . .
33	0.181
34	0.189

Above we have discussed the determination of cut-off scores for *relevant* levels. This issue may need some further elaboration. In the rater-agreement analyses for the pre-university examination in English, to take an example, we saw that judges considered the minimum CEFR level needed to master the sample of items taken from the pre-university examination was judged to be between B1 and B2. From other sources in the internal validation study we also know that the examination was *aimed at* a level that corresponds to B2. We therefore believe that the most relevant CEFR score is between B1 and B2. It is at this score that we indicate what minimum score the candidate needs to prove that he functions at B2.

It is also possible to compute cut-off scores at A2/B1 and at B2/C1 for the vwo examination. However, in the case of a cut-off score A2/B2 (*does the candidate function at the B1 level?*) we have more suitable instruments at our disposal, namely examinations that are geared towards a lower level than the pre-university examination. If we wish to determine if a candidate is at C1 level (at the cut-off score B2/C1), then we might be able to compute the cut-off score needed for C1 in the pre-university examination. However, from a validity point of view this is a debatable procedure as judges have indicated that in the present pre-university examination there are (considerably) fewer items at C1 level than at B2 level. We would run the risk of claiming *that a person functions at C1 level because he has mastered (nearly) all B2 items in a test, whereas in fact we should be showing that that person has mastered a sizable number of C1 items as well as some B2 items*). It is therefore important to choose the right instrument with sufficient items at a particular CEFR level to be able to give a reliable estimate on CEFR-level mastery.

In the present examination procedures applied in the Netherlands the State Examination Committee (CEVO) determines the cut-off score for each examination. When it is claimed that an examination is at a particular CEFR level, we need to look at where the CEVO cut-off score is positioned. At this point in time it has not yet been possible for either students or schools to claim that they are at a higher level than the CEFR level that corresponds to the CEVO cut-off score. If a candidate has managed to achieve a higher score than the scores that go with the cut-off score, one can of course conclude that his/her CEFR level will be higher than the level that goes with the cut-off score.

The judgements of the difficulty of the items measured can be validated empirically by comparing judgements with the answers of the candidates to the items. A complicating issue is that the examination results are sometimes difficult to compare because the examinations do not contain common items. Empirical validation can show if differences in judgements of a random sample of items by expert judges may result in that the estimated required level of mastery for a particular CEFR level in one examination is different from the required mastery of the same level in another examination.

In the following figures we will illustrate where CEVO cut-off scores and relevant CEFR cut-off scores are to be found in the Dutch pre-university examinations for English, French and German. As can be seen, the difference between the cut-off point with the CEVO cut-off score (pass/fail) and the cut-off score that goes with the relevant CEFR level of an examination, as concluded from the standard setting, may be considerable. We also give an indication of the score distribution (and consequently of the corresponding CEFR levels) of the sample student population for each examination.

In Figure 1 below, the distribution of scores and cut-off scores is given for the highest school level examination in English (pre-university).

Figure 1: Distribution of scores and cut-off scores in the highest school level examination in English (pre-university)

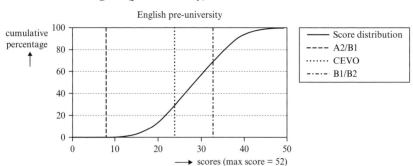

We see that cut-off scores with two CEFR levels have been computed: A2/B1 and B1/B2. That is to say that the scores to the right of the cut-off score line A2/B1, so scores of 8 and higher, belong to the B1 level. If candidates get scores higher than 33 this indicates a level of B2. On the basis of the internal validation process and from the estimates of judges we have concluded that this examination is aimed at students in the B2 to C1 range. We find that the CEVO cut-off score does not support this. Students can pass this examination with a score that is considerably lower than the score that judges expect at B2 level. However, a considerable percentage of students (circa 35%) do in fact reach B2 level on this examination. It needs to be said that it is not possible to prove with a high score on this examination that one has reached the C1 level: there were not enough items in the C1+ basket.

In Figure 2 below the distribution of scores and cut-off scores is given for the pre-university examination in French.

Figure 2: Distribution of scores and cut-off scores in the pre-university examination in French

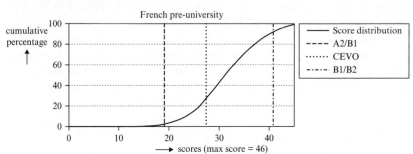

In Figure 2 we see that two relevant CEFR cut-off scores have been computed, at the level A2/B1 and at the level B1/B2. The CEVO cut-off score is positioned in between those two levels. The judges estimated at the standard setting that the minimum level for the pre-university examination in French is positioned just past B1. CEVO expects from candidates at pre-university level a minimum CEFR level that seems to correspond with the level that is estimated by the judges at the standard setting as the level of the pre-university examination.

In Figure 3 below, the distribution of scores and cut-off scores is given for the pre-university examination in German.

Figure 3: Distribution of scores and cut-off scores in the highest school level examination in German (pre-university)

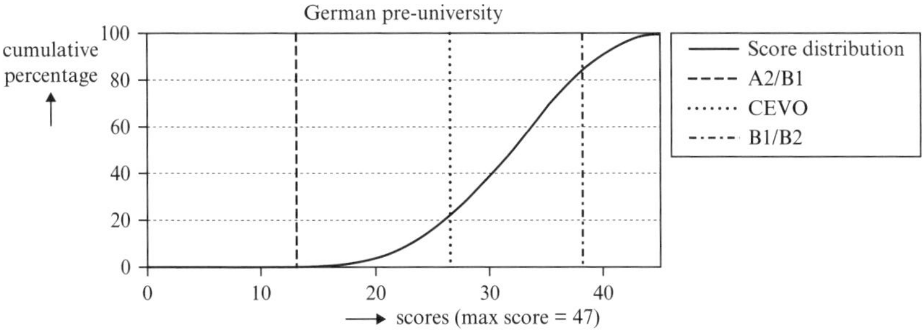

In this figure we see that two relevant CEFR cut-off scores have been computed, at A2/B1 and at B1/B2. The CEVO cut-off score is positioned exactly in-between. The judges estimate that the minimum level for the pre-university examination in German is positioned in between B1 and B2. It is clear that the CEVO cut-off score is positioned considerably lower. Only a small percentage of candidates achieve the B2 level in the pre-university examination.

General conclusions and recommendations

Below we give an overview of the general conclusions that we have been able to draw in this study. We should like to point out here that our task has been to link the current state examinations of reading comprehension in English, French and German to the CEFR. We leave it to others to draw conclusions as to the required content of and the required levels in the examination syllabuses and the state examinations of reading comprehension.

1. Following all the proposed steps in the draft Manual turned out to be a time consuming and costly process.
2. The linking process is a good way of critically reviewing and evaluating the content and statistical characteristics of the examinations in question.

3. From the content specification it appears that the emphasis in the state examinations of reading comprehension is on the global descriptor 'reading for information'. When the specific descriptors of the CEFR are taken into account, it is found that these specific descriptors are sufficiently represented in the examinations. It may be considered to include a few more texts for reading for correspondence and reading of instructions in the examinations, especially at the lower levels.

4. The examinations contain a variation in text sources, text types and topics as mentioned in the CEFR.

5. The examination texts, from low school level to high school level examinations, reflect the increase in linguistic and cognitive complexity, as supposed in the CEFR.

6. The variation in reading tasks which the candidates have to perform increases from low level to high level examinations.

7. The phases of specification and standardisation could best be carried out in both a national and an international context.

8. In many cases the State Examination Committee's cut-off scores (sufficient/insufficient) do not coincide with the cut-off points as estimated by judges for the relevant CEFR levels.

The project has formulated a number of recommendations, two of which follow below.

- Further research will need to be carried out to find out if examinations exist that have been calibrated in the way the draft Manual proposes. For a number of tests it is claimed that they have been linked to the CEFR in a valid and reliable way. However, we have the impression that often this is not done in the way the Manual proposes.

- Foreign test development organisations will have to be contacted for empirical validation. Since the full report was published, a number of such organisations co-operated in empirical validation of the Dutch foreign language examinations described above.

References

Alderson, J C, Figueras, N, Kuijper, H, Nold, G, Takala, S and Tardieu, C (2006) Analysing Tests of Reading and Listening in Relation to the Common European Framework of Reference: The Experience of the Dutch CEFR Construct Project, *Language Assessment Quarterly* 3 (1), 3–30.

CEVO (2006) *Syllabus voor het Centraal Examen Moderne Vreemde Talen*, Utrecht.

Council of Europe (2001) *Common European Framework of Reference for Languages: Learning, Teaching, Assessment*, Cambridge: Cambridge University Press.

Council of Europe (2003) *Relating Language Examinations to the Common European Framework of Reference for Languages: Learning, Teaching and Assessment. Manual Preliminary Pilot Version*, Strasbourg: Council of Europe.

DIALANG (2002) *Diagnostic tests in 14 languages on the internet*: www.dialang. org

Liemberg, E and Meijer, D (2004) *Taalprofielen*, Enschede: NaB-MVT.

Noijons, J and Kuijper, H (2006a) *De koppeling van de centrale examens leesvaardigheid moderne vreemde talen aan het Europees Referentiekader*, Arnhem: Cito.

Noijons, J and Kuijper, H (2006b) *Leesvaardigheidsexamens moderne vreemde talen in Europees verband*, Arnhem: Cito.

Notes on the volume contributors

Karen Ashton joined Cambridge ESOL in 2004 to work on the *Asset Languages* project. Her role included managing the research agenda, researching areas of comparability, the impact of assessments, and standard setting for performance assessments. She recently completed a PhD in this area. She is currently working at Cambridge ESOL as the Project Manager of SurveyLang, a European consortium implementing the European Survey on Language Competences.

Monica Barni is Associate Professor of Educational Linguistics at the University for Foreigners in Siena. She is currently Director of the CILS centre and co-ordinator of a research line at the Centre of Excellence for Research *Permanent Linguistic Observatory of the Italian Language among Foreigners and of Immigrant Languages in Italy*. Her main research interests and activities concern language teaching and learning, language assessment, language contact, and linguistic landscape.

Gergely A Dávid has worked on the measurement of foreign language proficiency for over 20 years now. In the 1990s he worked extensively on the internal filter exams at the Centre for English Teacher Training, Eötvös Loránd University, Budapest. As member of the Hungarian Accreditation Board for Language Examinations, he worked out the measurement requirements/conditions to be observed by test producers. In 2003, he acted as reader to the preliminary pilot edition of the Manual and launched the Hungarian Association of Language Examiners and Measurement Specialists. His chief research interests lie in test method effects, quality management for language tests and group oral techniques.

Nigel Downey obtained his BA from the University of Leicester, UK, and an MA in TEFL from St Michael's College, Vermont, USA. He is also a holder of the University of Cambridge DELTA and is currently researching for a PhD in Applied Linguistics from the University of Lancaster. He has been teaching English in the UK and Greece since 1987 and in 1999 joined the Hellenic American Union, where he is Head of Teacher Education. He is also joint Co-ordinator for Testing Development and teaches graduate courses in Applied Linguistics at the Hellenic American University. He has presented at international conferences in a number of European countries.

John O'Dwyer is Director of the Bilkent University School of English Language, General Director of the İhsan Doğramacı Foundation Primary and High Schools, and a lecturer in the Bilkent University Graduate School of Education in Turkey. He has held leadership roles in educational institutions in international contexts for over 20 years, striving to create generative organisations responsive to the challenges facing today's educators. He has worked in a range of countries on teacher training projects, project evaluation, and curriculum development projects. His PhD research focused on project evaluation, specifically the use of formative evaluation for organisational learning in a context of curriculum renewal.

Thomas Eckes has been at the TestDaF Institute in Hagen, Germany, since 2001. He is currently Deputy Director and Head of the language testing methodology, research, and validation unit. Dr Eckes has extensive teaching experience in educational measurement and statistics, as well as in cognitive and social psychology. He has published numerous articles in edited volumes and peer-review journals, including *Language Testing*, *Language Assessment Quarterly*, *Diagnostica*, *Journal of Classification*, *Multivariate Behavioral Research*, and *Journal of Personality and Social Psychology*. His research interests include: rater effects; many-facet Rasch measurement; polytomous IRT models; construct validity of C-tests; standard setting; computerised item banking; internet-delivered testing.

Angela ffrench holds an MEd in Language Testing from the University of Bristol, and an MA from the University of Cambridge. Having been involved in teaching and testing English for 20 years, both in the state and private sectors, Angela joined Cambridge ESOL in 1991 as an Examinations Officer, with special responsibility for Speaking. Since 2001 she has been responsible for the management of a suite of examinations ranging from upper intermediate to advanced levels. In this capacity she has been involved in all aspects of developing and administering tests and assessment criteria, in the training of item writers, in pretesting and analysing test material, and in the grading of the examinations.

Neil Jones is Assistant Director, Research and Validation, at University of Cambridge ESOL Examinations. His work includes innovative developments in item banking, computer-based testing, and the link between assessment and learning. Current interests are the construction of multilingual language proficiency frameworks including the development of Asset Languages.

Elif Kantarcıoğlu is an English language instructor at Bilkent University School of English Language, Turkey. She has an MA degree in ELT and her thesis was on test validation. She has been involved in language assessment for over 10 years. Her areas of interest are test design, validation and Rasch measurement techniques. She is currently doing her PhD on the subject of CEFR linking at Roehampton University, London.

Gabriele Kecker is currently Deputy Director and head of the test development unit at the TestDaF Institute in Hagen, Germany, focusing on issues of quality assurance, validation, research and test development. She is providing expert assistance at the German Institute for Educational Progress (IQB) and at the National educational board for German schools abroad (ZfA) for item development in alignment with the CEFR and standard setting. Since 2004 she has been in charge of the CoE Manual project at the TestDaF Institute. She previously taught German as a foreign language and worked for several years as a teacher trainer at the Ministry of Tourism in Morocco and as a lecturer at the University of Anananarivo in Madagascar.

Hanan Khalifa holds a PhD in Language Testing from the University of Reading, UK. Previously, she has worked within a university context and with international development agencies on the development of test batteries and item banks, ESP/EAP curriculum development, and educational reform. Hanan also has extensive experience in capacity building, programme evaluation, and in conducting impact studies. Her role as Assistant Director involves: setting the group's research agenda, assessing reading, ensuring alignment of products to the Common European Framework of Reference, and building validity arguments for assessment products. Her research interests include: standard setting, qualitative research, and ethical and fairness issues in educational assessment.

Charalambos Kollias received a BA in English Literature from Deree College, Athens, Greece, and an MA in TESL from St Michael's College, Vermont, USA. He is currently researching for a PhD in Applied Linguistics from the University of Lancaster, UK. He has been teaching English since 1989 and joined the Hellenic American Union in 1999, where he is a teacher and teacher trainer. He teaches on the MA in Applied Linguistics programme and is joint Co-ordinator for Testing Development at the Hellenic American University. He has presented at international conferences in Europe and has taken part in international CEFR linking projects.

Henk Kuijper is a senior consultant in the Adult and Vocational Education Unit at Cito, Institute for Educational Measurement in the Netherlands. He is involved in projects for language testing development for Dutch as a second language and Dutch as a mother tongue. He has worked in international consultancy projects on language testing. He has carried out research on computer testing and on relating language examinations to the CEFR. He is a member of the ALTE (Association of Language Testers in Europe) Standing Committee for Quality Assurance and of the ALTE working group for Language Assessment for Migration and Integration.

Sabrina Machetti is a researcher of Educational Linguistics at the University for Foreigners in Siena, Italy. She also works as a consultant at the CILS (Certification of Italian as a Foreign Language) examination centre. Her main research interests are language teaching and learning, language assessment, and linguistic landscape.

Waldemar Martyniuk is Assistant Professor (*Adiunkt*) of Applied Linguistics at the Centre for Polish Language and Culture of the Jagiellonian University in Krakow, Poland. Teacher trainer, author of textbooks, curricula, and testing materials for Polish as a foreign language; translator of the *Common European Framework of Reference for Languages* into Polish (2003); seconded to the Council of Europe, Language Policy Division (Strasbourg, France, 2005–06). Since October 2008 he has been Executive Director at the European Centre for Modern Languages (ECML) of the Council of Europe based in Graz, Austria.

José Noijons is a senior consultant at the International Bureau of Cito, the Institute for Educational Measurement in the Netherlands. He has been involved in many national and international CEFR-related projects. He has been a member of a number of working groups that have advised the Council of Europe on CEFR policies. He has been the co-organiser of a number of conferences that have focused on the impact of the CEFR. He is the Project Director of a number of international projects. He is now co-ordinator within the Consortium that is responsible for the development of background questionnaires in the PISA project.

Brian North is Head of Academic Development at Eurocentres, the Swiss-based foundation with language schools teaching languages where they are spoken worldwide, which has been an NGO to the Council of Europe for modern languages since 1968. The subject of his PhD was the development of the scale of language proficiency descriptors for the CEFR. He is co-author of the CEFR and of the prototype European Language Portfolio, co-ordinator of the 'CEFR examination manual' team and currently (2009) Chair of EAQUALS (European Association for Quality Language Services), the European accreditation scheme with over 100 member schools.

Johanna Panthier has been an Administrator at the Language Policy Division of the Council of Europe since 1992 where she accompanied the development of the Common European Framework of Reference for Languages (CEFR) from the very beginning. She has also been the member of the Division in charge of other projects building a toolkit around the CEFR, such as the Manual for *Relating language examinations to the CEFR*, the material illustrating the levels of the CEFR, compendia of case studies on the use of the CEFR and the Manual, the forthcoming (revised) Manual for language examining and test development, etc. Since 2006 she has been responsible for the Division's new project on the Languages of Schooling.

Spiros Papageorgiou is a language assessment specialist in the Testing and Certification Division of the English Language Institute at the University of Michigan, where he conducts research related to testing programmes and manages test development projects. His main interest is standard setting and he has consulted a number of examination providers about linking their examinations to the CEFR. His PhD thesis (from Lancaster University) investigated the judges' perspective in the CEFR linking process and was awarded the Jacqueline Ross TOEFL Dissertation Award in 2009.

Angeliki Salamoura holds a PhD in Second Language Processing (Psycholinguistics) from the University of Cambridge, UK, and has a number of publications in this field. She has worked as a postdoctoral researcher on English language processing in the same university where she developed a strong background in quantitative research. She also has experience as an EFL teacher overseas. Her current role at Cambridge ESOL involves working on state sector projects, on the development and validation of bespoke assessment products and on CEFR-related topics. Her research interests include methodological approaches to linking examinations and maintaining alignment to the CEFR, quantitative research methodology and bilingual/second language processing.

Anna Maria Scaglioso works at the University for Foreigners in Siena's CILS – Certification of Italian as a Foreign Language – department as an item writer. She also works as a teacher trainer, in Italy and abroad. Her main research interests are language teaching and learning, and language assessment.

Barry O'Sullivan is Professor of Applied Linguistics, Director of the Centre for Language Assessment Research (CLARe) at Roehampton University, London, UK. He has written two books on language testing, *Issues in Business English Testing* (UCLES/Cambridge University Press 2006) and *Modelling Performance in Tests of Spoken Language* (Peter Lang 2008). He has published widely in the area and has presented his work at conferences around the world. He is active in language testing globally, working with ministries, universities and examination boards. Recent projects include developing affordable tests for Mexico, CEFR-linking projects in the UK, Mexico and Turkey and a major international placement test for the British Council.

Gábor Szabó is Assistant Professor at the Department of English Applied Linguistics at the University of Pécs, Hungary. He has been advisor to the ECL examination system and has been involved in various other national and international language assessment projects. His main field of interest is the application of IRT in language assessment. He is currently member of the Hungarian Accreditation Board for Foreign Language Examinations.

Lynda Taylor is a Consultant to University of Cambridge ESOL Examinations and formerly Assistant Director of the Research and Validation Group there. She holds an MPhil and PhD in Applied Linguistics and Language Assessment from the University of Cambridge, UK. She has over 25 years' experience of the theoretical and practical issues involved in L2 testing and assessment, and has provided expert assistance for test development projects worldwide. She regularly teaches, writes and presents on language testing matters and has edited and written chapters for several of the volumes in the *Studies in Language Testing* series.

Carole Thomas has been involved in ELT for almost 30 years and has taught in Spain, the United Kingdom and Turkey. She has worked in the field of language testing for over 15 years and is currently working at Bilkent University in Turkey where she holds the post of Testing Development Co-ordinator. Her main responsibilities include the development of placement and proficiency tests, training and standardisation in assessment and co-ordinating the COPE–CEFR linking project.

Tamsin Walker has an MSc in Computer Science, taught English in Spain, and has worked at Cambridge ESOL, UK, for five years now, firstly on IELTS validation, then grading and other issues relating to the Validation of Asset Languages assessments and its alignment to the CEFR.

Jessica Wu is Program Director of the Research and Development Office at the Language Training and Testing Center (LTTC) where she handles test validation, research, and development for the various language testing and teaching programmes. She received her PhD from the University of Surrey in Roehampton (UK). Her research interests include oral assessment and the impact of large-scale language testing. She is currently a member of the Editorial Board of Language Assessment Quarterly.

Rachel Y Wu is Chief of the Division I, Testing Editorial Department, the Language Training and Testing Center (LTTC), and has been closely involved in the research and development, and validation of the General English Proficiency Test. She received her master's degree in Educational Psychology from the University of Illinois, Urbana-Champaign, and is now studying for a PhD in language testing.